Colonias in Arizona and New Mexico

Border Poverty and Community

Development Solutions

Adrian X. Esparza and Angela J. Donelson

The University of Arizona Press   Tucson

The University of Arizona Press
© 2008 The Arizona Board of Regents
All rights reserved

Library of Congress Cataloging-in-Publication Data

Esparza, Adrian X., 1957–
    Colonias in Arizona and New Mexico : border poverty
and community development solutions / Adrian X. Esparza
and Angela J. Donelson.
        p. cm.
    Includes bibliographical references and index.
    ISBN 978-0-8165-2652-9 (pbk. : alk. paper)
    1. Community development—Arizona. 2. Community
development—New Mexico. 3. Unincorporated areas—
Arizona. 4. Unincorporated areas—New Mexico. 5. Poverty—
Arizona. 6. Poverty—New Mexico. 7. Mexican-American
Border Region—Social conditions. 8. Mexican-American
Border Region—Economic conditions. I. Donelson, Angela J.,
1971– II. Title.
    HN79.A63C64 2008
    307.1′409721–dc22 2007021538

Publication of this book is made possible in part by a grant from
the Provost's Author Support Fund of the University of Arizona.

Manufactured in the United States of America on acid-free,
archival-quality paper containing a minimum of 50%
postconsumer waste and processed chlorine free.

13   12   11   10   09   08   6   5   4   3   2   1

Contents

Illustrations

Acknowledgments

We are indebted to many people who contributed to the research reported in the book. Foremost, we wish to thank the residents of Arizona and New Mexico colonias who shared lessons, challenges, and stories of hope as they have sought to improve their quality of life. As we discuss later in the book, these individuals remain anonymous because at times they shared sensitive information about their communities. We are inspired by their experiences and believe they will encourage other border-area leaders who seek to build community.

We also thank the Annie E. Casey Foundation and the Rural Poverty Research Center (sponsored by the U.S. Department of Health and Human Services) for their support for fieldwork and development of the case studies presented in this book. We also wish to acknowledge Esperanza Holguin, a friend and former colleague at the U.S. Department of Housing and Urban Development, for helping us conceptualize key challenges faced by colonias and introducing some remarkable community leaders interviewed as part of this research.

Finally, our deepest gratitude to *toda la gente* who understand life in the U.S.–Mexico border region.

Colonias in Arizona and New Mexico

Introduction

In recent years the U.S.–Mexico border region has become more visible across the country and even the world. The North American Free Trade Agreement (NAFTA), which reaches across the continent to ease trade between Canada, the United States, and Mexico, has had something to do with this. International attention continues to grow as the Central America Free Trade Agreement and the Free Trade Area of the Americas bring together dozens of countries to form the world's largest trade zone. These trade agreements will enhance the U.S.–Mexico border's reputation as the world's single most important transnational crossing point.

But mainly the border region captures the public eye because of drug trafficking and unauthorized immigration. In the first instance, drug traffickers find the border a convenient and easy port-of-entry to the world's most lucrative market, and, for this reason alone, the border region receives attention (Lorey 1999; Andreas 2000). In the second case, the number of unauthorized immigrants entering the United States continues to rise even though they face life-threatening conditions, paramilitary groups that aim to seal the country's southern border, and public outcries that call for stiffer government intervention. Despite these and other obstacles, undocumented immigrants continue to cross the border in search of something better (Conover 1987; Martinez 2001; Nevins 2002; Zúñiga and Hernández-León 2005).

Those more familiar with the U.S.–Mexico border region find deeper and more compelling reasons to embrace (or reject) the border experience. For them, it is a place where cultures meet, at times merging and forming a special vocabulary and lifestyle, at other times crashing head-on as cultural entrenchment and xenophobia carries the day. To still others it is simply where they live—the place they were born, raised, and came of age, just like people and places everywhere.

Each of these and other dimensions has been described, analyzed, and interpreted repeatedly, but in this book the U.S.–Mexico border region takes on a different meaning. It is defined by the poverty and disadvan-

tage that color many of the region's colonias. These are the places—large and small, remote and urban, old and new—that house a growing number of people in southern Texas, New Mexico, Arizona, and California.

Colonias rarely make the news, much less the headlines. This is understandable because, unlike drug trafficking or border security, poverty and deprivation are not engaging or controversial. Rather, they are troubling and make most people uneasy. Perhaps this explains why so few know about colonias and the people who live in them.

By definition, colonias are located in the border region, but the spatial dimensions of the region are unclear. While all agree that the U.S.–Mexico border spans the entire length from Texas to California, about 2,000 miles (approximately 3,200 km), its northern boundary is less certain. For example, the U.S. Department of Housing and Urban Development (2004a) says that the border region extends northward 150 miles (240 km), whereas the U.S. Environmental Protection Agency (2003a) indicates that the region runs 62.5 miles (100 km) north of the border. Despite these incongruities, it is safe to say that hundreds of colonias dot the border region, many within a stone's throw of the international border, others more distant.

Along with location, colonias are defined by their severe infrastructure deficiencies (Ward 1999; Donelson and Holguin 2001a, 2001b; Lemos et al. 2002). Many colonias lack the basics that nearly all Americans enjoy—access to on-site water, sewer, electricity, heat, and paved streets and roads. The poor infrastructure conditions in colonias are their most identifiable problem and drew the attention of the federal government some time ago. In 1989 federal legislation was passed that bestowed formal status to colonias in Texas, New Mexico, Arizona, and California. Thereafter, they were eligible for assistance that targeted infrastructure improvements.

Life in colonias is also defined by several economic and social characteristics (for detailed reports, see Peach 1997; Ward 1999; Driesen and Aguirre 2000; Pagán 2004). These include rapid population growth, persistently high levels of poverty and unemployment, comparatively large concentrations of Hispanics, limited English-language skills, and inadequate health care.

In addition, many colonias are unincorporated, which means that making things better is difficult.[1] Unincorporated communities rely on the services of county government, but with their budgets stretched thin and responsibilities mounting, assisting colonias is often not the coun-

ties' highest priority. Without the political clout needed to get things done and in the absence of local government, improving these unincorporated communities is challenging and frequently falls on the shoulders of colonia residents. It seems as though the political and social environments of the border region are always changing, constantly in flux as national and binational policies and agreements filter down to the local level (Massey et al. 2002). Colonias bear the brunt of these policies as quality of life is diminished.

The lack of attention devoted to colonias, especially those in Arizona and New Mexico, motivated our research and defines the book's objectives.[2] First, we seek to elevate the visibility of Arizona and New Mexico colonias with the hope that greater attention will mobilize action. To accomplish this, we provide a comprehensive picture of colonias and their context. This includes a summary of the region's past and a more detailed account of Arizona and New Mexico urban and economic history as it applies to the border region. We also describe recent patterns of growth and development to set the stage for avenues of investigation that follow later in the book.

Second, the book considers how national policies have affected colonias in Arizona and New Mexico. At issue is evaluating whether, and to what extent, policies unwittingly destabilize these communities even as agencies such as the Department of Housing and Urban Development and the Environmental Protection Agency work diligently to improve their quality of life. In short, at times the federal government works against itself by responding to pressures from multiple and competing interests. Numerous critical issues color the border, ranging from the death of unauthorized immigrants, public health, and border security to lesser-known concerns such as air quality and ecosystem sustainability. The federal government responds to these and many more issues, often with disastrous and contradictory results (Andreas 2000; Massey et al. 2002; Nevins 2002).

Policies that affect colonias, however, are imposed on both sides of the border. For this reason, we also look at policies handed down from Mexico City. They make their way to Mexico's northern border mainly through unauthorized immigration and the concentration of industry and labor in the region's major urban centers, such as Ciudad Juárez and Tijuana, which house the region's maquiladora economy. Literally hundreds of thousands work in maquilas, and policies that affect the maquilas and their workers also affect life in Arizona and New Mexico

colonias. We are especially interested in policies that led to recent peso devaluations. To get at the impacts of national policies on both sides of the border, we look closely at the social and demographic characteristics of colonia residents. We are particularly interested in understanding the ways in which changes in policy affect levels of unauthorized immigration, quality of life, and community development over time.

Our final objective is to consider the role of community development as it responds to poverty and the lack of resources. We present numerous examples of how colonia residents are working to improve their neighborhoods and communities, even as they face an uncertain political arena. Colonia residents are much the same as other Americans in that they desire a better life, especially for their children. And like most Americans, they have tried to take control of their lives and communities through local leaders and grassroots organizations that pursue community development. We showcase several examples of community-led initiatives that have responded successfully to specific problems and long-term development goals.

We also describe colonias that have fallen short of development objectives. Despite the best of intentions, not all communities have been successful, and a sample of these is brought forward with the aim of providing lessons for those contemplating or working through community development initiatives. Information for community case studies was obtained from on-site research.

Before describing the book's organization and content, a word about the focus on Arizona and New Mexico is warranted. First, Texas colonias are excluded because they have received far more attention in the research literature (e.g., Richardson 1996; Chapa and Eaton 1997; Ward 1999; Pagán 2004), and government agencies at state and federal levels have been involved with numerous initiatives and programs that target colonias in Texas. For example, the U.S. Census Bureau has been working in Texas to coordinate data and mapping (GIS) capabilities for colonia communities (Ratcliffe 2001). Colonias in Texas first drew attention in the early 1980s, after nongovernmental organizations and activists raised concerns about their third-world living conditions. However, after state and federal legislation was passed giving some—yet still seriously inadequate—resources to address infrastructure problems, the concerns of the colonias faded from the public consciousness.

Second, California is excluded from our analysis because there is only a handful of federally recognized colonias in the state (sixteen), and their

history, context, and setting differ significantly from other states (U.S. Department of Housing and Urban Development 2004a). In contrast, there are 87 and 140 federally recognized colonias in Arizona and New Mexico, respectively, and many of these settlements have been in place for well over a century.

Finally, it makes sense to combine the study of colonias in Arizona and New Mexico because their history, development, and border experiences are similar. At the same time, these states differ in substantive ways from Texas and California. For example, both Arizona and New Mexico were carved out of the Gadsden Purchase of 1853, the Arizona Territory was separated from the New Mexico Territory in 1865, and they became states at nearly identical times: New Mexico on 16 January 1912 and Arizona on 14 February 1912. In addition to these historic connections, the same 1989 federal legislation formally recognized colonias in Arizona and New Mexico. In contrast, Texas had colonias programs in place years earlier.

Chapter 1, "A Brief History of the U.S.–Mexico Border Region," provides a broad view of the border as it developed from the late 1500s to the present. Such a historical view is warranted because the sequence of exploration, wars, revolutions, and binational agreements all played important roles in defining the present-day character of southern Arizona and New Mexico.

In "Economic Development in Southern Arizona and New Mexico," we discuss the emergence of agriculture and mining early in the region's history, as well as the role that railroads played in the long-term development of these industries and the region. Networks of colonias first appeared and later grew as these industries spread throughout southern Arizona and New Mexico. This chapter also describes the near collapse of agriculture and mining during the mid-twentieth century and the growing military presence in the years that followed.

Chapter 3, "The Social and Economic Characteristics of Colonias," describes the quality of life for colonia residents. We examine social and economic conditions including income, poverty, educational attainment, language skills, housing conditions, and other indicators of quality of life. These characteristics are presented for 1990, 2000, and 2005 using data from the U.S. Census Bureau and our own estimates for 2005. We pay particular attention to changes during the years 1990 through 2005, when targeted federal policies sought to improve the quality of life for colonia residents.

In "Urbanization and Colonia Development" we focus on colonias as a set of villages, town, and cities and examine their diversity, growth, and morphology. Colonias are far more than places of poverty and deprivation. Like towns and cities everywhere, they have unique histories, locations, and economic and social functions. We highlight these differences by comparing several smaller and larger colonias. This chapter also looks at urbanization trends over the past several decades for Arizona and New Mexico, colonia counties, and a select group of colonias. We also show that long-distance commuting is common among colonia residents as they seek jobs outside local communities. The chapter concludes with a discussion of colonias' land use and morphology, in which we describe the spatial arrangement of land uses and neighborhoods in more rural and remote colonias and those located closer to larger towns and cities.

The second part of the book, "Policies and Community Development," shifts attention to factors that affect quality of life in colonias and local community development efforts. We look at the relationship between national policies and the social and economic characteristics of Arizona and New Mexico colonias. At issue is gaining an understanding of whether the constantly shifting array of national and binational policies disrupts the social and economic fabric of colonias, thereby hampering local community development. This part also examines approaches to community development and their outcomes in Arizona and New Mexico colonias.

Chapter 5, "National and Binational Policies in the Border Region," summarizes policy changes that have affected the U.S.–Mexico border region during recent decades. We focus on three policies, the 1982 and 1994 peso devaluations that fueled unauthorized immigration; the 1986 Immigration and Reform Control Act, which granted amnesty to long-term unauthorized immigrants living in the United States; and recent immigration policies that attempt to close the border to unauthorized workers. Although other policies on both sides of the border played a role in shaping the quality of life in Arizona and New Mexico colonias, we select these three because they have produced the most significant impacts.

In "National Policies and Colonia Development," we examine the effects of policies as they play out in Arizona and New Mexico colonias. The question guiding our analysis is whether policies have been detrimental to the quality of life in colonias. Our aim here is not to

place blame on the shoulders of colonia residents. Rather, we investigate whether national and binational policies undermine local development initiatives. To get at this issue, we look at border apprehensions over time to assess how changes in immigration policy channeled unauthorized immigrants to new gateways. We also examine the foreign-born population living in colonias and their effect on local quality of life.

Chapter 7, "The Challenges to Capacity Building in Colonias," explores why many colonias are unable to address quality-of-life issues. Our discussion centers on the importance of physical and civic infrastructure in colonia development. From this background, we illustrate how and why community development efforts in some colonias have failed by examining communities that have struggled to build and sustain improvements to physical and civic infrastructure.

In "Developing Community Capacity in Colonias," we consider how physical and civic infrastructure can be enhanced by building community capacity. We begin by defining capacity and capacity building, then explain how and why it emerged as an approach to community development. This chapter also discusses what community capacity building looks like in a rural context and why it is critical for colonias.

Chapter 9, "Strategies for Capacity Building in Colonias," describes how several colonias overcame quality-of-life issues. The discussion showcases community capacity building strategies that responded to quality-of-life concerns as well as long-term development goals. We identify and describe particular strategies, assets, and approaches that led these communities to a new and promising future.

The final chapter, "The Road Ahead," has two objectives. First, we continue the theme of community development by presenting a long-term colonia development plan, which uses the capacity building approach and sets out a sequence of short- and long-term activities to meet community development goals and objectives. Second, we identify policies, programs, and initiatives at federal, state, and local levels of government that have contributed to colonias' community development. The aim is to provide an inventory of agencies and programs that local leaders and community organizers can draw upon as they consider initiating community development plans.

Although the U.S.–Mexico border region has attracted the attention of scholars for many decades, the plight of colonias in Arizona and New Mexico has been largely ignored. Therefore, we provide the first compre-

hensive assessment of these colonias with the aim of raising their visibility in the public's eye, identifying and evaluating reasons why many remain outposts of poverty and deprivation, and describing particular community development efforts that have failed or succeeded. It is our sincere hope that readers will gain an appreciation of the depth of problems and issues that confront colonia residents and mobilize financial, political, and human resources accordingly.

Part I
Histoy and Background

1
A Brief History of the U.S.–Mexico Border Region

Southern Arizona and New Mexico are often seen as bit players on the stage of the U.S.–Mexico border, as both the popular press and scholars have focused on their more populous and politically and economically prosperous neighbors, Texas and California. Yet, southern Arizona and New Mexico are much more than the "vacant middle" of the borderlands. The two states are at the heart of the debate on current federal border enforcement and immigration policy that is increasingly impacting rural areas. Southern Arizona and New Mexico have been sandwiched by the pressures of increasing borderwide urbanization and industrial development taking place in neighboring states. As a result, these states now have rapidly growing communities unable to cope well with the stresses of growth. Between 1960 and 2000 the population of border counties in Arizona and New Mexico grew by 160 percent. Today, these counties are home to more than 1.6 million people, including residents of many poor colonias in the United States (U.S. Census Bureau 2000).

In defining southern Arizona and New Mexico, we generally refer to the 29,640 square miles (about 76,760 square km) of land contained within the 1853 Gadsden Purchase. This rugged desert land stretches south of the Gila River and west of the Rio Grande, from present-day Yuma, Arizona, to lands south of Phoenix and east to New Mexico's eastern border. In this chapter and throughout the book, we also include in our analyses several southern Arizona and New Mexico counties that lie just north and east of the lands of the Gadsden Purchase.[1] We include these counties because they also contain colonias recognized by the federal government.

This chapter outlines the unique and important history of border settlement in southern Arizona and New Mexico. We explore how settlements emerged and why they developed more slowly than and distinctly from more urbanized sections in Texas and California. We discuss how major events, policies, and developments from the Spanish colonial period in the late 1500s to the present day have shaped patterns of growth.

The remainder of the chapters in part I examine how colonias have grown and developed in more recent history (the 1880s through the present). Chapter 2 focuses on the economic history of southern Arizona and New Mexico, and chapter 3 examines the socio-economic characteristics of colonias. Finally, chapter 4 explores how Arizona and New Mexico colonias have changed in terms of growth, land use, and morphology.

This chapter, then, provides a historical context for a broad overview of border urbanization. We break the expansive 400 years of Spanish, Mexican, and American settlement history of the border region into four periods of development. For the first period, which spans the Spanish rule of the 1590s through the end of the Mexican era in 1853, we explore how strategic gateways came to be developed in California and Texas, while routes from Mexico into Arizona and New Mexico were largely ignored. The second period outlines the U.S. rule of New Mexico and Arizona Territories from 1853 to 1912. In this section, we illustrate how California and Texas continued to gain prominence, while Arizona and New Mexico struggled to attract population and investment. For the third period, from Arizona and New Mexico statehood in 1912 to the mid-1980s, we explain how population centers in California and Texas grew into major metropolises from World War I though the 1980s. At the same time, Arizona and New Mexico border settlements witnessed boom-and-bust cycles of growth that kept them small outposts of little strategic and economic importance. The final period of the mid-1980s through the present ushered in a new era of growth and instability for the entire border region. These decades have been marked by Mexican debt crises and massive changes in U.S. border policy. Debt and policy changes have transformed both urban and rural areas of the U.S.–Mexico border into socio-demographically different communities. As we will show, rural communities now face overwhelming quality-of-life problems that plague border urban centers. Both urban and rural areas have witnessed the expansion of poor colonia populations and have been unable to cope well with the stresses of growth.

The Spanish Conquest and the Mexican Period, 1598–1853

The Spanish first discovered the northern Mexican frontier in the late 1500s as they made their way north from Mexico City to secure their control of the Spanish empire. In doing so, they set the foundations for

the border's largest and most prosperous cities in present-day Texas and California. These foundations of urban wealth and preeminence persist today. Three of these cities remained the most economically important border cities through the end of the twentieth century—El Paso del Norte and the port cities of Matamoros and San Diego. Each city was founded off the routes of the three royal highways that the Spanish used to funnel military troops, missionaries, and settlers. Since their founding, El Paso/Juárez and San Diego/Tijuana have continued to dominate as points of border urbanization and commerce (Kearney and Knopp 1995).

The first gateway, El Paso del Norte, lies at the very center of the U.S.– Mexico border, in present-day Ciudad Juárez, Chihuahua (just south of El Paso, Texas). The Spanish-born explorer Juan de Oñate founded El Paso del Norte in 1598 and established the first European settlements in the upper Rio Grande Valley of New Mexico. Settling the area was an easy choice: it was a natural gateway—the lowest pass across the Rocky Mountains—and the area was a fertile river valley that had been home to Indian peoples for centuries. The pass quickly became a critical link in New Spain's central corridor, which was the only Royal Spanish Highway (or Camino Real) linking ranching and farming areas of the Rio Grande to north–south commerce with the Spanish seat of power in raw materials, foodstuff, livestock, and Indian slave trading (Arreola and Curtis 1993; Kessell 2002). The route ran from Chihuahua City to Santa Fe and then west to the Hopi mesas of northern Arizona.

The second gateway of Matamoros arose at the far eastern edge of the present-day border in 1689. Another route crossed Nuevo Leon, Mexico, up through San Antonio, Texas, and northeast toward Louisiana (Kessell 2002). Matamoros, later to become one of the three most economically strategic U.S.–Mexico border cities, was founded just east of this route on the lower Rio Grande and the Gulf Coast. It lies just south of present-day Brownsville, Texas.

The third gateway of San Diego is at the western edge of the border region on the Pacific Ocean. Another Spanish trade route was founded in 1697; it initially ran only from Sinaloa through the western edge of Sonora, then west along the Gulf of California into northern California, although it eventually extended to San Diego. This route crossed a small portion of Pimeria Alta, the present-day Santa Cruz River Valley of Arizona, which remained unsettled until 70 years later. The Spanish finally blazed the trail to San Diego when Carlos III realized the area

needed to be populated before the French, Russians, or Anglos could claim this important port for emerging international trade (Kearney and Knopp 1995).

The Spanish invested heavily in these three north–south routes at strategic sites. They engaged in a three-part settlement process: Jesuit, Franciscan, and Dominican missionaries established numerous Catholic missions; Spanish military garrison troops founded presidios; and settler families established villas or civil settlements with municipal councils to govern local affairs (Arreola and Curtis 1993). Given the expense of maintaining permanent settlement so far from the seat of power in Mexico City, the Spanish chose to develop few cities. They relied primarily on the three gateways and key cities off these trade routes, such as San Antonio, El Paso, Albuquerque, Santa Fe, Tucson, and Santa Barbara, to control the northern frontier (Hamnett 1999; Kessell 2002).

All three gateways grew in preeminence between the mid-1700s and 1821, when Mexico gained independence from Spain. By the late 1700s, the three largest and important border towns—El Paso del Norte, Matamoros, and San Diego—clearly dominated by engaging in an emerging contraband trade industry. Although Carlos III prohibited Mexico from trading with nations other than Spain, El Paso del Norte engaged in trade with Anglo merchants using the Santa Fe Trail, Matamoros with the merchants of New Orleans, and San Diego with the French, Americans, and Russians (Kearney and Knopp 1995). Unauthorized trade helped these cities grow and blossom into critical ports of commerce.

While these gateway cities grew, however, few explorers ventured into southern Arizona and New Mexico until the mid-1800s (Bancroft 1962). There are a few exceptions. Coronado made his famous 1540 expedition through northern Mexico into Cochise County to the Zuni pueblo on the border of central Arizona and New Mexico in search of the famed seven cities of Cibola (Bancroft 1962). He did not find gold and fame there, however, and the Spanish lost interest in this desolate land until the late 1600s. Between 1687 and the early 1700s, the Jesuit Eusebio Francisco Kino founded a cluster of southern Arizona missions, stringing northward along the Santa Cruz River toward Tucson. He was successful in converting the Pima Indians, who proved they were loyal to the Spanish as they fought the Apaches to the east. Kino also founded two other small missions: a lone mission called Quiburi in the San Pedro Valley and one in Sonoita, just south of Why, Arizona. Because they were located off

the main trade routes and therefore isolated from other settlements, these missions remained small service centers for farms and area mines (Bancroft 1962; Kessell 2002).

There were three reasons why the Santa Cruz Valley remained the only outpost in southern Arizona and New Mexico until the late 1800s. First, hostile Indians drove settlers away, making it difficult to open the region to roads and communication, with Apache raids blocking settlement efforts in the area. The Chiricahua Apache and Western Apache of southeastern Arizona and southwestern New Mexico and the Mescalero Apache of eastern New Mexico were perhaps the fiercest warriors among the Indian groups (Melody 1989). They were enemies of foreigners, probably beginning with the Spanish, who took members of their nation into the slave trade as workers for the silver mines and domestic help for wealthy Mexican families (Melody 1989). Fighting in small nomadic groups of about a hundred, the Apaches frequently attacked ranches in the Santa Cruz, San Pedro, and Rio Grande Valleys, creating little incentive to settle beyond the safety of the Spanish presidios (Melody 1989; Hamnett 1999).

Second, the harsh terrain made settlement of southern Arizona and New Mexico immensely difficult. Although various merchants in Santa Fe attempted to develop trade with Sonora in the mid-1600s, the distance and lack of an east–west road system frustrated these efforts (Simmons 2001). In 1795 José de Zúñiga, the captain of the Tucson presidio, set out to open this route. Although he sent out scouts from Tucson northeast to the Zuni lands in west-central New Mexico, they found the trail was too rough for wagon travel, with Apaches preventing establishment of a stable commercial connection (Simmons 2001). In the late 1700s and early 1800s, private groups of New Mexicans made occasional trips to Sonora, but they had to construct their own rough trails (Simmons 2001). Even in the mid-1800s, geography still made it difficult to create a connection between Texas, New Mexico, Arizona, and California because all had established north–south routes. For example, cloth produced in New Mexico had to be sent south to Chihuahua, then west to Arizpe, Mexico, and then north to Tucson (Kessell 2002).

Third, southern Arizona and New Mexico remained desolate because Spain simply lost enthusiasm for settlement efforts. Spain's money, power, and authority dwindled toward the end of its conquest in Mexico. Father Kino urged the Spanish authorities to invest in more missions in southern Arizona, pleading that the Pimas were different from the

raiding Apaches to the northeast (Bancroft 1962). But nothing came of this vision: the settlement frontier did not move beyond Tucson (Kessell 2002). During this period, only the three gateway settlements and major cities off these settlement routes were able to support a lucrative stream of trade and commerce and thus retain a strong Spanish presence. For example, the Franciscan and Dominican missionaries maintained a strong California presence in the 1700s by engaging in illicit fur trade with the Russians and Americans (Proffitt 1994).

When Mexico gained independence in 1821, the existing settlement patterns continued throughout most of the next 32 years of Mexican rule. Strategic gateways continued to gain importance in California and Texas, although they were destabilized during the last 14 years of this period, while Arizona and New Mexico remained sparsely settled. Mexico's Federalista government, in power from 1821 to 1830 and 1832 to 1834, instigated policies to foster trade, enabling El Paso del Norte, Matamoros, and San Diego to grow and prosper (Kearney and Knopp 1995). However, when Centralista Antonio López de Santa Anna launched a successful coup against the Federalista presidency in 1834, he led the effort to restrict and control the border region. The Centralistas were fearful of American encroachment and trade that pulled northern Mexican cities into greater American dependence (Kearney and Knopp 1995). This desire for greater control over the border, in part, led Mexico into war with an expansionist U.S. government in 1846. Mexico lost the war in 1848, along with half of its land. The final U.S.–Mexico boundary was settled in 1853, when Mexico sold a strip of land south of the Gila River in the Gadsden Purchase. Mexico saw this land as having little value because it remained an unsettled frontier for both the United States and Mexico (U.S. General Accounting Office 2004).

The Territorial Period, 1853–1912

The Gadsden Purchase completed the final acquisition of the New Mexico Territory. First created in 1850, the territory included the present-day states of Arizona and New Mexico, and in 1865 the Arizona Territory was separated from the New Mexico Territory. Over the next 60 years, settlers of the area struggled to attain recognition and investment.

Meanwhile, the new states of California and Texas achieved prominence. These more urban states gained influence as the West was opened to mining and the railroads. The gold rush in 1848 prompted the beginning of a mass settlement process in California. It drew miners from

Mexico through San Diego into northern California, stimulating development of San Diego hotels, retail stores, and supporting establishments (Taylor 2001). From 1851 through the 1870s, a steady stream of settlers continued to come to the Baja California area, where additional gold deposits were found (Taylor 2001). California's significant population growth prompted its admission to the union in 1850. Soon afterward, California sought to blaze communication and commercial connections through the New Mexico Territory that would link it to the state of Texas and the rest of the nation.

California got its wish in 1858 with the arrival of the Butterfield Overland Mail Stage. In 1856 the state had presented Congress with a petition requesting daily mail service (Trafzer 1980). John Butterfield received the federal contract to lay out the road through the New Mexico Territory and establish the way stations, which provided mail service between San Diego and El Paso (Trennert 1988). Two decades later, the Southern Pacific Railroad (the nation's second transcontinental railroad) was completed, spurring further settlement. By the 1880s, El Paso had become the most important smelting center in the Southwest (Kearney and Knopp 1995). During this time, San Diego also built new subdivisions and public works, including interurban rail and cable car lines, dams, schools, a public library, an opera house, and a dam that brought irrigation and electricity to the area (Taylor 2001). But San Diego's real economic boom occurred in 1896, when Congress decided to establish a major naval and military base there (Taylor 2001).

Southern Arizona and New Mexico were at last opened to permanent settlement in the 1850s, when the U.S. government developed military forts and camps to protect the New Mexico Territory. Yet, few settled the area until the military conquered the Apaches in 1886 (Goodman 1969). With the construction of the Southern Pacific Railroad in the 1880s, eastern mining companies set up profitable operations in Arizona and New Mexico to extract copper and other mineral deposits. The railroad and mining industries stimulated southern Arizona and New Mexico boomtowns, banking, and an emerging agricultural industry (Schweikart 1981). Settlers also continued to migrate to the area in yet another wave, prompted by the Mexican Revolution of 1910. Over the following decade more than half a million Mexicans crossed the border, with communities all along the U.S. border attracting more than their share of immigrants (Meyer and Garcia 1987).

Despite their increased population growth during this period, Arizona and New Mexico remained largely rural and of limited economic

importance.[2] Although both territories aggressively sought statehood, the process was delayed for two reasons. First, the remoteness and lack of development were perceived to be a financial drain on the United States, much as it had been on Spain and then Mexico. Second, the U.S. Congress held political prejudice against both Arizona and New Mexico. Arizona was accused of having a "weak and hastily cobbled constitution" (Wagoner 1970). Into the early 1900s, New Mexico was a primarily Spanish-speaking, Catholic territory perceived as threatening to the predominant white, Protestant culture (Gonzales-Berry and Maciel 2000).

Statehood through the Early 1980s

After decades of petitioning for statehood, both Arizona and New Mexico were finally admitted as states in 1912. They were the last of the continental states to join the union. Not surprisingly, they continued to fight for influence during the early years of statehood. Settlements of southern Arizona and New Mexico continued to have this problem into the 1980s, as they witnessed boom-and-bust periods of growth and decline. The southern halves of both states became increasingly dependent upon a narrow economic base, at a time when northern cities in these states and border gateway centers in Texas and California were able to diversify and grow steadily in international significance. By the early 1980s, El Paso/Juárez and San Diego/Tijuana became major metropolises and industrial centers, with the former having 800,000 and the latter nearly 1.3 million residents (Lorey 1990).

Four factors were responsible for the expansive growth of El Paso/ Juárez and San Diego/Tijuana. The first was the Volstead Act of 1919, which was responsible for pushing tourist-oriented bars, casinos, and other alcohol-related businesses out of U.S. cities into Mexico (Lorey 1999). Not surprisingly, tourism grew the fastest in the Mexican sister cities located across the border from the largest U.S. border cities at the time, San Diego and El Paso. Juárez grew from 10,621 residents in 1910 to 48,881 in 1940, while Tijuana grew from 733 residents in 1910 to 16,486 in 1940 (Lorey 1990).

Second, El Paso and San Diego grew rapidly because they benefited from military growth and related industries, prompted by World Wars I and II. Both wars enabled the cities to substantially expand and diversify their growing economic bases. During World War I, El Paso gained significant population as tens of thousands of troops were sta-

tioned at Fort Bliss (Kearney and Knopp 1995). During World War II, Fort Bliss obtained artillery and missile development specializations. After the war, El Paso expanded its existing industrial base of copper smelting and agriculture by adding food processing, petroleum refining, textile manufacturing, and construction (Kearney and Knopp 1995). Similarly, San Diego benefited from becoming a major naval base in 1919. World War II brought the city aircraft construction and government industrial contracts. After the war, the city diversified by also establishing itself as a tourist center (Kearney and Knopp 1995).

The third factor contributing to urban growth of these gateway cities was the Bracero Program, which gave U.S. farmers and industrialists legal access to approximately 200,000 low-cost Mexican workers annually from 1942 to 1964 (Calavita 1992). The Bracero Program was developed to address labor shortages in farms, factories, and railroads during World War II (Kearney and Knopp 1995; Weaver 2001). The program led to mass migration to border towns, especially established population centers.

The fourth factor that transformed San Diego/Tijuana and El Paso/Juárez from urban centers into internationally important metropolises was the industrialization of the border. By the early 1960s, mechanization of agriculture eliminated the need for so many workers, leaving many Bracero farm workers and laborers unemployed. In response, the Mexican government launched two new programs: in 1961 the Programa Nacional Fronterizo (PRONAF, the National Border Program) to promote tourism and in 1965 the Border Industrialization Program (BIP). The BIP spurred much larger scale development on the Mexican side of the border through incentives for establishing twin plant manufacturing operations. By 1970 the first of these operations, called maquiladoras, opened in Ciudad Juárez (Sklair 1989). The ability of U.S. plants to send parts and raw materials to Mexico and obtain finished goods duty-free prompted maquiladora operators to set up smaller-scale operations on the U.S. side of the border, with larger Mexican assembly operations on the Sonoran side. Drawn by the existing population bases, these operations were concentrated in urban gateway cities, especially Tijuana and Juárez. As shown in table 1.1, they overshadowed the population growth in Arizona and New Mexico's binational border cities.

During this time, southern Arizona and New Mexico border settlements witnessed boom-and-bust cycles of economic and population growth and decline. The dynamics of these cycles and their impacts

Table 1.1

Populations of Selected Binational Border Cities, 1930–1980

Border city	1930	1940	1950	1960	1970	1980
San Diego, CA	147,897	203,341	334,387	573,224	697,027	875,538
Tijuana, BC	8,384	16,486	59,950	165,690	340,583	429,500
El Paso, TX	102,421	96,810	130,485	276,687	322,261	425,259
Ciudad Juárez, CI	19,669	48,881	122,566	276,995	424,135	385,603
San Luis, AZ	n.a.	n.a.	n.a.	n.a.	189	1,946
San Luis Río Colorado, SO	910	2,364	13,593	42,134	63,604	92,790
Nogales, AZ	6,006	5,135	6,153	7,286	8,946	15,683
Nogales, SO	14,061	13,866	24,478	37,657	53,119	68,067
Douglas, AZ	9,828	8,623	9,442	11,925	12,462	13,058
Agua Prieta, SO	6,677	6,552	13,121	17,248	23,272	34,380

n.a., data not available

Sources: Modified from Lorey (1990, tables 105, 107, 110); Arizona Workforce Development (2000)

on specific places are detailed more fully in chapter 2. The population growth and decline of these border settlements can be tied to a simple cause: the demand for raw materials, especially copper, and agricultural products.

Given their smaller populations and few options for economic diversification, southern Arizona and New Mexico communities became increasingly dependent upon a narrow economic base. In the early 1900s these communities grew along with mining and agriculture, especially with the United States' involvement in World Wars I and II. The demand for copper—used in nearly every piece of war equipment—prompted settlement and development in rural Arizona and New Mexico. Economic growth in farming and ranching communities of southern Arizona and New Mexico also continued to blossom until the early 1960s with the low-cost labor of the Bracero Program (Seltzer 1959; Kent 1983; Ward 2000, 2003).

These settlements witnessed a major economic downturn, however, with the transition to a service economy in the early 1960s. Mining companies such as Phelps Dodge abandoned boomtowns like Bisbee, Arizona, and Silver City, New Mexico, because mining was no longer

economically viable. By this time, most mining operations had shifted overseas or north to new open-pit mining operations in Graham and Pinal Counties and portions of Pima County (*Arizona Statistical Review* 1952–1980). Similarly, the mechanization of agriculture eliminated the need for many of the workers required in the past. The PRONAF and BIP programs enabled some of the Arizona and New Mexico border communities, such as Nogales and Douglas, Arizona, and Columbus, New Mexico, to strengthen their position as tourism and trade centers. However, most of southern Arizona and New Mexico suffered economic decline due to the Mexican economic crises of the mid-1980s.

The 1980s through the Present: Mexican Crisis and Immigration Reform

Over the last two decades two related sets of events—economic crises in Mexico and dramatic shifts in U.S. border policy toward Mexico—have transformed the physical and socio-demographic landscape of the entire border region. These rapid changes have destabilized many small, long-standing southern Arizona and New Mexico settlements. Mexican debt crises and peso devaluations (described in greater detail in chapter 5) have contributed to borderwide industrialization, attracting millions of new workers. At the same time, sweeping U.S. immigration reform (also described in detail in chapter 5) has directed mass migration increasingly from urban to rural communities on both sides of the border. As a result, populations have exploded in southern Arizona and New Mexico communities, while resources are inadequate to meet their basic needs. Binational border cities like El Paso/Juárez and San Diego/Tijuana have been unable to provide many residents with basic infrastructure and decent living conditions (Esparza et al. 2004; Peña 2005). Similarly, many southern Arizona and New Mexico settlements have been transformed from sleepy rural communities into poor colonia subdivisions with unique infrastructure, health, and environmental challenges. This section outlines how economic crises and border policy changes have led to the creation and expansion of colonias.

Since the mid-1980s Mexican economic crises have prompted patterns of borderwide industrialization. Mexico's peso devaluations of 1982 and 1994, along with the country's increased economic liberalization after entry into the General Agreement on Tariffs and Trade in 1986, lowered the cost of Mexican labor (Lorey 1999). These events, along with

efforts of Mexican border states to promote maquiladoras and target economic infrastructure investments toward maquiladora industrial parks, prompted U.S. and foreign companies to relocate their assembly operations to the northern Mexican border (Lorey 1999; Pavlakovich-Kochi 2006).

Although maquiladoras had operated in Mexican urban areas since the 1960s, they did not grow rapidly until the mid-1980s and early 1990s. It was during this time that industrialization spread from urban to rural places. Plants in smaller urban centers, especially Nogales, Sonora, have grown quickly. For example, the number of maquiladoras in Nogales grew 65 percent from 1990 to 2000, from 65 to 107 plants (Twin Plant News 1990, 2000). Maquiladoras also opened in formerly rural Mexican towns along the border with Arizona and New Mexico. For example, San Luis Río Colorado (the twin city of San Luis, Arizona) had thirty-three maquiladoras by 2000, up from twelve in 1990 (Twin Plant News 1990, 2000). By 1995 the Mexican towns of Palomas (3 miles [about 5 km] south of Columbus, New Mexico) and Naco (a sister city to Naco, Arizona) had five and four maquiladoras, respectively (Twin Plant News 1995). Both towns had reported no maquiladoras in 1990 (Twin Plant News 1990). Therefore, it is clear that recent Mexican debt crises attracted maquiladora plants seeking low-cost labor to smaller Mexican towns across the border from Arizona and New Mexico.

While debt crises pulled immigrants to work in northern Mexican maquiladoras, massive changes in U.S.–Mexico border policy forced communities on both sides to address rapid socio-demographic changes. Three types of U.S. policies were influential, those relating to immigration, drug, and border control. All created impacts that have strained the ability of both metropolitan municipalities and rural counties alike to provide basic human and infrastructure services.

Massive immigration reform occurred in 1986, when the U.S. Congress passed the Immigration Reform Control Act (IRCA). The United States was witnessing increased unauthorized immigration due to the declining Mexican economy. President Reagan and U.S. politicians declared increased border control an issue of "national security" necessary to control an "alien invasion" (Massey 2005). The IRCA allocated increased funding to the Immigration and Naturalization Services' U.S.–Mexico border enforcement efforts and imposed sanctions on employers who hired undocumented workers. The law backfired. A legal provision created expectations of future amnesties, as it granted amnesty to

3 million existing agricultural workers and long-term U.S. residents (Massey 2005).

Today, more than 11 million unauthorized Mexican residents have crossed the border, making their homes in cities and rural areas in both the Southwest and throughout the United States (Durand et al. 1999; Pew Hispanic Center 2005). In southern Arizona and New Mexico, many of these families settled in places where laborers knew they could find work—agricultural settlements of the El Paso Valley in southeastern New Mexico and southwestern Texas, Cochise and Yuma Counties in Arizona, and the Hatch Valley and Luna County of New Mexico. This migration transformed sleepy farming towns from temporary settlements of male farm workers into permanent slums for poor Mexican families. Southern Arizona and New Mexico counties' inability and unwillingness to provide for the social needs of these immigrants has made conditions worse. Since the passage of the IRCA, entry-level wages for undocumented workers declined to $4.44 per hour for 1991–1996, compared to $4.81 for 1980–1986 (expressed in constant 1990 dollars; Durand et al. 1999). The IRCA caused wages to decline for two reasons. First, employers began to divert part of the employee wages to hired labor subcontractors, who provided specific numbers of workers for set rates and times. Second, employers paid their employees less because they were required to maintain significantly more paperwork under the IRCA (Durand et al. 1999).

The second set of policies that have destabilized border communities relates to U.S. drug policy, which has transformed many neighborhoods into havens for drug trade, or at least places marked by heightened federal drug surveillance. In the 1980s President Reagan launched the War on Drugs, dispatching the U.S. Drug Enforcement Agency and Department of Immigration and Naturalization Services to crack down on Colombian drug cartels that shipped drugs through Florida. But the drug traffic merely shifted to Mexico and the Southwest. Mexican drug lords, who now control eleven of the thirteen largest U.S. drug markets, began to take up the trade for heroin, cocaine, and, increasingly, methamphetamines, as reported in *The Economist* (Anonymous 2005). Mexican gangs smuggle these drugs through places such as ambos Nogales, which federal agents have named "cocaine alley" (Davidson 2000). By 1995 drug trafficking had so permeated rural areas along the U.S.–Mexico border that the federal government declared southern Arizona a "high intensity drug interdiction zone." In response, federal agents

installed monitoring equipment such as lights, sensors, and cameras in communities such as Nogales, as well as in San Diego and the El Paso area (Davidson 2000; Nevins 2002). More rural communities such as San Luis in southern Yuma County and Sasabe in southern Pima County, Arizona, are also now the sites of large drug raids (Hawley 2005; Marek 2005).

Perhaps most important in the destabilization and transformation of rural settlements in the border region of Arizona and New Mexico have been border control policies that have directed unauthorized immigration to these places. Beginning in 1993, the U.S. Border Patrol launched major crackdowns in urban centers such as El Paso (Hold the Line, 1993), San Diego (Operation Gatekeeper, 1994), and Nogales (Operation Safeguard, 1994). The idea was to direct efforts at urban centers to push immigrants to rural settings. This, it was believed, would make it easier to spot illegal immigrants and to make illegal immigration more costly to crossers forced to resort to remote areas (U.S. General Accounting Office 1999).

Yet, these border control policies have only frustrated apprehension efforts. The probability of apprehending Mexican unauthorized immigrants fell from about 20 to 30 percent prior to the implementation of the urban blockades to a low of 5 percent in 2002 (Massey 2005). Mexican towns catering to the burgeoning human smuggling industry have sprouted, seemingly overnight, across the southern Arizona border (Hawley 2005; Marizco 2005). Previously rural areas have suffered tremendous strains on social services. Numerous hospitals and emergency rooms in U.S. rural border communities have closed because they can no longer afford to absorb the cost of providing medical care to undocumented immigrants, many of whom now die in the desert (U.S.–Mexico Border Counties Coalition 2002). Social relations have also been strained to the breaking point. Nearly 500 volunteers have anointed themselves civilian border patrol agents—some of them moving from other parts of the country to the U.S.–Mexico border—in an attempt to apprehend unauthorized immigrants (Jordan 2005). In their determination to stop the flow of immigration, more than twenty chapters of Minutemen have sometimes created a climate of hostility and intimidation for legal Mexican American citizens in many communities of all four border states (Frontera NorteSur Online 2005; Marek 2005).

Immigration, drug, and border control policies have contributed to the expansion of border quality-of-life problems (chapter 6 addresses this

issue in greater depth). At the same time, various levels of government have failed to address the growing needs of colonia residents. Colonias suffer neglect for several reasons. For many decades, local governments in the border region have been persistently tax poor (see chapter 2 for a discussion of the historical roots of this economic problem). It should be no surprise, then, that local governments have neglected to provide basic infrastructure and social services in the colonias. In addition, federal resources intended to bolster local governments are seriously inadequate to meet the mounting challenges (see chapter 7 for a detailed discussion of this point). Finally, state governments have mostly been unwilling to confront colonias' concerns. As Wilson and Guajardo (2000) observed, border states have given counties only weak powers over land control and infrastructure financing issues and inadequate funding to build infrastructure and address housing needs. We discuss these challenges and their implications in greater detail in chapters 7 and 10.

In summary, Mexican debt crises and U.S. policies toward the border have transformed rural areas of the border since the 1980s. While previously rural areas were largely untouched by permanent migration, all areas of the U.S.–Mexico border are now forced to cope with the stresses of urbanization, growth, and socio-demographic change.

Summary

From the Spanish colonial period to the present day, California and Texas gateway communities have dominated as prevailing centers of commerce, trade, and population. Southern Arizona and New Mexico, for most of their history a remote region, remained primarily rural until the mid-1980s.

In the last two decades, the landscape of the southern parts of these states has been destabilized and radically transformed. Southern Arizona and New Mexico are anything but the vacant middle of the borderlands. They are populated by communities that have suffered the impacts of trends and policies of the 1980s: population growth and strains on social services due to economic crisis in Mexico and U.S. border policies that have pushed problems to previously rural areas. As a result, these areas have witnessed the expansion of colonias, both on the U.S. and Mexican sides of the border.

2

Economic Development in Southern Arizona and New Mexico

The origins and development of colonias in Southern Arizona and New Mexico are tied closely to the rise of the railroads and the mining and agriculture industries. When these industries emerged in the mid-1800s, they crossed much of the West and fueled urbanization in many places. From Butte, Montana, to Elko, Nevada, to Yuma, Arizona, mining, agriculture, and the railroads were instrumental in shaping urban futures. Why, then, does the connection between colonias and these industries take on added importance?

This chapter answers this question by looking back to when the railroads, agriculture, and mining industries were chiseled out of the vast desert wilderness of southern Arizona and New Mexico. We explain why extractive industries and the railroads had such a profound effect on colonias, and how this influence changed over time as the region's economy evolved.

The chapter begins by describing how early federal investments, beginning in the 1850s, contributed to development of the region. These origins are important because they led to the settlement of colonias and their growth in subsequent years. We explain how and why a narrow economic base in agriculture and mining was established from the early 1900s into the 1960s through investments of federal monies and eastern U.S. corporate capital. Finally, we demonstrate that in more recent years southern Arizona and New Mexico have had difficulty adjusting to an economy based on government employment and the service industry that caters to it. These recent changes are discussed as they affect colonias.

Early Economic Development, 1850s–1912

The federal government's earliest investment in the U.S.–Mexico border region took place in the 1850s. At the time, the border was far removed from the country's political and economic circles, and Anglos were just beginning to settle the region. The city of Phoenix, for example,

was founded in 1868, and Tucson, located 65 miles (104 km) north of the present-day international border, had reached a population of only 8,000 by 1880.

Apaches were dominant in the border region, roaming south into Mexico and as far north as Tucson. The Apaches were a fierce and independent people who resisted settlement in the region, and well-known leaders, such as Cochise, were organizing resistance as early as the 1830s.

Given the country's expansionist policies at the time, it comes as no surprise that the federal government established military forts and camps to protect the New Mexico Territory (of which Arizona was a part) after the Gadsden Purchase of 1853. By 1886 the forts were critical in putting an end to the "Apache menace." The outcome of controlling the Apaches was immediate, and settlers began to expand cattle ranching and irrigation-based farming projects into the region (Goodman 1969).

Although ranching and agriculture grew during this time, they were not new to the Southwest. Spanish American and Mexican American families had been raising livestock and working small-scale farms in the region since the 1500s. However, Aguirre (1975) observed that Mexican ranchers had abandoned many of their haciendas because of Apache plundering, made possible as the Spanish government withdrew protection.

The region remained isolated until improved transportation, communications, and capital investment led to population growth in the 1880s and 1890s (Lyon 1968). Federal subsidies of the railroad industry were especially important in transforming the region. In the 1880s the Southern Pacific Railroad opened Arizona and New Mexico to the extraction and transport of copper and other mineral deposits. Copper, which had been discovered in the Mule Mountains near Tombstone, Arizona, in 1877, was worth only pennies per pound. This meant that inexpensive and accessible transportation was needed to make mining profitable (Myrick 1967).

Arizona and New Mexico border towns and the surrounding unincorporated areas began to develop around the new transportation infrastructure. For example, the twin cities of Nogales, Arizona, and Nogales, Sonora, grew quickly—from a combined population of 2,700 in 1890 to 4,500 in 1898 to 8,000 by 1909. This growth occurred as the twin cities became railroad stops, and commerce grew with the establishment of a Mexican free trade zone for the border region (Sanborn Map

Company 1886–1939; Kearney and Knopp 1995). Similarly, Douglas, Arizona, and the nearby unincorporated communities of Pirtleville and Naco were founded in 1900 and 1901, respectively, to serve the surrounding mines (Arreola and Curtis 1993; Kearney and Knopp 1995). Both of these unincorporated communities are now classified as colonias.

Arizona and New Mexico communities slightly north of the Mexican border grew and prospered because of their location on the Butterfield Overland Mail Stage route. The Atchison, Topeka, and Santa Fe Railroad also contributed to growth because it connected the harbor of Guaymas, Sonora, to El Paso, Texas, which lies on the Rio Grande (Smith 1997). Railroad stops sprang up as trains crossed the rugged countryside and, in short order, became settlements and towns that catered to the surrounding territory. For example, Benson, Arizona, with a population of 600 by 1886, prospered as a shipping point for cattle on the railroad (Sanborn Map Company 1886–1939; Franke 1950). Willcox, Arizona, which was established in 1880 as an overnight stop on the Butterfield Stage route, grew to a community of 500 residents by 1893 as a supply point for rail construction (Sanborn Map Company 1886–1939; Franke 1950). These and other long-standing settlements with similar economic histories are now recognized as colonias by various federal agencies.

During these formative years, Chinese labor was essential for the construction of railroads, but the Chinese Exclusion Act of 1882 put a halt to their immigration. Chinese were smuggled into the United States from Mexico for years to come, as was opium, but the railroads and other industries in the region felt the brunt of the Chinese Exclusion Act because their pool of cheap labor had been cut off (Nevins 2002).

In response, employers sought Mexican laborers. Recruitment dipped well south of the border as Mexicans were brought northward to fill the labor gap. Labor contractors did the recruiting and were so forceful and aggressive in their jobs that they were labeled *enganchadores*, those who use the "hook" to snare workers (Galarza 1964; Massey et al. 2002). The recruitment of Mexican workers is critical to understanding the connection between economic development in southern Arizona and New Mexico and the establishment of colonias. While the Chinese Exclusion Act put an end to the reserve of cheap labor across the entire West, in the border region the Chinese were easy to replace with Mexicans—a cheap and accessible labor force. This distinguished the border region from other parts of the country.

Mexican workers found homes in colonias, which were initially worker

camps located at the fringe of established towns or well outside their environs. Pirtleville, Arizona, for example, is located just west of the larger city of Douglas, and Naco is located on the international border, 8 miles (about 13 km) south of Bisbee. These and numerous other camps became well known among Mexican workers who rarely ventured northward beyond the border region. In 1890, for example, nearly 96 percent of Mexicans in the United States stayed near the border—within 100 miles (160 km)—and this figure remained nearly constant for decades to come (Elac 1972). Thus, it was the recruitment of Mexican labor that led workers to present-day colonias and enabled expansion of the railroads.

The railroads, in turn, stimulated banking and an emerging agricultural industry (Schweikart 1981). For example, the Arizona Bankers Association, which was founded in 1903, fostered economic and population growth by backing mining mills, farmers, and projects such as railroad lines and important irrigation projects such as the Arizona Canal (Lyon 1968; Schweikart 1981). With the new form of transportation and sources of water, cattle ranching and farming became increasingly important in New Mexico and Arizona border counties (Kent 1983; Meyer and Garcia 1987).

Growing Dependence on Mining and Agriculture, 1912–1960s

After admission to the union in 1912, Arizona and New Mexico continued to prosper. But prosperity came at a price, as both states became increasingly dependent on agriculture and copper mining. This narrow economic base was fueled by federal investments and the government's demand for natural resources. Such an artificial (not market-driven) supply-demand relationship propped up the regional economy temporarily but foretold of hard times to come.

After construction of the railroads, Arizona began to dominate the domestic copper industry. Many of the copper production and smelting operations were located in southern Arizona, especially Cochise County (Smith 1934). A few other mining centers were based in western New Mexico, near Silver City, Deming, and Las Cruces (Smith 1934).

From 1880 to 1919, Arizona went from producing only 3 percent to more than 40 percent of the nation's copper (Smith 1934). The fast growth of telegraph and telephone systems during the late 1800s and

early 1900s provided the region with access to a rapidly expanding market. America's involvement in World War I and World War II fueled further copper production. Copper wires were essential to nearly every piece of war equipment, from coils to wires for electronic devices. After both wars, however, the military's need for copper declined significantly. At the same time, corporations based in the eastern United States became less dependent on domestic copper as they relied increasingly on foreign operations in Chile, Canada, and Africa (Austin 1992). By the 1930s, foreign copper mines accounted for one-half of production, and these operations slowly siphoned off Arizona's corner on the market (Smith 1934; Arizona Department of Mineral Resources 1957–1958).

Early indications showed that domestic copper would face mounting foreign competition in the years ahead, making it unwise to rely heavily on the copper industry. Despite this evidence, state agencies with significant political influence, such as the Arizona Copper Tariff Board and the Arizona Department of Mineral Resources, dismissed the need to diversify (Arizona Department of Mineral Resources 1957–1958). This attitude persisted in part because Westerners saw mining as an industry important to the region's economic development. Mining, it was believed, would promote economic diversification. This followed the long-held rationale that primary industries, such as mining, spur growth by stimulating investment in allied industries, such as the construction of processing and fabricating plants (Nash 1990).

Even as foreign operations were expanding, the federal government encouraged greater investment during the early 1950s by granting large subsidies to mining interests. For example, the Defense Production Act of 1951 certified a number of Western mines to participate in a special program that expanded copper output for the U.S. defense industry. The goal was to increase production of copper as quickly as possible. At issue was securing an adequate supply of metals and minerals that were "critical and strategic" to national security. In return, companies were guaranteed a market for their copper for the first few years of production, with a floor price at which the government agreed to purchase the metal. Yet, the program was cut in 1957, due to increased foreign production (Arizona Department of Mineral Resources 1957–1958).

This initial investment, along with the expectation for a defense-related copper market, left many Western mines unable to compete with foreign markets. It set in motion the decline of the southern Arizona and

New Mexico mining industry, which manifested fully in the 1970s. While decreased production led to fewer jobs and diminished incomes for colonia residents, an alternative industry arose.

Agriculture supplied and grew from the mining industry and the railroads that were brought in to serve mining interests. Federally subsidized irrigation technology helped farming develop in the middle Rio Grande Valley near Las Cruces, New Mexico, and the lower Rio Colorado Valley near Yuma, Arizona, as well as Cochise and Luna Counties, located in southern Arizona and New Mexico, respectively (Kent 1983). Irrigated agriculture was well established in the region by the 1920s (Kearney and Knopp 1995).

Agriculture in the border region depended on low-cost Mexican labor, and farming succeeded in the region because of the large labor reserve, comprised mainly of Mexicans who immigrated to the United States in response to the Mexican Revolution of 1910. The revolution proved advantageous for U.S. ranchers and farmers because the number of immigrants more than met the needs of recruiters who, at the time, were traveling deep into Mexico to satisfy labor shortages. During the years 1911–1915, for example, the United States accepted tens of thousands of Mexican immigrants, and by 1920 more than half a million had crossed the border (Lorey 1999; Nevins 2002). Immigration was such that it made an impact on the demographics of Arizona. By the time of the 1900 census, only 11 percent of Arizona's population was Mexican; by 1910, this figure had risen to 14.4 percent (Meyer and Garcia 1987).

Immigration was made easy by the near absence of regulations, and for decades Mexican workers crossed into the United States without constraint. The openness of the border remained until the Immigration Act of 1917, which, in effect, closed the border to Mexicans. Congress imposed literacy requirements and an $8 head tax that excluded nearly all from entering the United States (Geffert 2002).

During World War I, however, labor shortages deepened as many young men in the United States went off to war and others left farms for urban factories. These shortages raised the ire of ranchers and farmers throughout the West, which led the federal government to establish the first formal farm-worker program in 1917 (Geffert 2002). The program opened the border to legal Mexican immigrants once again, excluding them from the Immigration Act of 1917. The farm-worker program was extremely successful, with tens of thousands of workers entering the

country each year. An estimated 500,000 to 1.5 million Mexicans entered the United States during the 1920s (Kearney and Knopp 1995; Nevins 2002).

In the years ahead, agriculture prospered, especially during the Bracero Program, which lasted from 1942 to 1964. The program was developed to address labor shortages during World War II and to assist in the continued development of Southwestern agriculture after the war (Weaver 2001). The program gave farmers legal access to low-cost Mexican labor brought north through worker recruitment (Galarza 1964; Rothenberg 1998). For example, between 1942 and 1945, 168,000 braceros entered the country (Massey et al. 2002).

Even though the Bracero Program eased the northward flow of workers, it unintentionally spurred the flow of undocumented workers (unauthorized immigrants). This occurred because farmers and ranchers were not penalized for stepping outside the law, which meant that undocumented workers could be hired at lower rates and with no bureaucratic requirements (Elac 1972; Massey et al. 2002). The outcome was startling: the number of undocumented workers ousted from the country rose from 57,000 between 1940 and 1945 to 856,000 for the remainder of the decade (Nevins 2002).

The illegal practices of ranchers and farmers, especially those in Texas, developed a culture of unauthorized immigration that carried forward over the years. Given the ease of crossing the border, Mexicans had little incentive to follow the rules either (Massey et al. 2002). Even so, ranchers, farmers, and undocumented workers had no clue of the numerous impacts that would surface from their actions in the decades to come (Lorey 1999; Andreas 2000). Many Mexican farm workers, already familiar with communities north of the border, would permanently settle in colonias.

In addition to favorable immigration policies, the agriculture industry was assisted in other ways. Federal and state agencies were vital in helping agriculture prosper by providing infrastructure subsidies and by funding agriculture extension agents who identified appropriate crops, livestock, and other forms of agricultural development (Ward 2000, 2003). Although agriculture remains important today in southern Arizona and New Mexico, it employs few workers. Even with irrigation projects well established, employment in agriculture has declined since the late 1950s and early 1960s.

From the 1960s to the Present:
Difficult Transition to a Service Economy

The late 1950s and early 1960s marked a profound change in the economic base of southern Arizona and New Mexico. Employment in mining and agriculture declined significantly and was replaced by a service economy catering to border trade and government employment (Lorey 1999). But these industries have failed to compensate for losses in higher-paying jobs, especially in mining, which was nearly always unionized. Lower-paying jobs, in turn, contributed to the expansion of poor, informal settlements—colonias—on both sides of the U.S.–Mexico border.

The end of the Bracero Program in 1964 left many Mexican farm workers unemployed, up to an estimated 50 percent in Nogales, Sonora (Baerrensen 1971). This had significant adverse impacts on trade and commerce in U.S. border communities, where many Mexican agricultural workers traveled north of the border.

As discussed in chapter 1, the Mexican government responded to massive unemployment by launching the Programa Nacional Fronterizo (National Border Program) in 1961 for tourism development and the Border Industrialization Program in 1965 to promote maquiladora development. The programs began to stimulate growth in Mexican border cities by the mid-1960s (Kearney and Knopp 1995). Population growth helped transform the economic base of communities just north of the Mexican border, from extractive economies to more service-oriented ones (De Gennero 1987). Yet, these service and retail jobs have not compensated for losses in higher-paying industries. In the nine rural counties of Arizona and New Mexico that border Mexico, average per capita income in 1999 was 77 percent of the respective state average, down from 82 percent in 1989, according to the U.S. Census Bureau (1990, 2000).

Today, wages in the mining industry significantly outpace those in business services and retail trade (fig. 2.1). But most mining jobs in Arizona and New Mexico have disappeared and claim only a fraction of their previous level. At the same time, the number of jobs in services and retailing has grown but the wages lag well behind extractive industries such as mining. These trends hold for both Arizona and New Mexico.

What is perhaps most striking about the new, service-based economy of U.S. rural border counties is the prevalence of government employment. Approximately 25 percent of the Arizona rural border county

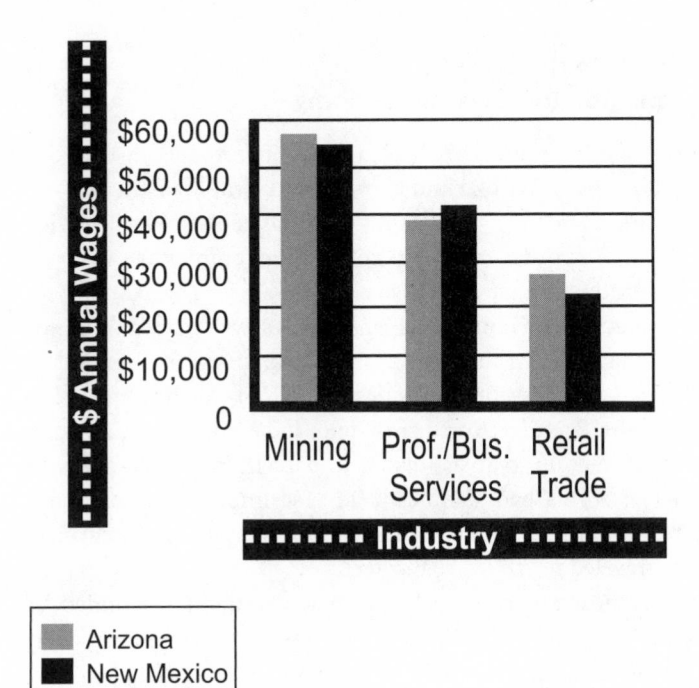

Figure 2.1 Average annual wages for selected industries in Arizona and New Mexico, 2005. Source: U.S. Department of Labor (2006)

workforce was employed in government-related employment in 2000, compared with only 15 percent for the nation and 15 percent for the state of Arizona.[1] New Mexico, a more rural state, has a larger proportion of government workers, at 23 percent of the workforce.

Many of the professional and service jobs created since the 1950s are tied to services required by government employees, especially the U.S. military. In the border region of Arizona and New Mexico, these places include Fort Huachuca in Cochise County, Arizona, Holloman Air Force Base and White Sands Missile Range in Otero County, New Mexico, and the Yuma Proving Ground and Marine Air Station in Yuma County, Arizona.

After World War II, Fort Huachuca expanded significantly. In 1954 it became the site of the U.S. Army Electronic Proving Ground. Its mission as a testing center for electronic devices spurred rapid population growth in Sierra Vista, Arizona, from 3,121 residents in 1960 to nearly 40,000

today (Patch 1962). Holloman Air Force Base, founded originally as the Alamogordo New Mexico Army Air Field in 1942, also gained prominence. The city of Alamogordo grew from a 1950 population of 6,783 residents to 35,582 in 2000 (U.S. Census Bureau 2000). Similarly, the city of Yuma grew from 6,000 residents in 1940 to 24,000 in 1960 to more than 75,000 residents today, due to employment of the Yuma Proving Ground and Marine Air Station in air force and military equipment testing equipment (Kearney and Knopp 1995).

Counties in all states bordering Mexico grew to be heavily dependent on defense spending. By the mid-1960s, the U.S. Department of Defense was spending $1.68 billion in counties along the Mexican border, more than the investments of all other federal departments and agencies in these counties combined (Nathan 1968). This defense-dependent economy has benefited narrow segments of the population, as the majority of high-paying jobs have gone to places with military investment and government income. For example, in 2000 the armed forces employed 22 percent of the population of Sierra Vista; 12 percent of the population of Alamogordo; and 7 percent of the population of Yuma. These figures compare with 3 percent for all rural border counties combined (U.S. Census Bureau 2000). Border communities and unincorporated colonias along the border have not enjoyed this targeted economic prosperity.[2]

At first glance, it seems that dependence on defense employment mirrors Arizona's early reliance on military forts and camps. Yet, today's situation is strikingly different. Whereas nineteenth-century forts protected Arizonans in areas plagued by the Apache raids, modern military installations serve a national purpose. As such, they are not closely connected to the region. For example, Holloman Air Force Base and Fort Huachuca are national testing and training facilities, and their infrastructure investments do not extend far beyond the installations. Military and defense investments have created dense clusters of wealth that exclude many people in peripheral communities. Employment and opportunity have been confined to a few.

Summary

Urban settlements have always had their roots in economic functions, from farming to manufacturing, commerce, and trade, and the colonias of southern Arizona and New Mexico are no exception. This chapter

explored the economic underpinnings of colonia settlement and development and traced the economic history of the region from the mid-1880s to the present.

This history builds on an economic rationale that swept across the United States during the second half of the nineteenth century and into the twentieth century. In the western United States (west of the Rocky Mountains), it involved satisfying the demand for minerals and food brought about by a rapidly growing population in the eastern half of the country that was becoming increasingly urban. Growth in the East and natural resources in the West led to a complementary supply-demand relationship, and the railroads were the critical link that brought supply and demand together. And all four industries, agriculture, ranching, mining, and the railroads, needed a vast reserve of labor.

The Chinese Exclusion Act of 1882 played a critical role in distinguishing the settlement and development of colonias in southern Arizona and New Mexico from other areas of the West. Chinese laborers, who were first brought to the United States at the close of the Civil War, were used extensively throughout the West, especially in mining and the railroads. But the Chinese Exclusion Act meant that this labor pool dried up, which led to labor shortages. In the border region, ranchers, farmers, and mining and railroad interests responded by bringing Mexican labor northward through aggressive recruitment programs, and this set in motion settlement of colonias, which in most cases were initially worker camps.

In the years that followed, the economies of southern Arizona and New Mexico evolved from a narrow base in mining and agriculture through the mid-1900s to a reliance on the Department of Defense and service industries more recently. Colonias have also weathered these changes, experiencing periods of prosperity through the first half of the twentieth century. In recent decades, however, the quality of life has suffered and in many cases continues to fall. This downward turn is linked to the changing employment base, which was dominated early on by natural resources extraction and the demand for unskilled workers but has become a specialized economy that requires a more educated workforce.

The worsening conditions in colonias are also anchored in immigration policies that have aggravated the situation over the years. There is no doubt that the United States has a long and contradictory relationship with Mexico, and immigration policy is just one way that it surfaces.

Policy has moved a long way from the Immigration Act of 1917. In these early years, Mexican immigrants crossed the border with little difficulty, mainly to serve the needs of agriculture. But over the years the U.S. government has repeatedly tightened, then eased, then tightened the flow of immigrants. Most recently, the border has become akin to a militarized zone, complete with flood lamps, high-technology surveillance equipment, and hundreds of patrol officers lining the border, all to keep workers on the southern side (Andreas 2000; Nevins 2002).

Ultimately, it is the human costs of immigration policy that are important, especially as they impact colonia residents. The nature and depth of these impacts are examined in the chapters to come.

3

The Social and Economic Characteristics of Colonias

There are 227 formally recognized colonias scattered across the rugged countryside of southern Arizona and New Mexico. Many of these colonias were founded more than a century ago and owe their origins to economic development in the region, especially the growth of agriculture, mining, and the railroads that required a vast reserve of Mexican workers. But these industries did more than shape the region's economy, they affirmed social norms of the day that called for the segregation of Mexicans (as well as African Americans, Native Americans, and Chinese) within neighborhoods of towns and cities, at the outskirts of town, or in more remote locations (Heyman 1993; Bustamante 1998; Chávez 2005). Many of these communities are now recognized officially as colonias.

These historic underpinnings were discussed in chapters 1 and 2, and this chapter turns to current conditions in colonias. Our aim is to provide a comprehensive assessment of the social and economic dimensions of colonias of southern Arizona and New Mexico. We also illustrate how these conditions have changed over time.

Bringing this information forward, however, is not an easy task. The reporting of social and economic data can mask the distinctive character of colonias and give the false impression that they are a homogenous group of communities. For example, poverty and deprivation apply to most colonias, but several have done quite well and others have been successful in promoting community development. While many colonias date back to territorial times, others are only a few years old. The majority are rural, agrarian settlements, although some are located near or adjacent to large cities. Chapter 4 discusses the diversity of colonias in more detail.

With regard to the changing conditions of colonias, the lack of data makes a comprehensive assessment of colonias difficult. Much of the problem results from the lack of formal enumeration districts (geographic units) called "colonias." That is, there is no spatial designation

comparable to the "county," "census tract," or "census block," and the U.S. Census Bureau is just now defining boundaries for colonias (Ratcliffe 2001). Although the state of Texas has made more progress in defining the spatial dimensions of colonias, this has not been the case in Arizona and New Mexico.

The difficulty in data compilation may explain, in part, why there is little published research that documents the quality of life in Arizona and New Mexico colonias. Specific characteristics, such as infrastructure and land development, have been dealt with (Donelson and Holguin 2001a, 2001b; Lemos et al. 2002), but by design these analyses were narrow in scope. Both the U.S. Department of Housing and Urban Development (HUD; 2004a) and the U.S. Environmental Protection Agency (EPA; 2003a, 2003b) have assembled some data that describe conditions in Arizona and New Mexico colonias but, by their own admission, data are sketchy at best.

Here we respond to this deficiency by describing the social, economic, and housing characteristics of colonias in 1990, 2000, and 2005. The chapter is divided into two sections. We first provide an overview of Arizona and New Mexico colonias and then turn to an assessment of unincorporated colonias. We focus on unincorporated colonias because they lack local government representation and often face the most difficult circumstances when launching community development efforts.

An Overview of Arizona and New Mexico Colonias

The formal designation or definition of colonias in Arizona and New Mexico follows guidelines set forth by the federal government. The U.S. Department of Agriculture Rural Development and HUD define colonias as incorporated and unincorporated communities near the U.S.–Mexico border that experience physical infrastructure deficiencies and/ or housing problems (U.S. Department of Housing and Urban Development 2004a). According to these two federal agencies, colonias must be located in one of the four states bordering Mexico and be within 150 miles (240 km) of the U.S.–Mexico border. The EPA uses different locational requirements. The agency has two programs for financing and implementing border infrastructure projects, the North American Development Bank and Border Environmental Corporation Commission,

which were funded with the passage of the North American Free Trade Agreement in 1994. These programs commit resources to communities within 62 miles (100 km) of the U.S.–Mexico border.

Given their infrastructure deficiencies, most colonias are very poor. The broad definition of colonias, however, has opened federal agencies to criticism. To obtain the colonia designation, counties or local governments simply pass a resolution that identifies specific neighborhoods or places as needing infrastructure. While the designation process provides flexibility, enabling counties and local governments to prioritize areas for federally funded infrastructure projects, critics charge the designation process is too open-ended. They argue that it enables wealthier communities that lack only minimal infrastructure to organize and lobby county governments for scarce resources. Critics believe that the colonia definition should be limited to the image popularized by the media and nongovernmental organizations, that of poor settlements of Mexican Americans living in shoddy housing, without clean water, electricity, and indoor plumbing.

Yet others say the broad federal definition is appropriate because it enables communities to mediate negative impacts brought by proximity to the border. They argue that communities near the border suffer from a lower quality of life because they take on the socio-economic problems brought by the growing integration of the U.S. and Mexican economies. For example, quality-of-life impacts include bankruptcies of community hospitals near the border that have had to treat unauthorized immigrants and strained public schools that have difficulty handling the complex educational needs of foreign-born residents.

Regardless of the critique, the definition of colonias has held since passage of the National Affordable Housing Act of 1990, which set aside funding for colonias. Given this definition, HUD designated a total of 87 colonias in Arizona and 140 in New Mexico (U.S. Department of Housing and Urban Development 2004a). Of those in Arizona, seven clusters of colonias are located on the sovereign lands of various Indian tribes and are excluded from analysis because of their special circumstances. Of the eighty colonias that remain, twenty-six are incorporated cities and towns and the remaining fifty-four are unincorporated. In New Mexico the distribution of incorporated versus unincorporated colonias is quite different. In this case, only thirteen incorporated villages, towns, or cities are colonias, one-half the number in Arizona. In New Mexico, there are 127 unincorporated colonias, nearly 2.5 times as

many as in Arizona. In sum, the analysis targets a total of 220 colonias across both states: 39 are incorporated and 181 are unincorporated.

Figure 3.1 shows the location of colonias in Arizona and New Mexico. The map illustrates the larger number of colonias in New Mexico versus Arizona. These are clustered near Interstate 10 from El Paso, Texas, to Las Cruces, New Mexico, then northward up the Rio Grande Valley and along the western boundary of New Mexico. Arizona colonias cluster in the southeastern corner of the state, but many are found in the western portion of the state in Yuma County. The appendix lists the names of Arizona and New Mexico colonias.

Tables 3.1 and 3.2 present population and income data for Arizona and New Mexico colonias for the years 1990, 2000, and 2005. Data for 1990 and 2000 come from the U.S. Census Bureau, while 2005 data are estimates.[1] Both tables report total population and the percentage of population that is Hispanic and foreign born. Hispanics are defined broadly by the Census Bureau to include all persons who claim Hispanic and/or Latino ethnicity. The Census Bureau is specific about the definition of the foreign population. In the simplest terms, it includes all persons who are not citizens of the United States at birth. In the U.S.– Mexico border region nearly all of the foreign-born population consists of Mexican nationals. In 2000, for example, Mexican nationals in the border cities of Nogales and Douglas, Arizona, accounted for 98 percent and 98 percent, respectively, of the foreign-born population. In New Mexico, 98 percent of Lordsburg's foreign-born population and 99 percent of Sunland Park's foreign-born population are Mexican nationals (U.S. Census Bureau 2000). All four of these cities are federally designated colonias. Tables 3.1 and 3.2 also list median household income (in current dollars), which serves as a measure of disposable income and earning capacity.

Table 3.1 presents data for Arizona colonias. The values listed include data for twenty-five incorporated and forty-eight unincorporated colonias, or more than 92 percent of the total number of colonias in the state. The demographics in Arizona colonias are quite dynamic (table 3.1). As of 2005 the total estimated population equaled 363,585, a 60 percent increase from the 1990 total population. This puts the growth trend on par with the state of Arizona, where total estimated population grew by 63 percent during the same period. But rates of population growth over time differ between incorporated an unincorporated colonias. Incorporated colonias grew by 56 percent, while unincorporated colonias grew

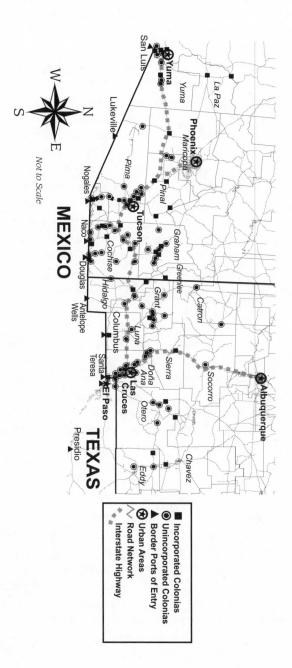

Figure 3.1 Location of the colonias of Arizona and New Mexico

Table 3.1

Population and Income of Arizona Colonias, 1990–2005

	Total population	Percent Hispanic	Percent foreign born	Median household income ($)
1990				
Colonias				
Incorporated	161,067	44.9	15.0	18,841
Unincorporated	66,456	38.9	14.9	19,592
Total	227,523	41.9	14.9	19,217
State	3,655,228	18.6	7.6	27,540
2000				
Colonias				
Incorporated	221,427	46.4	16.8	28,483
Unincorporated	96,804	43.2	17.6	29,516
Total	318,231	44.8	17.2	29,000
State	5,130,632	25.2	12.8	40,558
2005				
Colonias				
Incorporated	251,607	47.1	17.7	33,304
Unincorporated	111,978	45.4	19.0	34,479
Total	363,585	46.3	18.4	33,891
State	5,939,292	28.5	15.4	47,067

Data are for twenty-five incorporated colonias (one colonia was not included because its boundaries and legal status changed from 1990 to 2000) and for 44 unincorporated census units that comprise forty-eight unincorporated colonias. Six of the fifty-four unincorporated colonias were excluded because: (1) census boundaries overlapped with adjacent cities and towns; (2) census block group or census designated place boundaries for the same geographic location were substantially different between 1990 and 2000; or (3) the Census Bureau did not collect comprehensive demographic data for the area.

Source: U.S. Census Bureau (1990, 2000)

by 69 percent. This rate of growth is impressive, but unincorporated colonias claim only a small percentage of the total colonia population. In 1990 they accounted for only 29 percent of total population, reaching 31 percent by 2005.

Hispanics and the foreign-born population claim a significant share of the Arizona colonia population (table 3.1). This is demonstrated by examining differences between the percentage of Hispanics and foreign-born populations living in colonias versus the state as a whole. Hispanics

Table 3.2
Population and Income of New Mexico Colonias, 1990–2005

	Total population	Percent Hispanic	Percent foreign born	Median household income ($)
1990				
Colonias				
Incorporated	18,299	53.0	11.7	15,095
Unincorporated	71,253	47.2	10.5	22,015
Total	89,552	50.1	11.1	18,555
State	1,515,069	38.1	5.3	24,087
2000				
Colonias				
Incorporated	27,765	54.0	15.6	23,493
Unincorporated	92,091	51.2	13.8	29,401
Total	119,856	52.6	14.7	26,447
State	1,819,046	42.1	8.2	34,133
2005				
Colonias				
Incorporated	32,498	54.4	17.5	27,692
Unincorporated	102,510	53.3	15.4	33,094
Total	135,008	53.9	16.5	30,393
State	1,928,384	44.1	9.7	39,156

Data are for nine incorporated colonias in 1990 and ten in 2000. Four incorporated colonias are excluded for 1990 and three for 2000 because the Census Bureau did not compile data. The table presents data for 41 unincorporated census units that comprise ninety-three unincorporated colonias. Thirty-four of the 127 unincorporated colonias were excluded for the reasons listed in table 3.1.

Source: U.S. Census Bureau (1990, 2000)

accounted for 41 percent of the total colonia population in 1990 but only 19 percent of the total state population. Thus, the proportion of Hispanics in colonias was more than double that of the state average. By 2005 the difference had narrowed slightly: the colonia Hispanic population equaled 46 percent, while for the state Hispanics accounted for nearly 29 percent of the total population.

The percentage of the foreign-born population residing in incorporated and unincorporated colonias was nearly identical in 1990, equaling

15 percent. This was nearly twice the statewide value of 7 percent. Between 1990 and 2005 the foreign-born population rose in colonias, but it grew even faster across the state. By 2005, nearly 19 percent of colonia residents were foreign born, whereas over 15 percent of the Arizona population was foreign born.

The magnitude of these differences carries over to median household income (table 3.1). The 1990 median household income for colonias equaled $19,217 compared with $27,540 for the state (in current dollars). These figures indicate that colonia households would have to earn 43 percent more to equal the state median income. Colonia incomes grew over time and by 2005 equaled $33,891, but the gain was not nearly enough to offset the differential with the state. By 2005 median household income across Arizona was $47,067, meaning that colonia households would have to increase earnings by 39 percent to match statewide median household income.

The data reported in table 3.2 were compiled from 102 New Mexico colonias (73 percent of the total 140) for 1990 and 103 colonias (74 percent) for 2000 and 2005. The population in colonias of New Mexico is growing faster than the state overall. Between 1990 and 2005, total colonia population grew by 51 percent, while the New Mexico population increased by 27 percent. In absolute terms, most of this growth occurred in unincorporated colonias, which grew by 31,257 residents (44 percent) during this 15-year interval. In percentage terms, however, incorporated colonias grew the most, with a 78 percent increase.

The information in table 3.2 demonstrates that Hispanic and foreign-born populations play a critical role in colonia society, especially in New Mexico. For colonias the percentage of total population claimed by Hispanics rose from 50 percent in 1990 to 54 percent by 2005. For New Mexico, the Hispanic population grew from 38 to 44 percent of the total population. The foreign-born population grew by 5.4 percent in colonias during the 15-year period and by 4.4 percent for New Mexico.

In addition, the median household incomes in New Mexico colonias lag behind the state overall (table 3.2). This is especially the case in incorporated colonias. For the state, median household income grew by $15,069 (in current dollars) from 1990 to 2005, an increase of 63 percent. Incorporated colonias fared much worse. In 1990 median household income was $8,992 less than across the state. By 2005 incomes in incorporated colonias had risen by 83 percent from 1990 but the gap with state

incomes actually widened. This means that households in incorporated colonias would have to earn 41 percent more to equal median household income statewide.

The data reported above provide an overview of population and income characteristics for Arizona and New Mexico colonias. Populations in colonias of both states are growing rapidly, with those in Arizona on par with the state overall (one of the fastest growing states in the country), but in New Mexico population growth in colonias outpaced the state by a wide margin. The Hispanic and foreign-born populations are significantly larger than across both states, a characteristic that is common of all colonias in the border region. Yet, the Hispanic presence in Arizona and New Mexico is far less than in Texas colonias, where government sources place the percentage of Hispanics much higher.[2] Median household incomes in Arizona and New Mexico colonias lag well behind both states, indicating the economic hardships that confront residents.

The Characteristics of Unincorporated Colonias

The preceding discussion demonstrated that the population characteristics of incorporated and unincorporated colonias differ significantly. This is especially the case with income distributions. These differences are pivotal considering that incorporated colonias have local governments that, in many cases, provide more services, revenues, and opportunities than in unincorporated colonias. Therefore, in this section we provide a detailed analysis of unincorporated colonias. Social and economic characteristics are examined first, and a discussion of housing quality follows.

Table 3.3 presents variables that describe the quality of life in unincorporated colonias of Arizona and New Mexico. Two variables are economic measures: the percent of population below the poverty line and per capita income. Two impediments to upward mobility in the workforce are the lack of a high school education and the percent of population speaking Spanish at home, a measure that is highly correlated with the lack of English-language proficiency. The final two measures reveal additional challenges: the percentage of persons employed in farm work and the dependency ratio, which measures the social burden placed on the working-age population.

The quality of life in unincorporated colonias of Arizona and New Mexico lags well behind their respective statewide averages (table 3.3). As of 2005 over 21 percent of Arizona's unincorporated colonia population

Table 3.3

Social and Economic Characteristics of Unincorporated Colonias in
Arizona and New Mexico, 1990–2005

	1990	2000	2005	State 2005
Arizona				
Percent below poverty	23.3	22.0	21.3	13.0
Per capita income ($)	8,551	12,839	14,982	23,682
Percent high school	70.6	66.8	64.9	82.2
Percent Spanish spoken	35.0	38.0	39.6	22.2
Percent farm employment	14.6	6.1	1.8	0.01
Dependency ratio	78.1	76.2	75.2	59.2
New Mexico				
Percent below poverty	22.8	23.2	23.4	17.3
Per capita income ($)	9,221	13,981	16,361	20,269
Percent high school	67.4	69.9	71.1	80.8
Percent Spanish spoken	45.0	46.2	46.8	29.1
Percent farm employment	12.4	4.3	0.25	0.01
Dependency ratio	75.6	74.0	73.2	64.6

For Arizona, data are for 44 unincorporated census units that comprise forty-eight colonias; six of the fifty-four unincorporated colonias were excluded because data were unavailable. For New Mexico, there are 41 unincorporated census units, comprising ninety-three colonias. Thirty-four of the 127 unincorporated colonias were excluded for the reasons listed in table 3.1.

Source: U.S. Census Bureau (1990, 2000)

and 23 percent of New Mexico's colonia population lived below the poverty line. The federal government defines poverty levels on a sliding scale that depends on family size. For example, in 2005 the poverty line for a family of four was an annual income of $19,350 and the level for a single person was $9,570 (U.S. Department of Health and Human Services 2006).

Per capita income goes hand in hand with poverty statistics because it indicates the earning capacity of the colonia population. A wide gap exists between residents of unincorporated colonias and others living in Arizona and New Mexico (table 3.3). As of 2005, Arizona colonia residents earned $8,700 less per person than across the state, and in New Mexico the difference was $3,908. This means that colonia residents needed to earn 58 percent more income per person in Arizona and 24 percent in New Mexico to be on par with statewide averages.

Table 3.3 also reports the percentage of colonia residents 25 years and older who have earned a high school degree or general equivalency diploma. These data are important because many employers require high school diplomas and they are also essential for acquiring a college education. In 1990 over 70 percent of Arizona colonia residents had completed high school, but by 2005 this number had fallen to 65 percent. The decline in high school graduation may be connected to the growing foreign-born population in colonias, especially Mexican nationals. High school education is not provided by the government in Mexico, which means it is less common for Mexican citizens to complete high school (Massey and Liang 1989; White et al. 1990). It may also be the case that individuals and families migrating to unincorporated colonias are young and have not had an opportunity to complete high school. In any case, in 2005 17 percent fewer residents of colonias graduated than across Arizona. In contrast, high school graduation rates in New Mexico rose by over 70 percent between 1990 and 2005. Equally important, the gap between New Mexico colonias and the state is less than in Arizona.

English-language proficiency is critical to understanding the long-term social and economic complexion of colonias. Speaking Spanish at home is often used as a measure of social isolation because it approximates the degree to which households are integrated with (or isolated from) the broader Anglo society. In addition, the ability to speak and write English fluently is important in securing better-paying jobs and improving economic mobility through education. Table 3.3 lists the percentage of the population 5 years and older who speaks Spanish at home. In unincorporated Arizona colonias language barriers are substantial, with 35 percent of the population speaking Spanish at home in 1990, a figure that rose to 40 percent by 2005. These percentages are even more significant when compared to the state, where in 2005 only 12 percent of the Arizona population spoke Spanish at home. The problem of linguistic isolation in even more pronounced in New Mexico. In 1990 45 percent of New Mexico's colonia population spoke Spanish at home, and by 2005 this figure had risen to 47 percent, a value nearly 18 percent more than for the state overall.

The rise in linguistic isolation in Arizona and New Mexico's unincorporated colonias may be associated with the growing foreign-born presence (table 3.1). Nearly all of the foreign-born population is comprised of Mexican nationals, and many do not have well-developed English lan-

guage skills. This points to the importance of bilingual education in promoting social and economic integration.

The percentage of the workforce employed in farming (agriculture) is an indicator of education and skill levels among the unincorporated colonia population. Agricultural wages are the lowest in the country (on average) and the work is hazardous, with the rates of injuries and pesticide poisonings higher than in nearly all other occupations. For this reason, those employed in farming do so out of necessity and would likely seek out other employment if possible (Martin and Martin 1994).

Table 3.3 reports the percentage of the working-age population (16–64 years) employed in farming and agriculture in Arizona and New Mexico. In Arizona, 15 percent of colonia residents worked in farming in 1990, but this figure fell to 6.1 percent by 2000 and fell even farther by 2005. In New Mexico, farm employment in 1990 totaled 12.4 percent of the working-age population; by 2005 farm employment had fallen to less than 1 percent.

The decline in agricultural employment for both Arizona and New Mexico unincorporated colonias indicates that the labor force has shifted to other sectors of the economy, especially to urban-based employment. Zúñiga and Hernández-León (2005) documented these changes across the country, and chapter 4 discusses this shift in greater detail for Arizona and New Mexico colonias.

Figure 3.2 illustrates the decline in farm-worker employment. The map displays the percentage of the population employed in farm work in southern Arizona and New Mexico in 1990 and 2000.[3] The decline in agricultural jobs crosses a broad section of both Arizona and New Mexico, and by 2000 farm workers were clustered in only a handful of locations, including Yuma County in the southwestern corner of Arizona and New Mexico's Rio Grande Valley.

Finally, dependency ratios in Arizona and New Mexico are similar (table 3.3). The dependency ratio is a measure of the social burden placed on the working-age population. It is calculated by dividing the dependent-age population (0–15 years plus 65 years and older) by the working-age population (16–64 years). The larger the ratio, the greater the social burden because the working-age population provides day care and public schools for younger dependents and health care and special services for the elderly. For 2005, dependency ratios for unincorporated colonias in Arizona and New Mexico were similar but much higher than across

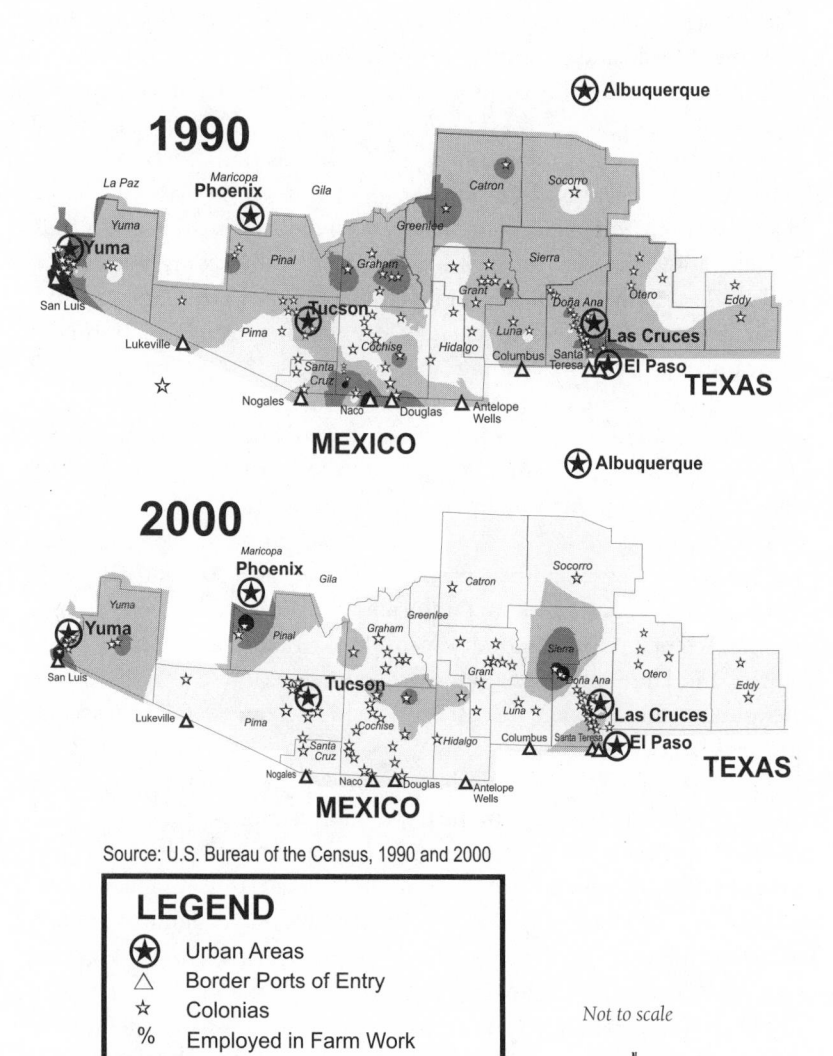

Figure 3.2 The location of farm workers in southern Arizona and New Mexico, 1990 and 2000

both states. For Arizona the dependency ratio is 16 percent lower than that of colonias; in New Mexico the ratio is nearly 9 percent lower. This indicates that working-age colonia residents support a greater number of dependents than other working-age residents across both states, a situation that is made worse by comparatively low incomes and employment mobility skills.

Housing is among the most important necessities, and the poor quality of housing in colonias (along with infrastructure) drew attention at the end of the 1980s. For this reason, federal programs often target housing and infrastructure improvements.[4] However, confronting housing problems is especially difficult in unincorporated colonias because they lack local funding sources and do not have local governmental developmental services such as low-income or affordable housing commissions. Housing is important as well because it offers colonia residents a means of gaining wealth and stability.

Characteristics of the unincorporated colonia housing stock include the number of housing units, housing tenure (owners versus renters), value, age, plumbing, and crowding (table 3.4). As of 2005, there were 46,540 housing units in the unincorporated colonias of Arizona, an average of 2.4 persons per household. Between 1990 and 2005, the number of housing units increased by 70 percent, which is on par with population growth. In New Mexico there were 42,394 housing units in 2005, or 2.4 persons per household. From 1990 to 2005, the number of housing units increased by 53 percent, which kept pace with colonia population growth.

The lion's share of colonia residents in Arizona and New Mexico own their homes (table 3.4). In Arizona 77 percent of unincorporated colonia residents owned their homes in 2005, up from 73 percent in 1990. The rates were even higher in New Mexico: 82 percent owned their homes in 2005, compared to 75 percent in 1990. Despite these high rates of ownership, housing values in unincorporated colonias lag well behind statewide averages. Thus, compared to the broader population, colonia residents derive less wealth from home ownership. For example, as of 2005 the median housing value across Arizona equaled $141,900, while in unincorporated colonias the median housing value was $95,148, or only 67 percent of the state average. Median housing values in New Mexico colonias were slightly higher than in Arizona, $105,406, and housing values increased by 81 percent from 1990 to 2005. As such, the median housing value in New Mexico colonias is 83 percent of the state average.

Table 3.4

Housing Characteristics of Unincorporated Colonias in Arizona and New Mexico, 1990–2005

	1990	2000	2005	State 2005
Arizona				
Total housing units	27,343	40,141	46,540	2,454,069
Percent owner occupied	73.1	75.4	76.6	69.9
Median house value ($)	56,068	82,121	95,148	141,900
Median year built	1974	1978	1980	1985
Percent without plumbing	1.9	1.9	1.9	0.7
Percent housing crowding	13.2	12.3	11.9	2.1
New Mexico				
Total housing units	27,697	37,495	42,394	868,205
Percent owner occupied	75.3	79.4	81.5	71.3
Median house value ($)	58,219	89,677	105,406	127,100
Median year built	1972	1979	1983	1980
Percent without plumbing	1.8	1.7	1.7	1.1
Percent housing crowding	10.0	10.3	10.5	1.3

For Arizona, data are for 44 unincorporated census units that comprise forty-eight colonias; six of the fifty-four unincorporated were excluded because data were unavailable. For New Mexico, there are 41 unincorporated census units, comprising ninety-three colonias. Thirty-four of the 127 unincorporated colonias are excluded for the reasons listed in table 3.1.

Source: U.S. Census Bureau (1990, 2000)

The age of the housing stock suggests the potential for wear-and-tear and obsolescence and, as such, is an important indicator of housing quality. Older housing, for example, is more likely to be equipped with outdated and inefficient heating and cooling systems, substandard insulation, and roofing materials that are weathered and in ill repair. Upgrading housing is costly and places an additional financial burden on homeowners, and such costs weigh heavily on the shoulders of colonia residents.

As of 2005, the median year in which houses were built in Arizona colonias was 1980 (table 3.4) and the colonia housing stock was 5 years older than across the state. In New Mexico, however, the colonia housing stock is younger than across the state. As of 2005, the median year that houses were built was 1983, while that for New Mexico was 1980.

The presence or absence of plumbing is another indicator of hous-

ing character. The presence of plumbing says little about its quality or whether in-house plumbing is connected to central sewer systems (versus septic tanks), but this variable indicates whether households go without plumbing facilities altogether—an important issue for family and public health. For Arizona unincorporated colonias, the percentage of housing units without plumbing remained constant at 1.9 percent from 1990 to 2005. This means that as of 2005, 884 housing units (of a total 46,540) were not equipped with indoor plumbing. In contrast, less than 1 percent of the Arizona housing stock lacked plumbing. In New Mexico, 2 percent of colonia housing units, or 721 dwellings, were without plumbing in 2005, indicating a slight improvement since 1990 and similar to the statewide average.

Finally, table 3.4 provides information on housing crowding, one of the most important indicators of housing quality because it indicates how well households "fit" with the housing they occupy and, as such, gets at issues of affordability and (un)met housing needs (Meyers et al. 1996). Crowding is measured by the number of persons per room, where one person or less (on average) per room is considered optimal and as more people occupy a single room, the level of crowding grows. Table 3.4 lists the percentage of housing units (owner and renter occupied) where the number of persons per room is greater than one. In Arizona's unincorporated colonias, crowded housing is common, accounting for 13 percent of units in 1990. The percentage of crowding fell to 12 percent by 2005 but still compares poorly with the state of Arizona overall, where only 2 percent of the housing stock was overcrowded in 2005. The situation in New Mexico unincorporated colonias is much the same. In this case, 10 percent of the housing stock was overcrowded in 1990, and this figure rose slightly to 11 percent in 2005. In the same year, only 1 percent of New Mexico's housing stock was considered overcrowded.

These data indicate that overcrowded housing is widespread in Arizona and New Mexico colonias. Even though overcrowding declined in Arizona and rose slightly in New Mexico in percentage terms, the number of dwellings increased significantly from 1990 to 2005, indicating that in absolute terms far more households are affected by crowding than in the past. These data also suggest that while the number of persons per household is nearly identical with state and national levels (2.4 persons), colonia housing has fewer rooms per dwelling. This raises concerns about the ability of colonia residents to buy or rent adequate housing, which is reflected in the lower median values of their homes.

Summary

Much of the poverty and deprivation of southern Arizona and New Mexico is found in the region's colonias. These are the settlements, small and large, rural and urban, that line the U.S.–Mexico border. Despite their numbers (86 in Arizona and 144 in New Mexico) and an estimated population of nearly half a million residents in 2005, little published research has examined quality-of-life issues in colonias.

This chapter responded to this deficiency by documenting the social, economic, and housing characteristics in Arizona and New Mexico colonias. Following HUD guidelines, the chapter began by enumerating colonias and their status as either unincorporated or incorporated communities. With these formal definitions and distinctions in hand, population characteristics were summarized, including total population, the percentage of total population that is Hispanic and foreign born, and median household income (tables 3.1 and 3.2). The total population counts that we report exceed those found in other published sources, even though our numbers likely undercount actual colonia populations. The same holds for the Hispanic and foreign-born population, both of which comprise a significant share of the total colonia population. Finally, even though median colonia household incomes continue to rise, they still lag well behind statewide averages.

While most colonias are confronted with severe poverty and deprivation, they are a diverse set of communities, with social, economic, and housing characteristics as varied as their background and histories. For example, populations range from 75,000 to just over 100 residents; some colonias are affluent and primarily Hispanic, while others house no Hispanics or foreign-born population. In short, it is easy and perhaps convenient to think about colonias as a homogenous group, but in many respects they differ considerably, with poverty and deprivation the common denominator.

The detailed analysis of unincorporated colonias shows that there are many obstacles to overcome as residents organize and mobilize community development efforts. Circumstances have led to lower incomes, fewer job skills, and less upward mobility than statewide populations in Arizona and New Mexico. This has led colonia residents to occupy less expensive (more affordable) housing, most of which is privately owned, rather than rented or leased. But some of this housing stock is of poor quality, with plumbing facilities lacking and overcrowding common.

Perhaps most important, this assessment of colonias reveals that population dynamics are driven in part by the growing presence of the foreign-born population, which is almost exclusively comprised of Mexican nationals. The processes driving the influx of immigrants are discussed in chapters 5 and 6.

4

Urbanization and Colonia Development

As of 2005 there were half a million residents living in 220 colonias in southern Arizona and New Mexico. The majority of these people earn far less than the national average, nearly 50 percent are Hispanic, and many occupy housing that is overcrowded and in ill repair. Given these characteristics, it is tempting to treat all colonias and the people who live in them as a homogenous group. But this perspective ignores the diversity of colonias and their residents.

This chapter examines the development of colonias as urban places and pays particular attention to the differences among them.[1] We begin by looking at the heterogeneity of colonias, especially their differences according to size, economic base, location, history, and interdependency in the regional urban system. We then consider the urbanization of colonias from a historical perspective and examine urbanization trends across Arizona and New Mexico, colonia counties, and a select set of colonias. The chapter concludes with a description of colonia land use and morphology, especially the form and function of rural, agrarian colonias and those near larger urban centers.

Colonia Diversity

A few colonias in Arizona and New Mexico are large incorporated cities, but over 50 percent have populations of fewer than 2000 residents. We begin by describing several of these smaller colonias and then turn to those that are comparatively large. The examples described below reveal the diversity among colonias. While only a few are larger cities, they all differ considerably in racial/ethnic profile, employment base, degree of remoteness, and future prospects. These characteristics point to the uniqueness of place and the importance of treating colonias as individual communities that stand alone, one from the other.

Small Colonias

Lake Arthur is a formally recognized colonia located in southeastern New Mexico. As of 2005, the town was home to 432 residents (U.S. Census Bureau 2006a), of which approximately 66 percent were Hispanic. The residents of Lake Arthur work in agriculture (the region is rich in dairy farming) or commute to jobs in Artesia and Roswell. Artesia is located 19 miles (30 km) south of Lake Arthur on New Mexico Highway 285 and is home to the Navajo Oil Refinery and a range of commercial and retail facilities. Roswell is located about 35 miles (56 km) north of Lake Arthur on New Mexico Highway 285. With a 2005 population of 45,199 (U.S. Census Bureau 2006a), Roswell is a regional center that provides numerous employment opportunities.

Virden, another formally designated colonia, is located in southwestern New Mexico in Hidalgo County, just a stone's throw from the Arizona border on New Mexico Highway 70. Virden is a small, rural village with a 2005 population of 118 residents (U.S. Census Bureau 2006a). Approximately 13 percent of the population is Hispanic. The village has experienced significant population loss in recent years: in 1980 the population was 246 (U.S. Census Bureau 2003a). Nearly everyone works in agriculture or in nearby towns such as Lordsburg, which is located about 32 miles (51 km) to the southeast. The village school has been closed for many years, and there is no indication that it will reopen in the near future—a sure sign of severe population decline.

Located near the California border, the town of Quartzsite, Arizona, is booming. Quartzsite is a designated colonia located in La Paz County, 2 miles (about 3 km) north of Interstate 10 and about 22 miles (35 km) east of Blythe, California. In 1990 the town's population equaled 1,876 residents; by 2005 it had grown to 3,397 residents, an increase of 81 percent (U.S. Census Bureau 2003b, 2006a). Approximately 95 percent of the population is considered "white," and only 5 percent is Hispanic. The town's growth owes much to its location near the interstate highway and its warm climate, which attracts a wave of "snow birds" during winter months. Many travel to Quartzsite in recreational vehicles and claim space in one of the town's numerous RV parks. The town hosts a rock and mineral show each year in January, which continues to grow in popularity, boosting the town's tourist and seasonal trade. Given the country's growing retirement-age population, the future looks bright for Quartzsite.

Many other smaller colonias acquire distinction by their regional setting and history. Those located in New Mexico's Mesilla Valley are a prime example. The Mesilla Valley is a rich agricultural region that stretches south along the Rio Grande from Las Cruces to the Mexican border. Home to about a dozen colonias, the Mesilla Valley is reminiscent of agricultural regions in other parts of the country where numerous small towns dot the landscape, only a few miles apart. The region has a long and colorful history, with many communities founded well over a century ago. Such is the case for Chamberino, which predates the 1853 Gadsden Purchase. Other colonias in the region, such as Anthony and San Miguel, date from the 1880s and served vital roles in the region's agricultural development.

Colonias of the Mesilla Valley are overwhelmingly Hispanic. Many Hispanics settled in the region long before statehood, while others were brought north from Mexico during the twentieth century to work on farms and ranches (see chapter 2). Thus, many families have lived in the valley for several generations. Other colonia residents remained in the region after the 1986 Immigration Reform Control Act granted them citizenship.

The history and agricultural character of many of New Mexico's smaller colonias extends north of Las Cruces through the region's Rio Grande Valley. Here, small and remote colonias such as Rincon, Garfield, and Salem are home to more recent Hispanic immigrants, who work the region's lucrative chile industry.[2] Processing plants and shipping facilities are scattered across the region's agricultural landscape and provide jobs for both long-term residents and migrant farm workers. Housing in these colonias is comparatively new, with manufactured homes comprising a greater share of the total housing stock.

In contrast to the older communities of New Mexico, many smaller colonias of southern Arizona were settled more recently as "wildcat subdivisions." These communities grew out of lax land-use regulations that apply to unincorporated areas of the state. Chapter 7 discusses wildcat subdivisions in greater detail, but here it is important to note that they have contributed to the growing number of colonias in Arizona. The comparatively high cost of urban living is largely responsible for the popularity of wildcat subdivisions because they offer land and housing at prices that lower-income segments of the population can afford.

Larger Colonias

There are only seven colonias in Arizona and New Mexico with populations that exceed 10,000 residents. Among these, Sunland Park, New Mexico, stands out because of its location near two major metropolitan regions. The city is located at the southernmost edge of the Mesilla Valley and abuts the U.S.–Mexico border. El Paso, Texas, hugs the city to the east and Ciudad Juárez (with a population nearing 2 million) is just miles away. For this reason, Sunland Park is far more urban than other New Mexico colonias and has the feel of a low-income suburban community. With a 2005 population of 14,089 (U.S. Census Bureau 2006a), approximately 98 percent of which is Hispanic, Sunland Park is economically diverse, with a wide range of commercial and retail outlets serving the city's population. Nevertheless, many critical problems confront Sunland Park's residents, including poor-quality housing, poverty, and a range of social service needs.

Other large colonias, such as Douglas, Nogales, and San Luis, Arizona, have long been known as border cities. Douglas and Nogales were settled before the turn of the twentieth century and received formal recognition as cities shortly thereafter: Douglas in 1901 and Nogales in 1922. San Luis was founded in 1930 as a port-of-entry to Mexico, and for several decades it remained a small and remote settlement.

Compared to other colonias, all three cities have maintained sizeable populations despite setbacks in the mining and agriculture industries, which played an important role in their growth and development. Census data indicate that as of 2005 the population of Douglas was 16,791, up from 13,058 in 1980 (U.S. Census Bureau 2003b, 2006a). The population of Nogales rose from 15,683 in 1980 to 20,833 in 2005. In San Luis, growth and development are more recent. In 2000 a total of 15,322 people lived in San Luis, and by 2005 the population had grown to 21,646.[3] Hispanics dominate in all these cities, claiming well over 90 percent of each of their populations. This is to be expected, given their settlement history and location on the U.S.–Mexico border. The importance of the transborder economy suggests that these cities will continue to grow for years to come.

Commuting Behavior

Interdependency is common for towns and cities everywhere (Krmenec and Esparza 1999; Esparza and Krmenec 2000), but it plays a critical role in the survival of Arizona and New Mexico colonias. By interdependency we mean that all colonias rely on larger towns and cities for goods, services, and places of employment. This holds especially for smaller colonias because only a few have shopping, commercial services, and jobs available locally, and interdependency keeps them afloat.

Thus, another common feature of colonias in Arizona and New Mexico is that they are tied to the broader urban regional system. Figure 3.1 illustrated the urban system in southern Arizona and New Mexico that serves the needs of colonias. Cities such as Tucson, Las Cruces, and El Paso are major centers, and a network of smaller towns and cities also provide services and job opportunities to colonia residents.

Given the degree of reliance on the urban system, it comes as no surprise that colonia residents spend quite a bit of time on the road. For example, some New Mexico farm workers refer to their cars as *muebles* (furniture), because they spend so much time in them. Tracing the commuting patterns of colonia residents is one way of gauging the extent of interdependence and connectivity in the regional urban system. Table 4.1 reports the commuting behavior of incorporated colonias for 1990, 2000, and 2005. These data show commuting patterns within and outside the county of residence and within and outside the place of residence. The distinction between these two commuting patterns is important because, in the latter case, commuters can leave their place of residence but still work in the same county. Thus, county size plays a role in understanding commuting patterns. While both states are similar in size, Arizona's territory is divided into fifteen counties, whereas New Mexico has thirty-three counties. This means that, on average, commuters in Arizona must travel a farther distance to leave their county of residence. The active working population (total workers) is listed for both states, and other entries represent percentages of the working population.

Commuting behavior differs significantly between Arizona and New Mexico colonia residents (table 4.1). As of 2005, nearly 90 percent of Arizona's colonia population worked in the same county they lived in, down from 93 percent in 1990. In contrast, only 60 percent of New Mexico colonia residents worked in their county of residence in 2005, a

Table 4.1

Commuting Behavior in Arizona and New Mexico Incorporated Colonias, 1990–2005

Commuting behavior	1990 (%)	2000 (%)	2005 (%)
Arizona			
Total workers	34,332	45,989	51,818
Worked in county of residence	93.1	90.2	89.2
Worked outside county of residence	4.8	7.4	8.3
Worked outside state of residence	2.1	2.4	2.5
Living in a place	100	98.2	97.6
Working in place of residence	57.4	65.6	68.3
Working outside place of residence	42.6	32.6	29.3
Not living in place	0	1.8	2.4
New Mexico			
Total workers	5,577	8,477	9,927
Worked in county of residence	69.4	61.7	59.5
Worked outside county of residence	3.8	4.6	4.8
Worked outside state of residence	26.8	33.8	35.7
Living in a place	100	100	100
Working in place of residence	32.5	29.1	28.2
Working outside place of residence	67.5	70.9	71.8
Not living in place	0	0	0

Data are for twenty-four incorporated colonias of Arizona and ten incorporated colonias of New Mexico. Data for 2005 were estimated using a linear extrapolation of 1990 and 2000 data. Yuma, Arizona (the twenty-fifth incorporated colonia), is excluded because of its size and biasing effect. Data limitations prohibited an assessment of commuting for smaller, unincorporated colonias.

Source: U.S. Census Bureau (1990, 2000)

decline of 10 percent since 1990. Over time, a growing number of colonia residents in Arizona and New Mexico traveled longer distances to employment sites. For New Mexico, however, nearly all commuting in 2005 was accounted for by out-of-state travel, where nearly 36 percent of total work trips leave the state. Workers living in Sunland Park account for nearly all (92 percent in 2005) out-of-state trips. This is to be expected due to Sunland Park's proximity to El Paso, Texas, which is a major urban center with more than 600,000 residents.

Table 4.1 also provides information about employment and commuting

by place of residence. As of 2005 slightly more than 68 percent of Arizona colonia residents worked in their place of residence, up from 57 percent in 1990. Although these figures suggest that over time a growing number of workers have found jobs locally, these aggregate trends hide the travel behavior of individual communities, where a sizeable proportion of local populations commute to work. For example, commuting beyond the place of residence was typical for people living in Eloy (67 percent, as of 2005), Gila Bend (58 percent), Mammoth (79 percent), and Marana (89 percent). Commuting beyond the place of residence is far more common among New Mexico colonia residents. For example, as of 2005 most Sunland Park residents worked outside the city (84 percent), and this pattern holds for smaller and more remote places such as Bayard (70 percent), Hope (94 percent), and Lake Arthur (74 percent).

The data presented in table 4.1 indicate that incorporated colonias of Arizona and New Mexico are reliant on the regional urban system, especially for employment. This is expected given the rural setting of many colonias, especially in New Mexico, where work is often found well beyond the local village, town, or city. But there is quite a bit of variability in commuting behavior. People living in smaller and more remote colonias are often forced to travel long distances, at times beyond the county of residence. In other cases, commuting distance is much shorter, especially for those colonias located near major urban centers and large employers, such as military installations, prisons, refineries, dairies, and mines.

Colonia Urbanization

The discussion above highlighted the diversity of colonias with regard to their size, location, history, and regional setting. However, little has been said about the process of urbanization that led to colonia development over a long period of time.[4] Moreover, there is little published research that documents the long-term urbanization of colonias in Arizona and New Mexico. For this reason, this section looks at urbanization patterns from a historic perspective. We begin by considering aggregate patterns of urbanization in Arizona and New Mexico, then turn to colonia counties and a more narrow set of colonias. Figure 4.1 shows the urbanization pattern (total state population that is urban) in Arizona and New Mexico for 1880 through 2000. For comparison purposes, the urbanization trend for the United States is also included.

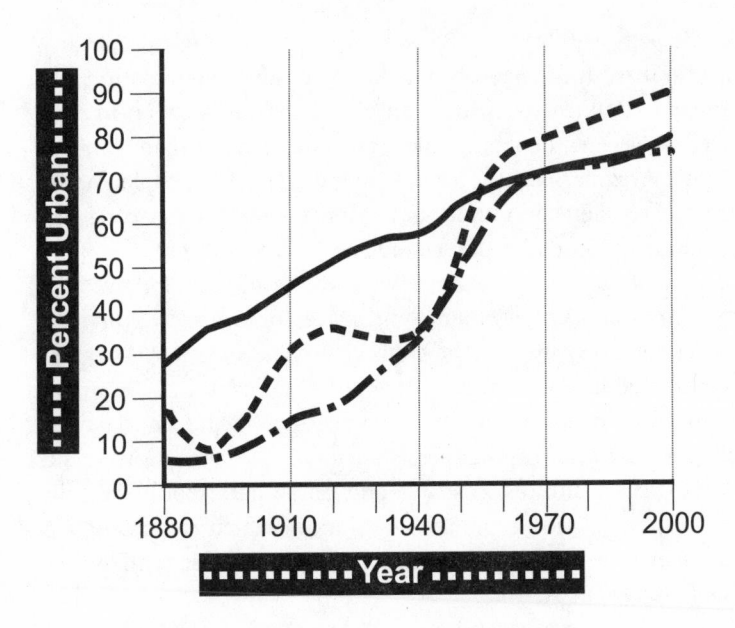

Figure 4.1 Urbanization trends in Arizona and New Mexico, 1880–2000. The figure shows urbanization data from the Census Bureau for 1880 through 2000. "Percent urban" refers to the percent of places that have a population of at least 2,500 residents. *Source:* U.S. Census Bureau (1920–1980, 1990, 2000).

During the past 120 years Arizona and New Mexico have experienced a dramatic transformation that led from predominately rural to urban communities. At the turn of the twentieth century Arizona's total population was about 123,000, with only 16 percent (about 19,700 residents) living in urban places of at least 2,500 residents. Urban settlement was so sparse that even the largest cities housed few people: in 1900, for example, Tucson's population was 7,531 and only 5,544 residents lived in

Phoenix. The picture in New Mexico is somewhat different because early on the state housed more people than Arizona, but the population was predominantly rural. In 1900, for example, slightly more than 195,000 people lived in New Mexico, but only 14 percent lived in urban communities. As with Arizona, even the largest cities claimed few people. In that year only 6,238 residents lived in Albuquerque, the territory's largest city, and 5,603 resided in Santa Fe, the second largest city.

The urban population grew rapidly in the years that followed, as agriculture, mining, and the military presence continued to grow (see fig. 4.1; Lorey 1999). By 1940, as the country prepared for war, Arizona's population neared half a million, with about 25 percent living in urban areas. New Mexico's population topped 531,000, with 33 percent classified as urban. The postwar years witnessed sustained urbanization as migrants flooded the Southwest (Esparza and Carruthers 2000). Thus, by 2000 Arizona's population topped 5.1 million, of which 88 percent was urban, and New Mexico's population exceeded 1.8 million, with 75 percent living in urban areas.

Urbanization in Arizona and New Mexico trailed national trends through the early decades of the 1900s (fig. 4.1). After the 1960s, however, the pace accelerated and mirrored nationwide urbanization rates. But these aggregate data say little about urbanization in Arizona and New Mexico colonias.

To get at this issue, we examine urbanization in counties in which colonias are located.[5] We look at colonia counties because historical urbanization data are unavailable for many colonias and, even at the county level, data prior to the 1940s are difficult to come by. While county-level data are not ideal, they are a good indicator of urbanization trends, especially in New Mexico, where county size is much smaller than in Arizona.

In New Mexico, urbanization in colonia counties has lagged well behind statewide trends over time, although this was not the case early on. As of 1940 the urban population in colonia counties surpassed the state: 35 percent versus 33 percent, respectively. This relationship soon disappeared, however, and by 1960 the percentage of urban dwellers across New Mexico exceeded that of colonia counties. For colonia counties, the urban population was 51 percent, but New Mexico's urban population totaled 66 percent. By 2000 only 57 percent of the population in colonia counties was urban, compared to 75 percent for the state.

Urbanization rates were similar in Arizona. In 1940 only 24 percent of

the population living in Arizona's colonia counties was considered urban, compared to 35 percent for the state overall. By 1960 this figure was 47 percent in colonia counties, while across Arizona 75 percent of the population lived in urban places. As of 2000, 62 percent of population of colonia counties lived in urban places, compared to 88 percent for the state.

This information illustrates the comparatively slow pace of urbanization in Arizona and New Mexico colonia counties. But this is to be expected because many of these counties, and the colonias within them, are rural and lack major employers (industry and services) that contribute to growth and development over time. These trends also demonstrate the dominance of large cities such as Phoenix, Tucson, Albuquerque, and Santa Fe, which draw much of the population growth in both states.

Although data limitations prohibit an examination of all colonias, we can point to the variability in urban growth among a select set of small and larger colonias for 1930 through 2005.[6] Urbanization rates are not available, but looking at absolute population change says much about the heterogeneity of colonias.

Hope and Columbus (located in Eddy and Luna Counties, respectively) demonstrate the differences among smaller New Mexico colonias. The village of Hope has experienced substantial population loss, falling from 275 residents in 1930 to 106 by 2005. Hope is a remote community located 21 miles (34 km) west of Artesia, and there is little to keep people from leaving. In contrast, the village of Columbus remained stable through much of this period, with population rising slightly from 391 in 1930 to 414 by 1980. In more recent years, however, Columbus has witnessed dramatic population growth. From 1980 through 2005 the population grew to 1,841 residents, an increase of 345 percent. Much of this growth is attributed to migration as people seek out rural lifestyles in the southwestern United States. Columbus is also located 3 miles (about 5 km) north of the Mexican border, which adds to its attractiveness.

In Arizona, the communities of Somerton and Thatcher are prime examples of the variability in population growth among smaller colonias. Both colonias were settled as agricultural communities even though they are located far apart (Somerton in the west of the state in Yuma County and Thatcher in the east in Graham County). In 1930 their populations were nearly identical: 891 residents in Somerton and 895 in Thatcher. For several decades population growth in both communities was similar, for

instance, by 1970 Somerton's population equaled 2,225 and Thatcher was home to 2,320 residents. But the similarities have disappeared in more recent years. As of 2005, Somerton's population totaled 10,071, far greater than Thatcher's population of 4,121 residents. The rapid rate of urban growth in Somerton may be explained by economic expansion in the region, especially agriculture, the military, and tourism.

There are few large colonias in New Mexico (Sunland Park is the only colonia with a population exceeding 10,000), but the Arizona cities of Douglas and Nogales demonstrate population growth trends in larger colonias. Douglas has a long history as a mining and border town, and by 1930 the population stood at 9,828 residents. In 1940 the population of Nogales was only 5,135 (data for 1930 were not recorded). This is not surprising, because Nogales served mainly as a point-of-entry to Mexico. But the economic fortunes of these cities led to divergent growth trends. The population of Douglas reached 13,058 by 1980 but fell to 12,905 residents by 1990, as copper mining and refining in the region dwindled. More recently Douglas has experienced a resurgence, and by 2005 the population had reached 16,791 as tourism, education (a community college), and a correctional facility repositioned the city's economic base. In contrast, the population of Nogales has grown steadily over time. By 1980 the city claimed 15,683 residents, and in 2005 the population reached 20,833, surpassing that of Douglas by a wide margin. This reflects the growing importance of border towns in more recent years.

Population data reveal much about the urbanization of colonias over time. While urban populations in Arizona and New Mexico grew rapidly during the twentieth century, colonia counties were left behind. This is not surprising because nearly all of these counties are located far from major urban centers that attract the majority of population growth. Examples of small and larger colonias demonstrate differences in population growth over time. These differences are tied to migration patterns and the economic fortunes of colonias.

Land Use and Colonia Development

While more attention is being focused on understanding the social and economic characteristics of colonias, far less is known about their land use and morphology. The final section of this chapter responds to this deficiency. Urban morphology is the study of places in two dimensions. It deals with the larger patterns of land use that fall within zones or

categories and the arrangement of buildings, streets, and other structures that together comprise the built environment (Gauthiez 2004). As such, local planning and zoning play a significant role in shaping urban morphology because they determine the use of land through zoning designations and height and bulk regulations. Other ordinances and regulations, such as subdivision regulations, housing codes, landscape ordinances, and architectural design codes, also affect the built environment (Hart 1998; Campoli et al. 2002).

The effects of planning and zoning on Arizona and New Mexico colonias are mixed and in many respects contributed to their divergent character. For example, the New Mexico counties of Hidalgo and Luna, which abut Mexico, have little or no land-use regulation that applies to rural areas; only state-level codes and ordinances regulate building standards and water and septic systems. In these counties there is little regulation to shape the form and function of urban places.

In contrast, Doña Ana County in New Mexico has developed a sophisticated system of land-use regulations that apply to unincorporated colonias. First, the county's Extra-Territorial Zoning ordinance regulates development around Las Cruces, one of the nation's fastest-growing metropolitan regions (Doña Ana County 1987). The ordinance established a 5-mile zone surrounding Las Cruces that, in effect, extends the city's jurisdiction well beyond its political boundaries. Second, the county recently established a Village District Zoning designation (Doña Ana County 2005) that bestows special status to historically significant unincorporated places founded prior to 1930. The Village District designation preserves historically significant places by regulating land development. The community of Doña Ana, an unincorporated colonia, has received such a designation. Third, the county regulates land use in the agriculturally rich Rio Grande Valley through its Performance District Zoning designation. Among other things, the Performance District Zone regulates parcel development in many New Mexico colonias, such as Berino, Chamberino, Vado, Rincon, Salem, and Garfield. It is important to remember, however, that many of these land-use regulations came on board long after communities were in place. As such, they will influence future growth and development but will not affect existing conditions.

Land-use planning and zoning also play an important role in Arizona colonias. Cochise County, for example, guides development in unincorporated places through its area plans. These include the Naco Area

Plan (adopted February 1998), Babocomari Area Plan (adopted September 2005), Tres Alamos Area Plan (adopted October 2005), St. David Area Plan (adopted December 2005), and others (Cochise County 2006). These plans regulate the density of development in pursuit of environmental and agricultural preservation. Yuma County uses a similar approach of land-use regulation in unincorporated places through its planning areas (Yuma County 2001). These plans regulate land use in specific corridors such as the Dateland East County Planning Area; Dome Valley–Wellton Planning Area; and the Yuma, Foothills, and South County Planning Area.

Land-use regulations play an important role in shaping the built environment. The examples described above illustrate that many colonias in New Mexico have few regulations, while others benefit from more recent land-use codes. Several counties in Arizona have recently put in place land-development plans that may well affect the future of unincorporated colonias, but the growing number of wildcat subdivisions, made possible by state-level legislation (see chapter 7), is problematic. Some of these wildcat subdivisions have received official status as colonias and help to account for the rising number of colonias in Arizona.

The Morphology of Colonias

Although colonias differ from one another, we develop generalized morphologies for two types of colonias. Our aim is to fill the gap left by the absence of research on the form and function of colonia communities. Our approach is informed by the study of older, more traditional rural subdivisions that are the core of many rural communities and apply to colonias as well (Arendt 1994; Campoli et al. 2002).

The morphology of the first type, the rural, agrarian colonia, is shown in figure 4.2, which summarizes the features of many rural colonias found in agricultural regions of southern New Mexico and Arizona and illustrates the physical characteristics of these older communities. They consist of similarly designed site-built homes (at times, manufactured homes) located on uniform lots that are connected by paved roads, with some having curbs and even sidewalks. It is common to find centralized water and electricity delivery systems in these communities, but septic tanks handle sewage for individual property owners. Propane gas also serves the heating and cooking needs of property owners. Newer residents often occupy manufactured homes or older trailers located at the

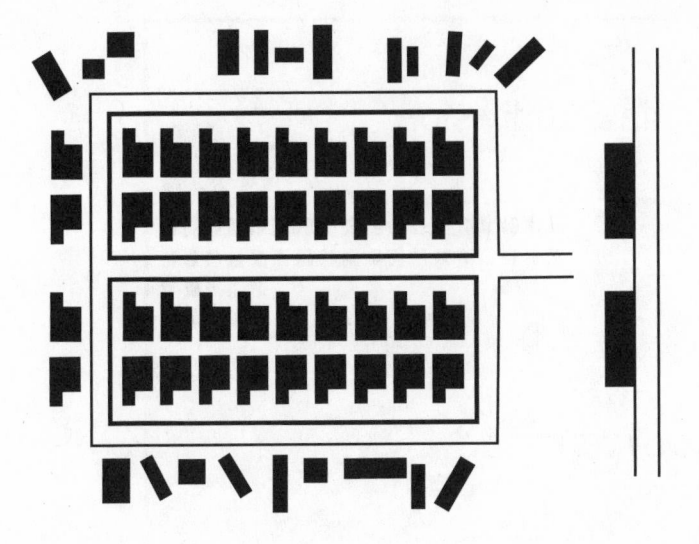

Figure 4.2 The typical morphology of rural, agrarian colonias

periphery of the core neighborhood, often without apparent regulation. As figure 4.2 illustrates, mobile homes are frequently situated ad hoc, unlike the core neighborhood. Access to this peripherally located housing is typically gained via unpaved roads.

A mix of land uses appears nearby, but outside of residential neighborhoods, often beside larger roads and even railroad tracks (shown to the right in fig. 4.2). These include limited retail and commercial land uses, such as local markets, gas stations, restaurants, cafes, laundromats, and the like. The diversity of retail and commercial land uses varies with the size and location of communities. It is common to find elementary schools and post offices in larger rural colonias. Agricultural production facilities may also be located nearby. These include food processing and storage facilities, especially for chile, cotton, and lettuce.

In other instances, colonias are more urban. These types of colonias are located near larger towns and cities. Many of them grew out of the mining industry, which forced Mexicans to live at the fringe of towns but not within them (Bustamante 1998). Thus, many colonias were founded as worker camps and over time grew into their more urban flavor.

Figure 4.3 shows a generalized layout of these urban colonias. Houses are often site built (at times, manufactured homes) and located on uniform parcels connected by improved roads. Some of these subdivisions

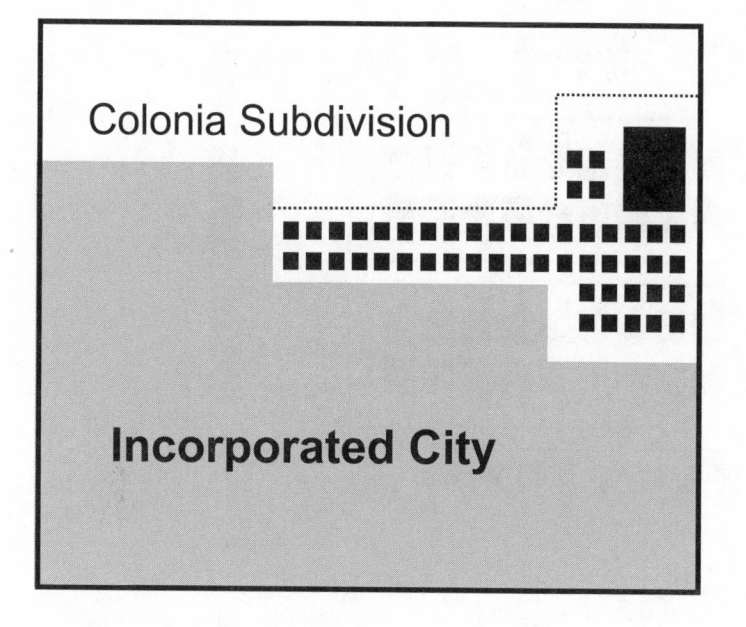

Figure 4.3 The typical morphology of urban colonia subdivisions

have centralized water delivery and sewer services connected to the incorporated city, as well as on-site electric and natural gas delivery. Schools, especially elementary schools, are often found in or nearby colonia subdivisions (upper-right corner of fig. 4.3). Depending on the situation, there may be retail and commercial land uses adjacent to colonia subdivisions, but often goods and services are obtained from the incorporated city.

Figure 4.4 shows representative urban and rural colonias of Arizona and New Mexico. Old Nogales is an urban colonia located adjacent to Tucson, Arizona. Its location near a major city has led to differences in land use and morphology compared to rural colonias. Chamerino is a colonia located in New Mexico's agriculturally rich Mesilla Valley. The older core of the community was developed decades ago and is surrounded by more recent fringe development consisting of manufactured homes. The positioning of these peripheral homes reveals little regularity and abuts the surrounding agricultural district.

Little published research has documented the morphology of colonia communities. The site maps presented in figures 4.2 and 4.3 respond to this deficiency by generalizing the form and function of rural, agrarian

Figure 4.4 The urban colonia of Old Nogales, Arizona (upper), and the agrarian colonia of Chamerino, New Mexico (lower)

colonias, as well as larger and more urban colonias. Given the diversity among colonia communities, subsequent research should consider a broader typology that is based on size, location, and regional setting.

Summary

A growing body of research has examined the social and economic complexion of Arizona and New Mexico colonias, but few studies have explored their diversity, urban roots, and urbanization patterns over time. In this chapter, we began by highlighting the differences between colonias, especially their size, location, history, and regional setting. At issue is ensuring that colonias are recognized as individual villages, towns, and cities, each with its own history, character, and future prospects.

We then assessed urbanization trends in Arizona and New Mexico, colonia counties, and a set of colonias. The pace of colonia urbanization lags well behind statewide averages. This occurs at the broader county level but also for individual colonias. The lack of urbanization is connected to the absence of local employment and the need for community development programs. Yet, other small and large colonias are prospering and their futures look bright.

Most colonia residents are dependent on the regional urban system and find themselves on the road much of the time. This chapter examined interdependency by looking at commuting behavior. We found that people often commute over long distances, especially those who live in small and remote colonias. But there are exceptions: residents of Sunland Park, New Mexico, live only a stone's throw from El Paso, Texas, and other colonias are near major employment sites. In most cases, however, colonia residents must commute longer distances.

Finally, the chapter looked at the morphology of colonias. Land development regulations are absent for many colonias, whereas others are affected by recently approved land-use codes. These diverging levels of local planning and zoning explain, in part, differences among colonias. We also presented two generalized morphologies that apply to rural, agrarian colonias and their more urban counterparts. These capture the rural setting of many smaller colonias and the more urban character of colonia subdivisions located at the fringe of larger incorporated towns and cities.

Regardless of size, location, or history, the majority of colonias are confronted by a range of problems that hamper growth and development. These issues are explored in the following chapters.

Part II
Policies and Community Development

5
National and Binational Policies in the Border Region

Many factors and forces bring growth and prosperity to towns and cities. Chief among these are local industries such as agriculture, manufacturing, and services that provide jobs within the community. Other local factors are important, such as educational facilities, infrastructure, and the quality of housing and amenities. In addition, external (nonlocal) factors such as regional and international competition, interest rates, inflation, and fluctuations in the national economy all affect the local development path. Although communities have some say in how local factors develop, they have comparatively little control over external conditions.

In the case of colonias, another tier of nonlocal factors influences growth and development: policies that affect the border region. These range from immigration and border security policies imposed by the U.S. government to issues of monetary solvency, especially currency devaluation. In the latter case, the Mexican government has devalued the peso twice in recent years, which produced enormous effects in the border region.

This chapter describes federal policies that affect quality of life in Arizona and New Mexico colonias, by providing a historical analysis of how these policies came to life and an indication of their likely effects on colonias. Four federal policies are discussed: the 1986 Immigration Reform and Control Act (IRCA), Operation Gatekeeper and related U.S. border control policies that came on board in the 1990s, and the 1982 and 1994 Mexican peso devaluations. There are certainly other federal policies that come to bear on the border region, but there is general agreement that these four have had the most substantial transborder impacts.

U.S.–Mexico Border Policy Revisited

Much of the turbulence that colors U.S.–Mexico relations is reflected in immigration policies, especially the tension between racism and the country's need for cheap, exploitable labor. Since its inception,

immigration policy in the United States has been positioned on a racist, or nativist, perspective in which the native-born (but not indigenous) population comprised of Anglo Protestants sought protection from what were considered undesirable immigrants, especially Catholics and those from southern and eastern Europe and China (DeLaet 2000; Hing 2004). At issue was ensuring that immigrants' numbers and power remained manageable by the ruling class of Anglo Protestants, who claimed the country as their own. This led to the imposition of quotas and the use of exclusionary devices such as literacy tests.

While nativist policies sought to restrict European immigration, they had an immediate and dramatic impact on the northward migration of Mexicans. The Immigration Act of 1917, for example, all but closed the southern border by imposing a head tax and literacy requirements. The act was met by stern opposition from ranchers and farmers, who forced passage of the country's first farm-worker program in the same year. The farm-worker bill excluded Mexican workers from the requirements of the Immigration Act of 1917, thereby ensuring a sufficient reserve of cheap labor (Geffert 2002; Nevins 2002; Hing 2004).

Restrictive policies that supported a racist agenda culminated in the Immigration Act of 1924, which imposed a strict quota system and required visas to enter the United States (Livingston 1993; Miller and Miller 1996; Magaña 2003). While aimed mainly at Europeans and Chinese, it succeeded in slowing immigration from Mexico, in part because the $10 visa fee excluded many from the formal immigration process. But restrictive policies inadvertently fueled the flow of unauthorized immigrants. This led Congress to establish the U.S. Border Patrol in 1924. The patrol had predecessors; in 1904 the Commissioner General of Immigration appointed seventy-six inspectors who monitored the border on horseback (James 1991; Nevins 2002). But unauthorized immigration escalated precipitously in response to the Immigration Act of 1924, which, in turn, called for increased border security.

While immigration policies sought to sustain the power and authority of the Anglo majority, severe labor shortages pushed policies in other directions. Labor shortages arose during World War I, but it was during World War II that they became critical. This led to the Bracero Program, the largest sustained guest-worker program in U.S. history.

The Bracero Program responded to the demands of farmers and ranchers who sought to keep labor costs low by bringing Mexican workers northward through a formal guest-worker program (Massey and

Liang 1989). The Bracero Program took effect in 1942 and was terminated in 1964, largely because of lobbying efforts by human rights groups that responded to racial tensions with Anglos, substandard housing, and the exploitation of workers, especially poor pay and health issues. During its history the Bracero Program brought more than 4.5 million Mexicans into the United States, where they worked in the agriculture sector (Langham 1992).

The success of the Bracero Program caused the demand for worker visas to outpace the supply by a wide margin. This led to a significant rise in unauthorized immigration and the subsequent imposition of Operation Wetback in 1954. Operation Wetback reflected the country's growing concern with unauthorized immigration, as witnessed by the 1952 Immigration and Naturalization Act (also known as the McCarren-Walter Act). The 1952 act emphasized the control of unauthorized immigration, citing as motivation labor market competition and the burgeoning cost of welfare programs (Miller and Miller 1996; DeLaet 2000). Operation Wetback, therefore, intended to reduce the number of unauthorized immigrants in the country through a deportation program that sent more than a million Mexicans back south of the border (Copp 1963; Massey and Liang 1989; Langham 1992; Magaña 2003).

Operation Wetback proved successful for several years, but termination of the Bracero Program in 1964 sent unauthorized immigration soaring. For example, U.S. Border Patrol apprehensions rose from 110,000 in 1965 to more than a million in 1977 (James 1991). Unauthorized immigration continued at high levels even though subsequent legislation sought to resolve the problem. For example, the Hart-Cellar Immigration Act of 1965 responded to the escalation of unauthorized immigration but with limited success (DeLaet 2000). For years to come, unauthorized immigration from Mexico would remain a sore spot and the cause of much debate at the highest levels of government.

The 1986 IRCA was the country's next major legislation that affected the border region. By this time, the foundations of immigration policy had evolved. Foremost, the racist (nativist) motivations of immigration policy were downplayed because human rights concerns had grown in the public's eye, especially issues of discrimination, equity, and social justice.[1] Second, the IRCA retained the emphasis on controlling unauthorized immigration, but these efforts were stepped up considerably (DeLaet 2000).

Garnering congressional support for the IRCA was difficult, however,

with two opposing forces at the center of conflict: satisfying agriculture labor demands and coping with the costs and consequences of unauthorized immigration. Problems arose because legal and unauthorized immigration are connected. Formal guest-worker initiatives, such as the Bracero Program, set the stage for unauthorized immigration that functions as a black market (Bailey 2004) because farmers and ranchers can employ unauthorized workers for less pay and without footing the bill for supplemental costs such as transportation, health care, and adequate housing. Such costs were spelled out in the Bracero Program agreement with Mexico (Elac 1972; Massey et al. 2002; Hing 2004). In effect, formal worker programs create an informal labor market, which benefits ranchers and farmers, and it is in their best interest not to shut the door on unauthorized immigration. In the meantime, the society at large carries the cost of providing unauthorized immigrants and their families with life's basic needs: health care, education, and adequate housing.

When working on the IRCA, although Congress was well aware of the benefits that unauthorized immigration offers the agriculture sector, its members could not avoid the problems associated with unauthorized immigration. For several decades, public opinion polls and congressional subcommittee reports identified unauthorized immigration as the country's number one immigration policy issue (Espenshade and Calhoun 1993; DeLaet 2000; Hing 2004). High among the concerns were the social costs of unauthorized immigration: health, welfare, education, and housing (Vernez and McCarthy 1996). Given this background, it is not surprising that the IRCA was conflicted and contradictory.

On the surface, the act appeared to address the problems of legal and unauthorized migration adequately, but over time problems arose. The IRCA provided for a formal guest-worker program, employer sanctions, an amnesty program, and increased funding for border security, especially technology-based surveillance. The guest-worker program sought to meet the needs of the agriculture sector but, even so, ranchers and farmers were concerned that the supply of labor would fall short. For this reason, the IRCA provided additional stop-gap programs (the Seasonal Agricultural Workers and Replenishment Agriculture Workers programs) that increased the number of farm workers available for hire (North 1987; Massey and Liang 1989; Donato et al. 1992; Miller and Miller 1996).

At the same time, employer sanctions were supposed to stop farmers and ranchers from hiring unauthorized workers: in effect, they sought

to eliminate the black market (Crane et al. 1990). Sanctions required that employers hire authorized workers only, and penalties were used to enforce compliance. This called for the inspection of worker documents (visas and passports), but sanctions were either poorly enforced or not enforced at all. In California, for example, estimates indicate that even with sanctions in place, 30 to 50 percent of the agricultural labor force consisted of unauthorized immigrants. One way that farmers side-stepped the verification requirement was to hire labor contractors (labor market intermediaries) who assumed the responsibility of hiring farm labor. Labor contractors, therefore, were responsible for checking and validating worker documents, not farmers themselves (Martin 1999). Labor contractors served a similar role in New Mexico's agriculture industry (Eastman 1991).

Other IRCA policies reveal that efforts to stop unauthorized immigration were contrived, at best. For example, the act banned unannounced raids on fields and food-processing facilities. Instead, the U.S. Border Patrol was required to give advance notice of their pending visits, which essentially nullified the enforcement of employer sanctions (De-Laet 2000; Hing 2004). Unannounced raids had proven to be the border patrol's most effective method of locating unauthorized workers, but under the IRCA raids were prohibited.

The amnesty program was supposed to stop the flow of unauthorized immigrants by granting them legal status. That is, once unauthorized workers were granted amnesty, they could cross the border legally, thereby lowering the number of unauthorized border crossings. While apprehension rates fell immediately after the IRCA was enacted, they rose in subsequent years (Stoddard 1989; Orrenius and Zavodny 2001; Krikorian 2005).

The effects of amnesty were complicated by unintentional impacts to urban labor markets. As unauthorized workers became legitimate, they left farms and ranches and sought out urban-based employment because wages, benefits, and job security were better than in the agriculture sector (Eastman 1991; Donato et al. 1992; Linton 2002). This led to competition with other low-skilled workers, especially African Americans (Bailey 2004), and to the diffusion of Mexican workers across the United States (Massey et al. 2002; Zúñiga and Hernández-León 2005).[2]

Finally, the IRCA sought to curb unauthorized immigration by improving border security, which was accomplished by increasing the number of U.S. Border Patrol agents and investing in technology-based

surveillance. These approaches had an immediate positive impact on slowing the pace of unauthorized immigration, but within a few years apprehensions were again on the rise (White et al. 1990; U.S. Office of Border Patrol 2004). In addition, it is not at all clear whether the decline in apprehensions is attributable to increased border security or the amnesty program.

Ratification of the 1986 IRCA required presidential support in addition to congressional approval. This led the act even further from its stated goals and objectives. The Reagan Administration had long championed the War on Drugs and saw the IRCA as an opportunity to advance its cause. It was widely known that the U.S.–Mexico border was ripe with drug traffickers, and Reagan saw the IRCA as an opportunity to broaden drug interdiction. This was accomplished by redefining the role of the U.S. Border Patrol through the IRCA so that, for the first time, agents were allowed to apprehend drug smugglers (DeLaet 2000).

Although the IRCA represented a substantial commitment to curbing unauthorized immigration, the 1990s witnessed a new approach to border control. For example, the Immigration Act of 1990 and the Illegal Immigration Reform and Immigrant Responsibility Act of 1996 responded almost exclusively to unauthorized immigration. But the toughest efforts to seal the border came from the Clinton Administration, especially those beginning with Operation Gatekeeper.

In some respects, the Clinton Administration's get-tough approach— and Operation Gatekeeper, in particular—built on policies and programs coming out of California years before (Wolf 1988). For several decades San Diego, southern California's gateway to Mexico, had been a favored point of entry for unauthorized Mexicans, so much so that the public begrudgingly accepted it as a matter of course. But in the mid-1980s much of the San Diego citizenry was enraged to a boiling point when the local press reported that unauthorized immigrants were responsible for rising crime rates in the city. Questionable press reports also noted that unauthorized immigrants were known to rob school children of their lunch money, which stirred emotions even more. Even though these reports were later proven inaccurate, they were easy for many to believe because Anglos had longed viewed Mexicans with suspicion (Espenshade and Calhoun 1993). This led local politicians to enter the fracas as they sought the limelight in bringing resolution to the situation. They turned to the U.S. Border Patrol, which launched Opera-

tion Clean Sweep in October 1986. Operation Clean Sweep aimed to eliminate the problem by clearing the streets of the "Mexican menace"; it led to the arrest of nearly 3,000 unauthorized Mexicans and managed to scare away many more (Wolf 1988).

Following a similar approach in the early 1990s, the Clinton Administration turned to the U.S. Border Patrol for assistance in slowing the flow of unauthorized immigration. The administration urged a strategy of "control through deterrence" and emphasized preventing undocumented crossings rather than apprehension (Hing 2004). This led to the construction of metal walls at principal access areas, especially in the San Diego and El Paso border patrol sectors, which had long been prime points of unauthorized entry. The Clinton Administration also turned to high-technology surveillance, arguing that it held much promise for sealing the border.

With the deterrence strategy in mind, the El Paso border patrol sector launched Operation Blockade in 1993. It increased significantly the presence of border patrol agents along the Rio Grande and proved to be successful, with the number of apprehensions falling considerably. A year later, the program was replicated in the San Diego sector under the title Operation Gatekeeper. Such efforts required additional funding, and between 1993 and 1997 the Immigration and Naturalization Service budget in the San Diego sector rose from $400 million to $800 million, with the number of agents growing from 3,389 in 1993 to 7,357 in 1998 (Hing 2004). The Clinton Administration was clearly responding to California's own efforts to handle unauthorized immigration, earlier through Operation Clean Sweep and in 1994 through Proposition 187, which attempted to prevent unauthorized immigrants from receiving any kind of public assistance (Massey et al. 2002; Nevins 2002).

With deterrence programs in place in El Paso and San Diego, it comes as no surprise that unauthorized immigrants looked elsewhere for places to enter the United States. By design, this is exactly what the Clinton Administration's get-tough policies sought to do: channel immigrants away from highly publicized points of entry, especially San Diego, to Arizona and New Mexico. This followed from the emphasis on deterrence rather than apprehension. In this case, entering the United States required crossing over remote and rugged terrain that served as natural barriers to entry (Nevins 2002; Hing 2004). The Clinton Administration and the Immigration and Naturalization Service believed that, confronted with

severe hardship and even the risk of death, Mexicans would not travel northward. But this was an ill-conceived and inhumane policy, given the history of deaths on the border in the years that followed.

The American Friends Service Committee's third annual report documented the loss of life as Mexicans tried to enter the country (American Friends Service Committee 1992). The report indicated, for example, that 117 bodies were retrieved from the lower Rio Grande in 1989 as Mexicans drowned trying to cross northward into the United States. The group also reported that in 1991 six bodies were found in the Tijuana River. In sum, there was ample evidence to suggest that forcing Mexicans to remote areas would not thwart efforts to enter the United States. Even so, the Clinton Administration moved ahead, which over the years led to the death of hundreds of immigrants. Nevertheless, unauthorized immigration continues to rise.

The history of U.S.–Mexico relations often reveals the unequal distribution of power that separates the two countries. This is especially the case with immigration policy, where the United States has clearly held the upper hand. From the beginning, U.S. immigration policies sought to exploit Mexican labor while excluding them from the broader social, political, and economic foundations of American society. In more recent years, human rights concerns shifted immigration policy somewhat. At the same time, however, concerns over unauthorized immigration grew, which placed decision-makers in a precarious situation. This led to ineffective and contradictory legislation that, by design or not, often failed.

While much has been said about the scope and failures of U.S. immigration policy, far less is known about its impacts on colonias of southern Arizona and New Mexico. There is every reason to believe that the ebbs and tides of both legal and unauthorized immigration have left their mark on colonias, given their history and location in the border region. But there is virtually no documentation of these impacts. In chapter 6, we look more closely at this issue.

Devaluation of the Mexican Peso

Policies coming down from the Mexican government have also affected colonias north of the border. Economic policies, especially those involving peso devaluations, are particularly important because their impact is far-reaching on both sides of the border. Peso devaluation has been linked to Mexico's recent economic history and the development path

the country has taken. During the twentieth century, Mexico evolved from an agrarian society to a manufacturing-based economy that was international in scope (de la Madrid 1984). But the transition did not come easily. As with many Latin American countries, Mexico's growth and development has come at a great cost.

Although Mexico struggled through the depression of the early 1930s, by the 1950s the country was on solid economic ground. Indeed, the years 1950–1970 are often called Mexico's "golden years" because of sustained growth and sound economic fundamentals (Morgan 1979; Kalter and Khor 1990; Patrick and Renforth 1996). Oil revenues, a commitment to import substitution (producing goods locally instead of importing from abroad), and a privatization program contributed to the country's economic success.

During the 1970s, however, the Mexican economy unraveled. Several factors contributed to the country's economic woes, including overspending on domestic programs, a growing deficit, inflation, and a deteriorating balance of payments (Galbis 1982; Harrell and Fischer 1985; Lustig 1998). In the last case, revenues received from exports fell, while the money spent on imports increased, producing a negative balance of payments on current accounts. To some extent, the rise in imports was caused by the government's single focus on developing the industrial sector while ignoring the commercial sector (de la Madrid 1984). This led industry and consumers to seek goods and services from outside the country. In short, Mexico sold fewer goods and services to other countries than it purchased from them, resulting in a foreign trade deficit.

Balance-of-payment problems are tied to Mexico's use of a fixed exchange rate after the 1973 termination of the Bretton Woods Agreement, which had guided the international monetary system since World War II (Griffith-Jones and Sunkel 1986; Kalter and Khor 1990; Aghevli et al. 1991; Edwards 1996). At the time, most industrially advanced countries adopted a floating exchange rate that responds to market forces. Many developing countries, however, especially in Latin America, moved to fixed exchange rates that are set by the government, not the market. When governments set exchange rates, currencies tend to become overvalued because they are seen as a policy instrument that can promote economic growth, rather than as a medium of exchange in global economies. When fixed exchange rates are coupled with negative terms of trade, overvaluation of currency becomes even more likely, which often necessitates devaluation (Bond 1980; Galbis 1982; Nashashibi 1983).

Such was the case in 1976, when the peso had become overvalued and was affecting the country's terms of trade. The Mexican government responded by allowing the peso to float on the international market, which led to a 40 percent reduction in value (Harrell and Fischer 1985; Lustig 1998). The devaluation triggered an economic crisis as investors lost confidence and pulled capital out of the country. This, in turn, exhausted the Central Bank's reserves. Mexico turned to the International Monetary Fund and World Bank for relief.

Propped up by rising oil prices, Mexico recovered from the crisis and as the 1980s approached the country's economy stabilized. The discovery of vast reserves of oil fueled high expectations by the Mexican government because it bolstered the country's position in the global economy. Coming out of the international oil crisis of the early 1970s, Mexico believed it was well positioned for long-term growth and development. Exploitation of oil reserves required massive capital investments, which were obtained from international financial markets. With the peso devaluation in place and an aggressive austerity program playing out, investors returned to Mexico and the country's situation continued to improve (Harrell and Fischer 1985; Kalter and Khor 1990; Lustig 1998).

But the recovery was short lived, as the country experienced a series of economic setbacks. Foremost was the external shock exerted by plummeting oil prices on the global market, which led to a severe problem with balance of payments. At the same time, Mexico had not invested oil revenues or external capital in upgrading plants and equipment, choosing instead to spend on domestic social programs. This meant that tax revenues were not generated from investments, nor did they contribute directly to the future economic growth of the nation. Investors grew leery of future economic prospects, which ignited capital outflows. Capital flight during 1982 and 1983 was estimated to be $100 billion (Adams 1997). The Mexican gross domestic product fell, foreign debt totaled $77 billion, and inflation rose from about 30 percent during the first months of 1982 to over 150 percent by the close of the year (de la Madrid 1984; Harrell and Fischer 1985; Kalter and Khor 1990; Lustig 1998). Facing another downturn, in 1982 the Mexican government once again devalued the peso, which fell by about 600 percent. The devaluation led to another economic crisis.

During the years that followed, Mexico endured rough economic times, but by the end of the 1980s future prospects looked much brighter.

Inflation fell and remained under control, the country pursued an aggressive privatization program that removed government from all but the
provision of basic services, and foreign debt obligations were on the
decline (De Long et al. 1996; Ramírez 1996; Whitt 1996). Direct foreign
investment surged from $14.5 billion in 1991 to $17.2 billion the following
year, and by 1993 it had risen to $22.5 billion (Adams 1997). The promise of
the impending North American Free Trade Agreement (NAFTA) made
the future look even brighter. With NAFTA melding trade partners from
across the continent, Mexico's position seemed more secure, especially
because of closer and more formal association with the United States.

But by 1994 the country was once again forced to devalue the peso, as
a series of setbacks drove the country to its most severe economic crisis
since the Great Depression of the 1920s and 1930s. Numerous economic
and political factors undermined the country's recovery. In economic
terms, the peso had become overvalued once again, which affected Mexico's terms of trade. As in the past, overvaluation of the peso meant that
Mexico's goods and services were comparatively more expensive, while
consumer and industrial goods in other countries became more affordable. This led to the deterioration of the balance of payments on current
accounts. To make matters worse, capital investments in the country
were not sufficient to generate long-term growth, manufacturing production peaked and then leveled off, and industrial wages fell (De Long
et al. 1996; Ramírez 1996; Blecker 1997; Lustig 1998).

The economic crisis was also affected by political events that set the
country on its heels. Foremost among these are the Chiapas peasant
revolt, which began on 1 January 1994, the same day that NAFTA came
into effect, and the assassination of presidential candidate Luis Donaldo
Colosio in March 1994. Colosio's assassination was especially upsetting
because he was the favored candidate and by all reports would have
become the next president. Foreign investors viewed these political problems as signs of long-term instability, which precipitated capital outflow
from the country (Ramírez 1996; Lustig 1998).

There are some opposing views, however, on Mexico's crisis of the
early 1990s. According to Blecker (1997), Mexico's involvement with
NAFTA played a significant role in peso devaluation. He argued that,
by design, devaluation was critical to NAFTA's success because Mexico
sought to improve its economic position by following a policy of export-
led growth. To make this happen, the country needed to attract direct

foreign investment, which meant that the peso needed to fall to its lowest possible level. Ultimately, devaluation served the needs of the United States and U.S. corporations, while Mexico and its citizens paid the price.

Regardless of the causes, the outcomes of the 1994 devaluation were severe. The value of the peso fell by 50 percent, far more than the 20 percent sought by the Mexican government (De Long et al. 1996; Whitt 1996). This triggered another national recession that plunged the country into crisis. A series of adjustments followed, however, such that more recently Mexico appears to be on more stable ground (Gurría 2000).

The peso devaluations of 1982 and 1994 had a tremendous impact on the U.S.–Mexico border region, which played out in three principal ways. First, the social costs of economic crises have been enormous. Even though the Mexican government has long sought to improve quality of life for its citizens, devaluations triggered deep recessions that weighed heavily on the Mexican population. This led to the reduction in social services, declines in per capita income, and a general lowering of the country's well-being (MacDonald et al. 1991). Critical questions arise from these social impacts. To what extent did the 1982 and 1994 peso devaluations send Mexicans north of the border in search of a better life? Moreover, to what extent have peso devaluations and their subsequent economic crises influenced quality of life in colonias of Arizona and New Mexico? This second question is difficult to answer because it has received virtually no attention in the research literature, although we discuss these issues in greater detail in chapter 6.

Second, peso devaluations have affected the maquiladora economy that crowds Mexico's northern border. From Ciudad Juárez to Tijuana, maquiladoras have been a major source of employment and wages for several decades and play a critical role in the region's economy. Economic recessions set in motion by devaluations trickle down to the local level in the form of lost manufacturing productivity, depressed wages, and reduced export trade (Lustig 1998). This reflects poorly on the country's long-term economic stability, which lowers investor confidence. One outcome of this is that investors seek out alternative locations. This explains, in part, the outflow of investment from Mexico to other regions of the world (Audley et al. 2003). Critical questions surface from the impacts of devaluation on the maquiladora economy. To what extent has unemployment in the northern border region forced Mexicans northward to Arizona and New Mexico colonias? In addition, how has this affected quality of life? Chapter 6 examines these questions as well.

Third, the 1982 and 1994 peso devaluations affected retail trade and commerce on both sides of the border because devaluation lowered the purchasing power of the peso. In effect, goods and services on the U.S. side of the border became more expensive, while the opposite holds for Mexican goods and services. The impacts of peso devaluation varied along the border, depending on the degree of cross-border interaction and the size and diversity of border towns and cities (Davila 1990). For example, the 1982 peso devaluation set in motion a frenzy of bargain hunting on the Mexican side of the border that required government intervention to avoid the depletion of basic foodstuffs (Harrell and Fischer 1985). Following the 1994 peso devaluation, retail sales in southern Texas fell between 20 percent and 50 percent, depending on the community (Patrick and Renforth 1996). Did the reduction in retailing north of the border slow the pace of unauthorized immigration to Arizona and New Mexico colonias? This may have occurred as the slowdown trickled through local economies, decreasing the demand for Mexican workers. Getting at this issue is difficult, however, because of the lack of data, but it is an important question for future research.

Summary

Years of research have shown that several factors promote growth and development in towns and cities. Foremost is the ability to employ the local workforce in basic industries such as agriculture, mining, refining, and manufacturing because these goods are sold outside the community and, in return, bring revenues back to the community, where they are spent on local goods and services. This process sets in motion a series of direct and indirect effects that promote economic growth. The quality of support services such as schools and health care also contributes to local growth by building human capital and attracting employers who value these services.

In the border region, national policies also play an important role in local growth and development. North of the border, U.S. immigration policies exert an influence by fueling or dampening unauthorized immigration. These patterns were set in motion decades ago as U.S. businesses sought cheap and exploitable labor from deep within Mexico. But informal or black-market immigration was produced in the process and remains a critical policy issue at the highest levels of government. Specific immigration policies, especially the 1986 IRCA and 1994 Operation

Gatekeeper, are of particular interest because they escalated unauthorized immigration and channeled it across the border with New Mexico and Arizona.

South of the border, economic policies put in place by the Mexican government may have influenced quality of life in Arizona and New Mexico colonias as well. The outcomes of the 1982 and 1994 peso devaluations were especially important because their effects were far-reaching. These impacts served as push factors that motivated migration because of declining wage rates, inflation, and cutbacks in social services.

In the next chapter, we look more closely at the relationship between federal policies and quality of life in Arizona and New Mexico colonias. Three issues guide the analysis. First, to what extent have immigration and border security policies affected unauthorized immigration and quality of life in Arizona and New Mexico colonias? The impacts of the IRCA, Operation Gatekeeper, and related policies of the mid-1990s are of particular interest. Second, have the 1982 and 1994 peso devaluations influenced quality of life in Arizona and New Mexico colonias? At issue is whether and to what extent turmoil in the Mexican economy led to unauthorized immigration and subsequent settlement in colonias. Finally, the impact of peso devaluation on the border region economy is well documented. However, little research has examined its impact on colonias.

6
National Policies and Colonia Development

Although history, location, and size distinguish one colonia from another, the vast majority struggle with fundamental problems such as infrastructure deficiencies, poor-quality housing, and limited health care and educational opportunities. Community development attempts to solve these problems but at times meets with limited success.[1]

This chapter examines one possible reason why community development is so difficult in colonias: the instability introduced by national policies on both sides of the border. Some of these policies apply directly, such as immigration reform, whereas the effects of others are indirect, such as Mexico's peso devaluations. Our objective is to understand whether the inconsistency in national policies works against community development efforts in colonias. This occurs as policies such as peso devaluation send unauthorized immigrants north of the border, where they often take up residence in colonias. We do not wish to hold unauthorized immigrants responsible for the challenges that confront these communities. Rather, we seek to determine whether national policies are a deeper source of the problem.

The chapter begins by documenting the relationship between national policies and the flow of unauthorized immigrants into the United States. We single out unauthorized immigration because it is the focus of recent U.S. policies and has been exacerbated by Mexico's peso devaluations. We then look more narrowly at the foreign-born population residing in colonias, with the aim of understanding how transborder migration has played out at the local scale. In this case, we evaluate the relationship between the imposition of policies and the flow of immigrants to Arizona and New Mexico colonias. Finally, quantitative methods are used to assess the relationship between the foreign-born population residing in colonias and quality of life. We evaluate the degree of association between the foreign-born presence and three quality-of-life indicators, median household and per capita income and educational attainment.

National Policies and Border Apprehensions

For much of the twentieth century, the U.S. government struggled to balance the competing objectives of supplying cheap labor for the country's economy (agriculture, mining, and railroads early on and a range of industries more recently) while clamping down on unauthorized immigration (DeLaet 2000; Hing 2004). Achieving these objectives has been difficult because they point out contradictions endemic in American society. On the one hand, nearly everyone in the country agrees that economic interests come first, which means that providing a reserve of cheap labor is paramount. On the other hand, many Americans have been reluctant to accept unauthorized immigrants as equals. The rationale for exclusion builds on either racist attitudes or an economic "pay as you go" motive that leads many to resist contributing to worker maintenance, especially health care and education. In the first instance, immigration policy has long reflected the racial bias against Mexican workers. Programs such as Operation Wetback, passed by Congress in the 1950s, and Operation Clean Sweep, which responded to the "Mexican menace" in southern California during the 1980s, confirm the racist basis of immigration policy (Wolf 1988; DeLaet 2000; Hing 2004). In addition, survey research by Espenshade and Calhoun (1993) noted issues of mistrust of Mexicans in general. In the second case, much of the public and congressional outcry that calls for a crackdown on unauthorized border crossings hinges on economic motives that are rooted in ideology. This holds especially for more recent years, when the country's dominant conservative ideology called for a broad-based reduction in federal spending, including the withdrawal of support for social programs. This "pay as you go" mentality applies to anyone who cannot afford basic needs, not just unauthorized immigrants. The federal government's retreat from social programs shifted responsibility to state governments, which politicized the "border problem" even more as state legislatures entered the policy-making arena (Carroll and González 2005; Nash 2005).

In any case, immigration reform over the years has clearly favored supplying U.S. businesses and households with cheap labor, despite public sentiments that call for a halt to unauthorized immigration. This is to be expected because the benefits to U.S. business are far-reaching. Mexican labor is comparatively inexpensive and, because workers are unauthorized, there is no need to cover additional costs such as health

insurance, education, and retirement benefits. Although seldom mentioned, American society is expected to subsidize the business community by covering these costs for Mexican workers.

Here, however, we are interested in understanding how national policies on both sides of the border have affected colonias of southern Arizona and New Mexico. Chapter 5 provided a summary of immigration policies in more distant years, and here we begin our assessment with the 1980s.

The recent history of the border has been complicated by a sequence of policies in Mexico and the United States, one responding to the other without cooperation or coordination. The story begins south of the border, where the Mexican government has dealt with a host of economic problems as the country pursued short- and long-term development goals. Peso devaluation has played a key role in shaping the country's economic fortunes, especially the devaluations in 1982 and 1994 (Harrell and Fischer 1985; Adams 1997; Lustig 1998). Devaluation was called for because overvaluation of the peso sent the country's balance of payments on current accounts well into the red. This means that Mexico's products became comparatively expensive, while the cost of foreign goods and services fell, which led to a decline in exports and a rise in imports. The effects of devaluation were severe as the country struggled to regain momentum and reestablish its position in the global economy.

These peso devaluations south of the border shaped the timing and flow of unauthorized immigrants. Apprehension data provided by the U.S. Department of Homeland Security (2004) indicate that 759,420 apprehensions were made along the country's southern border in 1980. Mexican nationals accounted for 97 percent of these apprehensions.[2] Over the course of the 1980s, however, the number of apprehensions became erratic and seemingly random, although they were clearly anchored to Mexico's devaluation policies. For example, from 1982 (the year in which the peso was devalued) to 1986 apprehensions more than doubled, rising from 819,919 to 1,692,544. More apprehensions were made in 1986 than in any year in recent history.

The cyclical nature of apprehensions during the 1980s illustrates the impact of Mexico's 1982 peso devaluation. The blow to the Mexican economy was severe and sent unemployment soaring across the country. This set in motion a massive northward migration that grew in subsequent years as the economy showed few signs of recovery. It comes as no

surprise that border apprehensions skyrocketed in response to the growing number of immigrants attempting unauthorized entry to the United
States in search of jobs.

The rise in apprehensions ignited concern in the United States, which
led to the 1986 Immigration Reform and Control Act (IRCA). This act
called for substantive immigration reform that sought to dampen the
flow of unauthorized immigrants, while ensuring an adequate reserve of
cheap labor. To satisfy these competing objectives, the IRCA called for an
amnesty program, farm-worker programs, tighter border security, and a
broadening of the border patrol's role in drug interdiction, a carryover
from the Reagan Administration's War on Drugs. The impact of the
IRCA was immediate and dramatic, with a 90 percent decline in apprehensions from 1986 through 1989. The Immigration and Naturalization Service responded by declaring the IRCA a resounding success (U.S.
Office of the Border Patrol 2004).[3] This success was short lived, however,
with apprehensions rising by nearly 43 percent from 1989 through 1993.

The failings of the IRCA led to even more restrictive measures as
Congress responded to public concerns by seeking stern resolution to
unauthorized immigration. In 1994, during the Clinton Administration,
Operation Gatekeeper came on board. Operation Gatekeeper pursued a
far more heavy-handed approach to border security, favoring control
through deterrence rather than apprehensions, meaning that the government sought to prevent border crossings rather than apprehend unauthorized immigrants after they entered the United States. The change
in policy signaled a decisive shift in border security, where the emphasis
was now placed on preventing border crossings altogether.[4]

The timing of Operation Gatekeeper was propitious because in 1994
the Mexican government was forced to devalue the peso once again. This
sent unauthorized immigration soaring, as Mexico's economy staggered
under the weight of a full-blown depression. Operation Gatekeeper managed to slow unauthorized immigration, with apprehensions declining
by more than 230,000 from 1993 to 1994. Even so, the success of Operation Gatekeeper was temporary, and the focus on deterrence fell well
short of expectations. Apprehensions increased by 50 percent during the
years that followed: from 1994 through 1996 they rose from about 1 million to more than 1.5 million.

While Operation Gatekeeper played only a minor role in stopping the
flow of unauthorized immigrants, it succeeded in altering immigration patterns along the country's entire southern border. This occurred

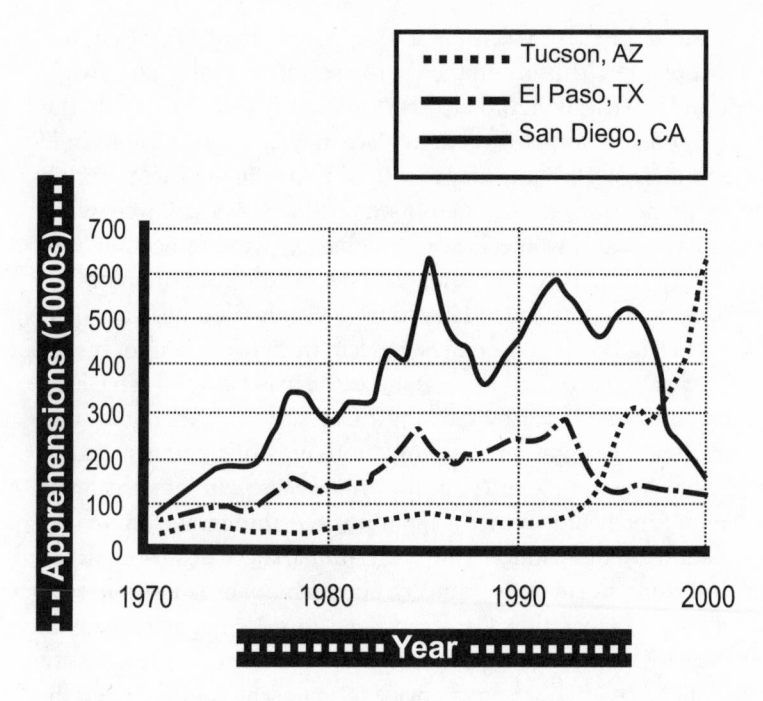

Figure 6.1 Apprehensions of unauthorized immigrants in the southern border patrol sector, 1970–2000. *Source:* U.S. Department of Homeland Security (2004)

because Operation Gatekeeper pursued an aggressive strategy of "control through deterrence" and targeted highly visible crossings in El Paso, Texas, and San Diego, California (Nevins 2002; Hing 2004). To accomplish this, measures aimed at deterrence (mainly by adding U.S. Border Patrol personnel) were beefed up at popular points of entry. Policymakers pursued this option because they believed that crossing the rough, rugged, and remote deserts of Sonora, southern Arizona, and New Mexico would discourage immigrants from traveling northward.

The migratory adjustment to Operation Gatekeeper is illustrated in figure 6.1, which displays apprehension data for selected sectors of the southern border. These sectors are geographic subdivisions defined by the Department of Homeland Security. The figure shows apprehensions for Tucson, El Paso, and San Diego during the period 1971 to 2000; these three sectors are the most active along the southern border.

Prior to Operation Gatekeeper, apprehensions in El Paso and San

Diego outpaced the Tucson sector by a wide margin. In 1990, for example, the number of apprehensions in the Tucson sector was only 53,061, while in El Paso and San Diego they totaled 223,219 and 473,329, respectively. But after Operation Gatekeeper was put in place in 1994, apprehensions in El Paso and San Diego fell, while they rose significantly in the Tucson sector. By 2000 apprehensions in the Tucson sector totaled 616,346, well over a ten-fold increase during the previous decade. At the same time, apprehensions in the El Paso and San Diego sectors dropped dramatically. By 2000 they equaled 115,696 in El Paso (a 48 percent decline from 1990) and 151,681 in San Diego (a drop of 68 percent from 1990). This occurred because the strategy of deterrence was successful in El Paso and San Diego, but immigrants responded by crossing the desert into Arizona. Along with these new immigration patterns, thousands of migrants died in desert regions attempting entry to the United States. In fact, the harsh desert environment did not stop unauthorized immigrants, a serious miscalculation by the Clinton Administration. These deaths continue unabated and are the subject of concern among human rights groups.

The failure of Operation Gatekeeper led to subsequent reforms in border security, with the Illegal Immigration Reform and Immigrant Responsibility Act (IIRIRA) put in place in 1996. The act continued the strategy of control through deterrence by increasing the commitment to high-technology surveillance, the construction of physical barriers, and enlarging the U.S. Border Patrol presence (see chapter 5 for a fuller discussion). The IIRIRA slowed unauthorized immigration momentarily but apprehensions were soon on the rise. In 2000 more than 1.6 million apprehensions were made, nearly the same number as in 1986, when the IRCA was introduced. Border security was tightened once again in 2001, in response to terrorist attacks in New York City and Washington, D.C. Heightened security was successful in slowing unauthorized immigration, with the number of apprehensions falling from approximately 1.3 million in 2001 to 931,557 by 2003. More recently, however, the number of apprehensions was once again on the rise.

The discussion above shows how national policies have affected unauthorized immigration to the United States. Peso devaluations in Mexico sent immigrants northward in search of jobs and set in motion a succession of immigration reforms in the United States. But they did little to stop unauthorized immigration. In the end, U.S. business profited from the failings of immigration reform, while public concerns have not been satisfied.

Colonias and the Foreign-Born Population

There is no doubt that the problems confronting colonias are caused by many factors, some longer term and other appearing more recently. Although numerous grassroots organizations, nongovernmental organizations, and government agencies work tirelessly to remedy these problems, we argue that national policies on both sides of the border hamper these efforts at a deeper and more fundamental level. Thus far, we have demonstrated the cyclical nature of unauthorized immigration, but we have yet to establish the impacts to colonias themselves. This is critical because the localized effects of unauthorized immigration receive only scant treatment in the research literature (Clark and Schultz 1997). In addition, coverage by the popular media tends to highlight newsworthy stories that dramatize the border, most often the drug trade or the financial burdens placed on state and local governments (Marizco 2005; Nash 2005). There appears to be little concern, however, for the localized problems that may arise from national policies.

To get at this issue, we examine the foreign-born population residing in unincorporated colonias of southern Arizona and New Mexico. The foreign-born population is comprised almost exclusively of Mexican nationals who were not U.S. citizens at the time of birth. Unincorporated colonias are singled out because they are confronted by the most challenging community development problems and often have fewer resources available to mount development initiatives. As such, grassroots organizing is often the only approach to community development. In addition, their small size and comparative remoteness suggests that unincorporated colonias are less likely to receive attention.

The analysis focuses on the timing of arrival and size of the foreign-born population living in unincorporated colonias, which enables us to evaluate whether changes in the foreign-born population parallel the broader pattern of immigration and apprehensions along the southern U.S. border described above.[5] While we anticipate growth of the foreign-born population in response to Mexico's peso devaluations in 1982 and 1994 (which were countered by the IRCA in 1986 and Operation Gatekeeper in 1994), there has been little systematic analysis of these relationships.

Figure 6.2 shows the foreign-born population residing in unincorporated colonias of Arizona and New Mexico for the years 1970 through 2005. The U.S. Census Bureau asks respondents to indicate their year of

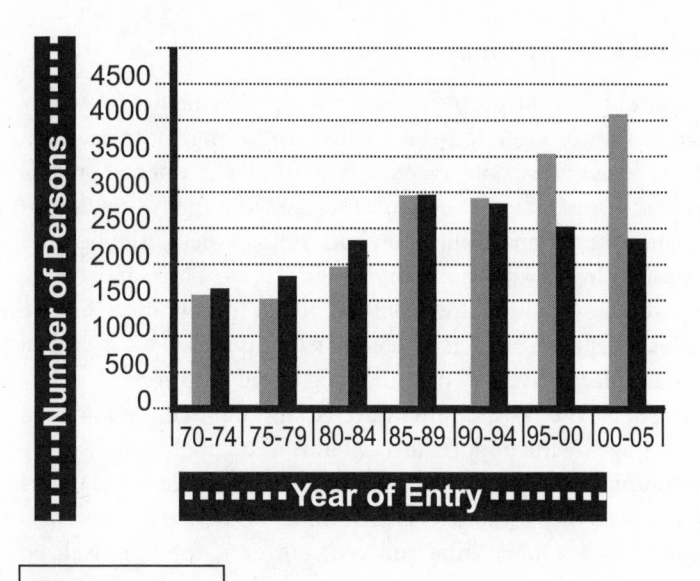

Figure 6.2 The foreign-born population in unincorporated colonias, 1970–2005. The figure reports data for 44 unincorporated census units that comprise forty-eight colonias in Arizona. The New Mexico data covers 41 census units that comprise ninety-three unincorporated colonias. Data for 2005 were estimated using a linear extrapolation of 1990–1994 and 1995–2000 census data. *Source:* U.S. Census Bureau (1990, 2000)

entry to the United States and then compiles these data at 5-year intervals. Figure 6.2 follows this convention. The vertical axis indicates the total number of foreign-born residents for all colonias collectively.

National policies have been instrumental in shaping the size of the foreign-born population living in unincorporated colonias of Arizona and New Mexico. During the 1970s the foreign-born population was comparatively small and similar across Arizona and New Mexico's unincorporated colonias, for example, 1,637 in Arizona in 1970 and 1,700 in New Mexico (fig. 6.2). During 1980–1984, however, the foreign-born population had grown significantly. During 1970–1974 and 1980–1984, Arizona unincorporated colonias experienced a 22 percent increase in the foreign-born population, and those in New Mexico witnessed a 38

percent increase. This growth captures the initial impact of the 1982 Mexican peso devaluation. The growth during subsequent years is even more substantial. During 1980–1984 and 1985–1989, the foreign-born population living in unincorporated colonias rose by an additional 47 percent in Arizona and 25 percent in New Mexico. Thus, between 1970 and 1989 the size of the foreign-born population nearly doubled.

The United States responded to the rise in unauthorized immigration with the 1986 IRCA, and its impact was felt in Arizona and New Mexico's unincorporated colonias. By the 1990–1994 time period the foreign-born population had fallen slightly from previous levels. But figure 6.2 shows that patterns of immigration began to shift in 1990–1994, with Arizona's foreign-born population inching ahead of New Mexico's. This is a result of the U.S. response to the 1994 Mexican peso devaluation, which led to the implementation of Operation Gatekeeper in the same year. As indicated in figure 6.1, Operation Gatekeeper diverted immigrants from Texas and California to Arizona. The program succeeded in slowing border crossings, but only for a short time. After 1994 the foreign-born population living in Arizona's unincorporated colonias soared to new heights, leaving New Mexico well behind. Even the IIRIRA, put in place in 1996, did little to stop the rise of Arizona's foreign-born population.

According to Martinez (1990), in transborder society Mexican immigrants are more likely to seek out places to live where the proportion of Hispanics is comparatively high, because long-term Hispanic residents ease socialization for new arrivals. Socialization is especially important in overcoming language barriers and fostering awareness of cultural values and norms. For this reason, the foreign-born population should be even more prevalent among colonias that house a greater number of Hispanics.

Figure 6.3 reports data for unincorporated colonias of Arizona and New Mexico that have Hispanic populations of 50 percent or greater. While these colonias are few in number, they speak of the role that social and cultural identity plays in shaping migration behavior. The 1982 peso devaluation sent a large number of Mexican nationals north of the border, where they took up residence in colonias dominated by Hispanics (fig. 6.3). This applies especially to Arizona, where the foreign-born population grew consistently from 1970 through 2005. But during the period 1985–1989, when the 1986 IRCA was implemented, a significant shift occurred in which the foreign-born population in Arizona colonias pulled well ahead of New Mexico's colonias. During this period, Arizona

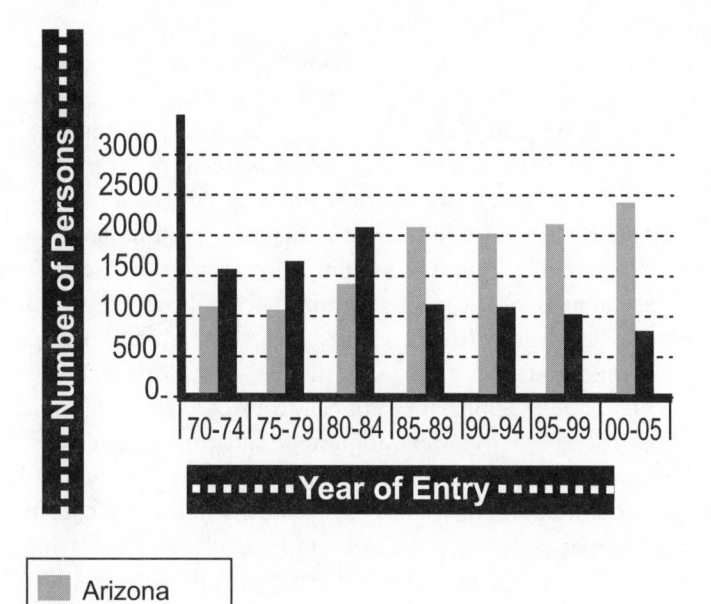

Figure 6.3 The foreign-born population in Hispanic unincorporated colonias, 1970–2005. The figure includes data for sixteen Arizona unincorporated colonias with Hispanic populations of at least 50 percent. In New Mexico, 20 census units comprise thirty-four unincorporated colonias with Hispanic populations of at least 50 percent. Data for 2005 were estimated using a linear extrapolation of 1990–1994 and 1995–2000 census data. *Source:* U.S. Census Bureau (1990, 2000)

colonias housed 907 (43 percent) more foreigners than did New Mexico colonias. In the years that followed, the foreign-born presence in Arizona's unincorporated colonias continued to grow, especially after enactment of Operation Gatekeeper in 1994 and the 1996 IIRIRA. Both these policies fueled the rise in the foreign-born population as unauthorized immigrants abandoned popular crossing points in Texas and California in favor of those in Arizona.

Figures 6.2 and 6.3 provide evidence of the impact of peso devaluations and immigration reform on unincorporated colonias of Arizona and New Mexico. Growth of the foreign-born population in these colonias mirrored broader trends, including the shift to Arizona following

Operation Gatekeeper in 1994. It is also apparent that the foreign-born population sought places to live where the Hispanic population was comparatively high. But it is important to acknowledge that the data reported in these figures are indicative rather than definitive. By this we mean there is no way of knowing the proportion of the foreign-born population accounted for by unauthorized immigrants. These data are unavailable from any source. Nevertheless, there is sufficient evidence to suggest that the rise in the foreign-born population is associated with the national policies of both Mexico and the United States.

The Foreign-Born Population and Colonia Quality of Life

This section investigates whether growth of the foreign-born population over time has affected quality of life in colonias. To get at this issue, we examine the strength of association between the foreign-born population and three quality-of-life indicators: the percentage of the population 25 years and older who have completed high school (including general equivalency diplomas), median household income, and per capita income. High school graduation is a good indicator of social mobility because it is often required by employers and is necessary for advanced education. Median household income is useful because it indicates the earning capacity of households, which often consist of multiple wage earners. Per capita income, in contrast, is an indicator of earning capacity across the entire population.

The correlation coefficients used in our analyses do not indicate causality. Instead, they measure the strength of a linear association between variable pairs, with values ranging from +1 to −1. A coefficient of +1 means that as one variable increases the other also increases in a perfectly linear fashion, whereas a coefficient of −1 means that as one variable increases the other decreases in a perfectly linear fashion. Values near zero indicate the lack of an association between the two variables.

Table 6.1 indicates the 5-year interval during which foreigners moved to a colonia, including incorporated, unincorporated, and predominantly Hispanic colonias (population at least 50 percent Hispanic, regardless of whether incorporated or unincorporated), as well as important national policies enacted during each period, including the 1982 and 1994 peso devaluations, the IRCA (1986), Operation Gatekeeper (1994), and the IIRIRA (1996). The foreign-born population entering the United

States during the years 1980–1984 and 1985–1989 were obtained from 1990 census data, and those entering from 1990–1994 and 1995–1999 were obtained from 2000 census data.[6] The values in the table are the coefficients for quality-of-life indicators.

The coefficients in table 6.1 indicate a strong negative relationship between the foreign population and quality of life in Arizona colonias. (The results of *t*-tests, which measure the strength of association, appear in parentheses.) For incorporated colonias these relationships were strongest for the foreign-born population entering the country during 1990–1994 and the percentage of residents 25 years and older who completed high school as of 2000. The relationship is negative, indicating that as the number of foreigners increased, the percentage of high school graduates declined. There were no statistically significant relationships between the foreign-born population and median household and per capita incomes across all time periods.

The negative association between the foreign-born population and high school graduation is especially prominent in unincorporated colonias. In this case, larger foreign-born populations were significantly associated with lower high school graduation rates in both 1990 and 2000. The relationship between the foreign population and median household income was not significant, but there was a statistically significant relationship with per capita income. This indicates that as the foreign-born population living in unincorporated colonias increased, per capita incomes fell. This is especially true in more recent years, as more aggressive immigration policies (Operation Gatekeeper and IIRIRA) came into effect.

Within colonias where Hispanics claim the majority, there are fewer significant associations between the foreign-born population and quality of life. In these colonias, however, the foreign-born population entering the country during the 1990s was associated with lower high school graduation rates and lower median household income.

Table 6.2 indicates statistically strong negative relationships between the foreign-born population and quality-of-life indicators in New Mexico colonias. The strongest relationship appears between foreigners entering during all time periods and the percentage of population completing high school. This relationship existed across all colonias but was especially pronounced for incorporated colonias. High school graduation and per capita income were also significantly related to the foreign-born population in unincorporated and Hispanic colonias. In these cases, correlation coefficients were negative, meaning that as the foreign-

Table 6.1

Policies, Foreign-Born Population, and Quality of Life in Arizona Colonias

Date of entry	Policy	Percent completing high school	Median household income	Per capita income
Incorporated colonias (n = 25)				
1980–1984	1982 peso devaluation	−0.303	0.118	−0.058
		(1.53)	(0.57)	(0.28)
1985–1989	1986 IRCA	−0.333	0.113	−0.084
		(1.69)	(0.55)	(0.40)
1990–1994	1994 peso devaluation and Operation Gatekeeper	−0.533	−0.138	−0.389
		(3.02)*	(0.67)	(2.02)
1995–1999	1996 IIRIRA	−0.453	−0.093	−0.314
		(2.43)**	(0.45)	(1.59)
Unincorporated colonias (n = 44)				
1980–1984	1982 peso devaluation	−0.485	−0.115	−0.147
		(3.59)*	(0.75)	(0.96)
1985–1989	1986 IRCA	−0.498	−0.136	−0.337
		(3.72)*	(0.89)	(2.32)**
1990–1994	1994 peso devaluation and Operation Gatekeeper	−0.628	−0.292	−0.460
		(5.22)*	(1.98)	(3.35)*
1995–1999	1996 IIRIRA	−0.623	−0.179	−0.365
		(5.16)*	(1.18)	(2.54)**
Hispanic colonias (n = 25)				
1980–1984	1982 peso devaluation	−0.256	−0.297	−0.252
		(1.27)	(1.49)	(1.25)
1985–1989	1986 IRCA	−0.301	−0.382	−0.331
		(1.51)	(1.98)	(1.97)
1990–1994	1994 peso devaluation and Operation Gatekeeper	−0.359	−0.429	−0.221
		(1.85)	(2.28)**	(1.09)
1995–1999	1996 IIRIRA	−0.430	−0.488	−0.254
		(2.28)**	(2.68)*	(1.26)

Data are for twenty-five incorporated colonias, 44 census units comprising forty-eight unincorporated colonias, and twenty-five colonias (incorporated and unincorporated) with Hispanic populations of at least 50 percent.

IRCA, Immigration Reform Control Act; IIRIRA, Illegal Immigration Reform and Immigrant Responsibility Act

* Significant relationship, $p < 0.01$; two-tailed t-test

** Significant relationship, $p < 0.05$; two-tailed t-test

Source: U.S. Census Bureau (1990, 2000)

Table 6.2

Policies, Foreign-born Population, and Quality of Life in New Mexico Colonias

Date of entry	Policy	Percent completing high school	Median household income	Per capita income
Incorporated colonias (*n* = 9 or 10)				
1980–1984	1982 peso devaluation	−0.732 (2.84)**	−0.530 (1.65)	−0.906 (5.65)*
1985–1989	1986 IRCA	−0.764 (3.13)**	−0.614 (2.06)	−0.886 (5.07)*
1990–1994	1994 peso devaluation and Operation Gatekeeper	−0.645 (2.39)**	−0.292 (0.87)	−0.465 (1.48)
1995–1999	1996 IIRIRA	−0.717 (2.46)**	−0.365 (1.11)	−0.545 (1.83)
Unincorporated colonias (*n* = 41)				
1980–1984	1982 peso devaluation	−0.466 (3.29)*	−0.306 (2.01)**	−0.450 (3.15)*
1985–1989	1986 IRCA	−0.478 (3.40)*	−0.338 (2.25)**	−0.492 (3.53)*
1990–1994	1994 peso devaluation and Operation Gatekeeper	−0.757 (7.23)*	−0.488 (3.49)*	−0.661 (5.50)*
1995–1999	1996 IIRIRA	−0.590 (4.82)*	−0.398 (2.99)*	−0.536 (4.41)*
Hispanic colonias (*n* = 26)				
1980–1984	1982 peso devaluation	−0.538 (2.71)*	−0.233 (1.02)	−0.520 (2.58)**
1985–1989	1986 IRCA	−0.492 (2.40)**	−0.185 (0.80)	−0.481 (2.33)**
1990–1994	1994 peso devaluation and Operation Gatekeeper	−0.604 (3.20)*	−0.332 (1.49)	−0.511 (2.52)**
1995–1999	1996 IIRIRA	−0.590 (3.10)*	−0.398 (1.84)	−0.536 (2.69)*

Data are for nine incorporated colonias for 1980–1989 and ten incorporated colonias for 1990–2000, 41 census units comprising ninety-three unincorporated colonias, and 26 census units comprising forty colonias (incorporated and unincorporated) with Hispanic populations of at least 50 percent.

IRCA, Immigration Reform Control Act; IIRIRA, Illegal Immigration Reform and Immigrant Responsibility Act

* Significant relationship, $p < 0.01$; two-tailed t-test

** Significant relationship, $p < 0.05$; two-tailed t-test

Source: U.S. Census Bureau (1990, 2000)

born population increased in size, the percentage of residents completing high school dropped and per capita incomes declined.

The data in tables 6.1 and 6.2 indicate that national policies impact quality of life in Arizona and New Mexico colonias and hamper efforts aimed at community development. This occurs because national policies influence transborder migration, which leads Mexican nationals to colonias north of the border. The foreign-born presence, in turn, affects quality of life as community resources, such as high school education, are strained. In addition, there is ample evidence to suggest that incomes, especially per capita incomes, decline as the number of foreign-born residents in colonias increases. We believe median household income may remain high, compared with per capita income, because compared to other types of communities more members of the colonia household work.

But the most significant impact results from the inconsistency in national policies as they change over time, as these policies affect the timing of entry to the United States and the size of the foreign-born population living in colonias. As the population characteristics of colonias changed over time, the magnitude and extent of impacts varied accordingly (tables 6.1 and 6.2). Thus, the demographics of colonias are always in flux. This complicates community development efforts, because the needs of new arrivals change over time and their needs often do not coincide with the development goals and objectives of long-term colonia residents. In chapters 7, 8, and 9, we explore the problems that arise from these conflicts.

Summary

The task of providing America's economy with cheap labor while controlling unauthorized immigration is difficult, perhaps impossible, to accomplish. Congress has tried to balance these competing objectives, but it is clear that U.S. business interests prevailed while public concerns took the back seat. The drive of business interests is understandable because unauthorized immigration rewards the business community in many ways.

In this chapter, we looked at some causes of unauthorized immigration and how the United States responded to it. Our aim was to evaluate whether unauthorized immigration affects colonias and complicates community development. On the Mexican side of the border, peso devaluations in 1982 and 1994 forced unauthorized immigrants northward.

The United States responded with a sequence of immigration reforms that met with varying degrees of success. For the most part these reforms, especially Operation Gatekeeper, only managed to reshape immigration patterns.

We also found that immigration plays a critical role in shaping the demographics of Arizona and New Mexico colonias. Data limitations necessitated an examination of the foreign-born population, rather than unauthorized immigrants explicitly. Even so, the timing and size of the foreign-born population living in colonias paralleled broader trends in unauthorized immigration. As such, there is clear evidence that national policies play an important role in shaping the population characteristics of colonias. As policies on both sides of the border change over time, the demographic composition of colonias change as well. As much as anything, the foreign-born presence points to the localized effects of border policies.

The most significant impacts, however, arise from instability and uncertainty as organizers and activists confront needs that change with time. In the simplest terms, it is difficult to work toward a vision of the future when instability abounds and the needs of new arrivals clash with those of long-term residents. Thus, it comes as no surprise that conflicts arise. These issues are addressed in the following chapters.

7

The Challenges to Capacity Building in Colonias

In chapters 5 and 6, we examined how recent border policies have induced waves of unauthorized immigrants to settle in many Arizona and New Mexico colonias. New waves of settlement have put tremendous stress on these places, and leaders in many colonias are finding it extremely difficult to meet additional demands for basic living conditions. In chapters 7 to 9, we examine the complexity of community development challenges in colonias and how residents have organized to address them. This chapter examines why many local community improvement efforts fail. Chapter 8 builds from this understanding to show how colonias can build community capacity, especially when aided by various institutions, and chapter 9 considers how leaders in some colonias have adopted strategies of effective capacity building to improve the quality of life.

Throughout these chapters, we use three sources of information: our direct experience working with colonias, practical knowledge related by other capacity builders, and lessons from a comparative capacity building study of five colonias (Donelson 2005). Our direct experience includes both local and federal perspectives. One of the authors, Angela Donelson, helped Arizona colonia residents and organizations obtain infrastructure and services, assistance in planning, and capacity building resources as a staff member in a local government agency and as part of the U.S. Department of Housing and Urban Development (HUD) Southwest Border Region, Colonias, and Migrant/Farmworker Initiative.

We also draw on knowledge related by field staff working in U.S.– Mexico border communities. These include capacity builders at HUD's Southwest Border Region, Colonias, and Migrant/Farmworker Initiative; the U.S. Department of Agriculture–Rural Development (USDA-RD); and two intermediaries, the Housing Assistance Council and the Rural Community Assistance Corporation. Intermediary organizations are national nonprofit organizations that act on behalf of the federal government by distributing resources to poor communities. We

especially owe thanks to Esperanza Holguin, HUD's New Mexico colonia specialist, who shared lessons learned from decades of experience working in dozens of these communities.

Finally, we relate the comparative capacity building experiences of five Arizona and New Mexico colonias. We chose them from among all the Arizona and New Mexico unincorporated colonias described in chapter 3. We selected two colonias that demonstrated the greatest socioeconomic strengths and improvements and three exhibiting the most stress and decline on quality-of-life indicators from 1990 to 2000 (Donelson 2005). Our intent was to understand how colonias working on quality-of-life improvements differed from those in decline. With generous support of the Rural Poverty Research Center and the Annie E. Casey Foundation, we interviewed sixty-five colonia residents in the five colonias who were identified by their peers as leaders. In interviews typically lasting several hours, we asked these leaders to reflect on their colonias, their development priorities, and their ability to solve problems. The responses of these leaders revealed how colonias have sometimes succeeded and other times struggled to mobilize to bring quality-of-life improvements.

As their stories are shared, we change the names of both leaders and the colonias in which they live to protect the identity of people who sometimes shared sensitive information. Furthermore, there is no reason to label certain colonias as "underperforming" because they continue to undertake efforts to improve the quality of life.

The Challenge of Building Physical and Civic Infrastructure

Although the federal government began to make funding available for colonia infrastructure in the 1990s, today many of these places remain deprived, if not in worse condition. Many families in the poorest colonias still live in condemned trailers or homes constructed with salvaged materials. Some colonia residents still have no local water service and are forced to truck in water at exorbitant costs. Children in several colonias regularly miss class when the school bus cannot cross their flooded, muddy roads.

Why do these places still lack services that most Americans take for granted? This chapter explores this question. We first address the structural reasons for the persistence of physical infrastructure deficiencies in

Arizona and New Mexico colonias. Next, we examine civic infrastructure, which refers to the quality of local leaders and their ability to organize networks to address community development needs. When civic infrastructure is strong, it enables a colonia to more easily obtain resources and influence political channels of decision-making. Therefore, a strong civic infrastructure enables leaders to build greater community capacity, that is, to mobilize effectively for short- and long-term priorities and opportunities to improve the quality of life.

Why Physical Infrastructure Deficiencies Persist

Physical underdevelopment in Arizona and New Mexico colonias persists for three reasons. First, weak state land-use laws and their lax enforcement are to blame. Land-use laws relating to land subdivision are weak, especially in Arizona, and developers are allowed to split lots without providing essential services. In Arizona, for example, landowners can subdivide their property up to five times without putting in basic services, so successive landowners can split property indefinitely. This practice has contributed to the rapid growth of unplanned colonia settlements in Arizona, particularly during the 1990s (Carroll 2006). The expansion of so-called wildcat subdivisions is costly to taxpayers. For example, a Pima County, Arizona, study conducted by the county administrator's office in 2000 estimated that bringing infrastructure up to county minimum standards would cost $35 million to $55 million per year (Davis 2000). In 1995 the New Mexico legislature banned a similar lot-splitting practice, and in 1996 an amendment to New Mexico subdivision law took effect that forced New Mexico developers in the southern part of the state to comply with subdivision regulations. However, past lot-splitting practices have left New Mexico with many colonias that lack infrastructure (Donelson and Holguin 2001a). Many of these colonias have since expanded because New Mexico counties have provided few staff to enforce existing land-use laws. Furthermore, neither state requires landowners to inform buyers about the availability of basic services. Many residents discover they lack services only after they have purchased their home.

Infrastructure problems also persist because colonias continue to attract poor people. When the poor seek homeownership—as more than three-quarters of Arizona and New Mexico colonia residents do—many become locked into substandard living conditions. Inadequate

infrastructure and services, compounded with poor housing, tend to force the poor to overspend on basic needs, trapping them in deeper poverty.

This predicament is best illustrated with a story. Pedro Reyes lives in the unincorporated colonia of Cerrito. A construction worker in his mid-thirties, Pedro moved to the area with his wife and two young daughters from an interior state of Mexico in 2000. He was lured by the prospect of a better life, abundant work, and affordable homes. Pedro, like many of his neighbors, is a relative of former Mexican farm workers. Many of the farm workers began to settle in the Cerrito area after the Bracero Program ended in 1964.

In just four years, Pedro saved what he thought was enough to purchase a decent home. He worked long hours and cut expenses by purchasing a beat-up old trailer and renting the lot on which it was sited from a local Mexican American landlord. The bank told him he needed a 20 percent down payment, or $10,000, if he wanted to buy a new mobile home and purchase the two acres of land he was renting. So Pedro sold his old trailer to make up the difference. With the cash in hand, he was devastated when the bank told him they had made an error: he did not have enough of a credit history to qualify for a loan. Having sold his home, Pedro had to find a new one quickly. He rented another trailer that sits on the property he is still trying to purchase.

Pedro wonders if he will ever qualify for a loan. He cannot get federally subsidized financing because the property is in a floodplain, like most of those in Cerrito. Because of his limited credit history, he is tempted to go to what some call "predatory" lenders, but they charge exorbitant fees.[1] In this area, subprime lenders charge typically between 18 to 50 percent in annual interest for home loans. While they do provide a source of financing to people who could otherwise never qualify for homeownership, their tactics are frequently abusive. Some offer "contracts for deed" or "owner carrybacks" that often take 10 to 20 years to pay off, with penalties for prepayment.[2] If he enters into such a contract, Pedro will have no ownership rights to the land or to anything built on it until he pays the contract in full. If he misses a payment, loses his job, or is forced to move before the contract is up, he will lose all equity in the property.

Pedro's dilemma is not uncommon. When colonia residents seek homeownership, infrastructure repairs and high housing financing costs consume their earnings. Instead of putting money into home equity, which they could later borrow against to finance an education or start a

business, they might spend thousands of dollars each year to truck in water, heat drafty homes with propane tanks, make flood repairs to their uninsurable homes, and pay interest on a home they may never own. These problems, which stem from exclusion from conventional housing markets, are not impossible to solve. However, they do take political will to address. So far, this will has been weak in Arizona and New Mexico. Little is known about the extent of contract for deed practices and predatory lending fees in the colonias of Arizona. Although in the past several years New Mexico legislators have begun to recognize how lenders and developers target colonia residents, by 2005 they had yet to pass a bill to protect them from these practices.

The state of Texas has made more progress. Since the mid-1990s the Texas Department of Housing and Community Affairs has successfully worked with the federal, local, and nonprofit sectors to convert many contracts for deeds into federally subsidized, low-interest loans. The state has also developed a contract-for-deed consumer education curriculum and passed a law requiring greater consumer protections relating to these contracts. Furthermore, in 2001 the Texas governor passed into law antipredatory lending statutes that require housing lenders charging interest rates of 12 percent or more to notify borrowers about housing counseling resources (Thacher, Proffitt, and Wood, LLP 2001).

Even when political will is strong, the Texas experience reveals it is difficult to design effective programs that give colonia residents access to conventional mortgage financing. For one, colonia residents must be willing and able to rehabilitate substandard housing units to federal health and safety standards. Residents rarely can do so when they lack access to adequate water and sewer infrastructure, and colonia residents may choose not to do so if they have to tear down their homes and rebuild to qualify for federally subsidized financing. Many families would rather keep a substandard home rather than give it up to make long-term payments on a new home they might not be able to afford, especially if they lost their jobs.

The third reason infrastructure problems persist is that resources for colonias are inadequate and poorly distributed. There are simply not enough funds to address basic needs. No one has estimated the costs in Arizona and New Mexico, but the needs for water and wastewater in Texas colonias alone are projected at least $777 million, not including the cost of individual hookups, indoor plumbing, and water supply acquisition (U.S. Department of Housing and Urban Development 2003).

Border counties and local governments lack the tax base and fiscal resources to keep up with the growing demands of infrastructure and human services (Wilson and Guajardo 2000). Federal resources bridge only a portion of this gap. The 1990 National Affordable Housing Act required HUD and USDA-RD to set aside funding for colonias. The USDA-RD has since provided tens of millions of dollars annually for colonia water and sewer grants, but these resources are not adequate for the needs of more than 2,000 colonias throughout the border region. HUD has made 10 percent of border states' HUD community block grants available to colonias, but this is merely $1 million per year in Arizona for the state's 86 colonias and $1.5 million annually for New Mexico's 144 colonias. Other federal entities also provide resources, although they are similarly inadequate. In the early 1990s, the Environmental Protection Agency funded a one-time grant allocation of $20 million for colonia infrastructure deficiencies in New Mexico (U.S. Environmental Protection Agency 2003a). Texas colonias also obtained $315 million of the agency's resources, but Arizona failed to pursue them because at the time state officials did not acknowledge the presence of colonias. Finally, the North American Development Bank and its sister institution, the Border Environmental Cooperation Commission, which were both created as environmental side-agreements of the North American Free Trade Agreement, have provided approximately $190 million for water, sewer, and landfill improvements in the border region of Arizona and New Mexico (North American Development Bank 2006a, 2006b). However, only fourteen projects have been funded as of 2006. Many colonias do not apply because grants must be combined with loans. Moreover, cash-strapped border counties are unwilling or uncertain to repay these loans.

In addition to being inadequate, resources for colonias are poorly distributed. As figure 7.1 illustrates, distribution channels are complex, with multiple levels of government and jurisdictions providing services. Each of the jurisdictions shown in the figure requires a fee for administrative services: state governments, regional councils of governments that oversee multiple-county areas, technical assistance providers that assist in project implementation, and county and local governments.

Moreover, the pass-through nature of the funding system is slow and cumbersome, making it difficult to implement projects quickly and effectively. The local population tends to perceive that funding goes to political favorites of county elected officials. For example, the former director of a locally run community water system in a New Mexico

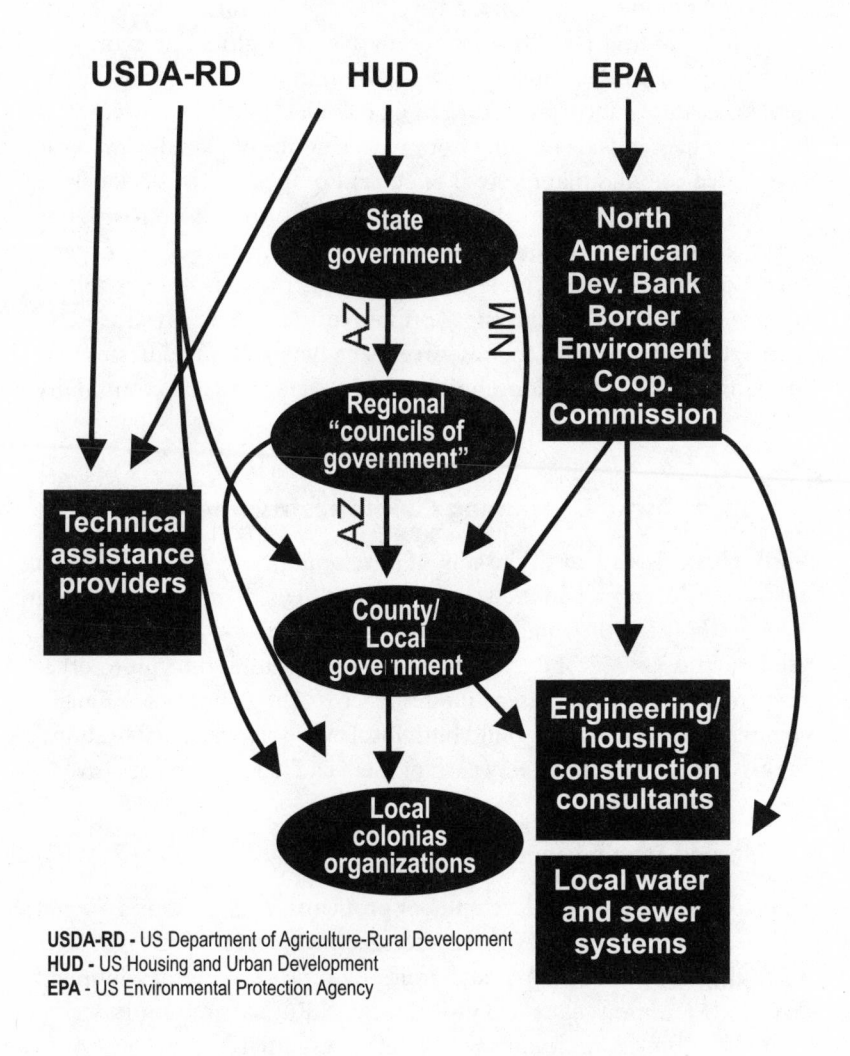

USDA-RD — US Department of Agriculture-Rural Development
HUD — US Housing and Urban Development
EPA — US Environmental Protection Agency

Figure 7.1 The flow of infrastructure funding from federal agencies to colonias

colonia voiced a complaint common among local community-based organizations, "It's not how well you prepare [the application]. It's who you know. If you go back and look at the record, the 'who you know' have gotten funded every year, and everybody else hasn't."

Even if political favorites are not always the victors, the more politically well-organized (incorporated) communities receive more funding. For example, incorporated Arizona colonias obtained 81 percent of HUD colonia set-aside funding from 1993 to 2001, compared with unincorporated colonias that received 19 percent of the resources (Donelson and Holguin 2001a, 2001b). In New Mexico the comparison is not as direct, since nearly all colonias are unincorporated. Based on our experience, however, colonias with strong civic infrastructure—leaders able to organize local residents and engage resource and policy networks—also receive the lion's share of the resources. The next section addresses why so many colonias struggle to build effective leadership on community development issues.

The Challenge of Developing Civic Infrastructure

Three challenges stand in the way of developing civic infrastructure in colonias of Arizona and New Mexico. First, few colonias have strong leaders who have the time and energy to advocate for community development issues. Second, colonia leaders often find it difficult to organize collectives that represent interests across the community. Finally, colonia leaders struggle to build both local and nonlocal collaborations. In this section, we discuss why each of these challenges is so pervasive.

Developing Strong Leadership

Some of the community development problems facing colonias are not unique to rural areas. Many rural places lack human and fiscal resources and suffer from inadequate economies of scale, making development difficult (McGuire et al. 1994; Fine et al. 2001). Rural communities struggle to develop strong leadership, which is essential if residents are to advocate for their own interests.

Yet, colonias tend to shoulder a heavier burden than most rural areas because they face additional leadership development challenges. First, because many colonia residents are poor, multiple priorities compete for

their time, which often leaves little energy to lead community efforts. Second, many colonias have a predominantly minority, Hispanic population. Residents' experiences with ethnic marginalization and discrimination tend to intimidate or discourage them from taking leadership positions. In addition, some colonias are deeply divided about community priorities along both class and generational lines. This thwarts potential leaders because they doubt that local interests can be unified and set in motion.

In these circumstances, leadership development is difficult because many colonia residents struggle to make financial ends meet. The experiences of seven Mexican women whom we interviewed from the colonia of San Cristobal illustrate this point well. All have been involved in their children's elementary school; they participate in a weekly parenting support program and volunteer in some of their children's after-school activities. Yet, they are part of only a small, motivated minority. Only 3 percent of colonia families volunteer at the school. Few can be involved, school administrators say, because both parents in most families are working. The seven women agree that things were not this bad economically even a decade ago. Employment has become increasingly scarce. The agricultural plant adjacent to the community has steadily laid off several hundred workers since the 1980s. Most agricultural jobs in the entire area have disappeared because the peso crisis of 1994 made it more profitable for Mexican farmers to sell their crops to the United States (Ford 2000). In addition, employment in maquiladoras, or twin plant operations, has been on the decline. Between 2000 and 2004 the area's maquiladora industry had laid off 18 percent of the workforce, due to the recession in the United States and the fact that many manufacturing operations have relocated to other parts of Mexico and Southeast Asia (Audley et al. 2003; Maquila Portal 2005).

Dwindling local work opportunities have forced families to pursue other options: they now drive farther, take multiple jobs, and/or supplement income with informal cottage industries. Whatever time is left in the day is devoted to the family or to improving skills to get a better job: learning English as a second language or taking general equivalency diploma classes. Although there is concern about the larger community, the women say that the lack of employment opportunities limits their own involvement in other activities. Even so, these seven women have a clear sense of priorities: affordable housing, access to health care,

after-school programs, more food and clothing assistance for their children, and a domestic violence program. But they do not have the time for leadership training to take on such large tasks.

Second, leadership is difficult to build and sustain because many Hispanic colonia residents are hesitant to lead. As Fredericksen and London (2000) noted, trust does not come easily to U.S.–Mexico border residents due to perceived and real discrimination based on citizenship, ethnicity, and economic status. Many Hispanics move to colonias to become homeowners and to flee problems of exploitative rental housing, urban crime, and related concerns (Burns 1996). These forces weigh upon residents, making it difficult to build a sense of community. Foreign-born Hispanics, many of them undocumented, worry they will be deported if they become visible in community affairs, and foreign-born Mexicans make up a substantial portion of new colonia residents (see chapter 6). In Texas, this population comprises an estimated one-third of colonia residents (May et al. 2003).

This second point—the challenge of building Hispanic leadership—is well illustrated in the unincorporated colonia of Solano. A community of about 2,000 residents, Solano is almost entirely Hispanic. It was settled at the turn of the twentieth century by a family of Anglo landowners who subdivided the community into small lots and sold them to Mexican families working in the mining industry and construction of the railroad. Solano, then, shares similarities with several Hispanic colonias in Texas that Ward (1999) and Saenz and Ballejos (1993) noted were created by Anglo developers seeking to isolate Mexican workers. Until the end of World War II, Solano was a vibrant community, with many Mexican-owned businesses, including a theater, skating rink, grocery store, dance hall, and several taverns. After the war, many Mexican families began leaving the area for better opportunities in urban areas.

Yet, the demographic complexion did not change dramatically until the 1990s. Large numbers of Mexican immigrants began to move in after the 1994 Mexican peso devaluation, so that by 2000 slightly more than one-third of residents were foreign born, up from one-quarter in 1990. The recent immigrants who came to Solano echoed the same motivations for moving there: they like the fact that the community is "calm" and "peaceful" and a place with "enough space" so that "everyone can live as they please."

Although extended families provide one another with support and neighbors sometimes help with needs, locals say it is nearly impossible to

recruit leaders for community development. Most alliances lie along family lines. The only local leadership exists within a small volunteer fire department, led by about a dozen Hispanic residents who have had some success bringing in sewer infrastructure to parts of the community, as well as road and lighting improvements. But most volunteer firefighters do not think much of recent Mexican immigrants. They believe many are undocumented loners who shun involvement. Long-term Hispanic residents similarly have given up on addressing persistent problems, such as illegal dumping of chemicals in washes, zoning complaints about dilapidated mobile homes and junked cars, and lack of a county law enforcement presence. Many believe the county elected officials—all of them Anglo and living in mostly Anglo communities—have little regard for the interests of a poor, Hispanic colonia several miles from the Mexican border.

Third, leadership is difficult to build and sustain in colonias because class and generational divisions confound community priorities. Class-based divisions are particularly evident in Solano. According to a survey of local needs conducted by a community health organization, recent Mexican immigrants expressed needs for community parks and infrastructure.[3] These priorities are very different from those named by financially better-off long-term leaders. Leaders complain that new immigrants "bring the community down to their level" by acquiring junked cars, horses, and other animals on small lots and playing loud music until early hours of the morning. In Solano, one volunteer firefighter expressed his frustration, "Many newcomers are here illegally, and they don't want to be too noticeable. Many [are not citizens and] do not vote, which means a loss of political power here. This community used to be a voting block. But since that generation moved away, politicians don't care any more about coming here."

Thus, Solano has two marginalized classes, recent Mexican immigrants and older Hispanic families. Class-based divisions are common in colonias. As Earle (1999) noted from his research in Texas, these types of divisions tend to center around the level of one's integration into U.S. culture, such as knowledge of English and citizenship status. Therefore, cohesive, representative leadership is difficult to build because these groups share few priorities.

In other colonias, leadership challenges are further complicated by cleavages not only along class but also generational lines. The colonia of San Cristobal (discussed earlier in this chapter) provides a good

illustration. San Cristobal is an almost entirely Spanish-speaking colonia of approximately 1,000 residents that was settled at the turn of the twentieth century by Mexican families who worked in agriculture and railroad construction. About half a dozen extended Hispanic families have multiple-generational roots. The Martinez family is the most prominent, having the largest land holdings. They have platted much of the land and, in the past decade, provided road easements and access to water and natural gas to a growing number of foreign-born immigrants who moved to the area after the Mexican peso devaluation in 1994. The Martinez family is selling most of these lots under "contracts for deed" to both Mexican-born immigrants and Mexican Americans seeking homeownership.

In the late 1990s, San Cristobal obtained sewer service for most of the developed area, an upgraded water system, better roads, and legal access to utilities. This attracted a third group of residents: bilingual, middle-class Mexican Americans employed as teachers, administrators, engineers, and other professionals. They see San Cristobal as an up-and-coming bedroom community offering affordable homeownership.

Since the 1990s, San Cristobal has been plagued by conflict as two groups, the middle-class professionals and the Martinez family, have battled for control. Problems first arose when a group of four middle-class residents won elected positions to the board of the only locally led organization, a community water cooperative. The Martinez family had run the cooperative since the 1960s. At that time, they created it to provide water service to the colonia. The Martinez family contested the win because they had much to lose. Prior to the election, they had agreed to provide water service to a family member who had just platted dozens of new properties. The new board refused to provide service to the area because the water system was over capacity. The Martinez family sued for breach of contract, but a county judge dismissed the lawsuit.

Undeterred, the Martinez family waged a war against the new board. They filed a complaint with the state, alleging they had been barred from voting. The state ruled that the association had, in fact, denied some the right to vote. As a result, the state ordered the board to adopt and implement written procedures to ensure fair elections in the future.

The level of conflict has drained local energy and enthusiasm for participation in public affairs. At the last water board election, current board members say they felt compelled to shut off the public water supply to generate the 5 percent quorum of water association members

required to keep federal funding. San Cristobal's leaders note that low citizen commitment has made it difficult to create a shared vision for the community. Several years ago, San Cristobal launched a local committee to install street lighting and attract industry to the area. The committee was abolished within two years, however, before it accomplished its objectives. The large group of citizens who initially expressed interest dwindled to two people. Conflict among generational and class factions has created an environment of distrust and fear. As in many colonias, these types of divisions have discouraged potential leaders from stepping forward to lead.

Building Sustainable Community Development

Colonias with community development success have more than just strong leaders, because individuals alone cannot carry long-term community development initiatives. However, leaders can create sustainable initiatives by organizing associations of residents who work for collective purposes, either as formal nonprofit organizations or informal grass-roots cooperatives.

Colonias struggle to organize for collective goals because they lack basic organizational competencies. This problem plagues both formal and informal associations. Informal associations—those that do not deliver infrastructure and social services—are particularly threatened. Most have no hired staff and rely entirely on volunteers who receive little, if any, board training or skills development. The ambiguous and loose-knit status of these informal cooperatives can compound their lack of credibility with stakeholders.

This is well illustrated by the case of the volunteer fire department in Solano, which is like many of the informal associations we have worked with. Volunteers would like to exert a greater presence in the community by building a community center and a new fire station. However, they lack the confidence, skills, and training to write proposals for financial and technical assistance. Because of this, they failed to apply for county-administered HUD community development block grant funding or a USDA-RD grant, which could have helped them pay off their $165,000 fire truck. Other rural communities in the county successfully applied for these resources to fund community centers and fire trucks. Instead, Solano's fire department took two decades to pay off the loan, relying on local fundraising.

Solano's fire department volunteers also would like to coordinate community cleanups and assist the county in remedying zoning violations, but they fear they lack the necessary power and credibility to do so. They believe residents targeted with zoning violations will retaliate by organizing local residents to overturn the fire department's tax. Solano's volunteer firefighters say they are exhausted from doing their work alone. Yet, they do not know how to build skills necessary to help them carry out their work.

The absence of basic organizational competency also challenges more formally organized nonprofit organizations operating in colonias. Like grassroots associations, they tend to lack the skills necessary to carry out their core mission. For example, in their study of eighteen housing nongovernmental organizations in the El Paso area, Fredericksen and London (2000) found that all but one lacked organizational capacity. They lacked skills in building leadership and vision; management and planning; fiscal planning and practice; and operational support, which refers to skilled staff and adequate infrastructure and support. Glaring problems included failure to include adequate minority representation on boards, an inability to retain skilled employees, the absence of stable funding and sound fiscal practices, and inadequate equipment and space (Fredericksen and London 2000).

Organizational problems in the water cooperative of the colonia of San Cristobal illustrate these challenges. After the state investigated voting fraud in the water board election, they asked a regional intermediary organization to help create proper election procedures. As the intermediary worked with San Cristobal, they found other problems they say are common to colonia utility cooperatives. The cooperative had no current membership lists to determine who should be billed for services. They also lacked descriptions of qualifications for the manager or board members; at the time, the cooperative's full-time manager also served as financial secretary, a clear conflict of interest. Moreover, the association also had poorly crafted policies and procedures that contradicted the bylaws.

Perhaps one of the worst predicaments facing colonia nonprofit organizations is financial management and accountability practices. Members of small organizations, in particular, often have little training in this area and can unintentionally misuse funds. In addition, the larger regional organizations that claim to represent their interests sometimes struggle with these issues.

The disappointing history of a micro-credit small business venture operating in the colonia of Josefito, located on the U.S.–Mexico border, illustrates this point. In the late 1990s, an urban-based, regional micro-credit association won a federal welfare reform grant to organize a sewing cooperative in Josefito. The colonia residents were excited. Micro-credit loans provided new employment opportunities to women who worked in the garment industry until the 1980s. At that time, maquiladora garment manufacturers began to relocate to the interior of Mexico and Southeast Asia for cheaper sources of labor. By the late 1990s, unemployment in Josefito had climbed to 25 percent, due to additional layoffs in natural resource–based industries and the service sector.

The sewing cooperative had an encouraging start. In three years, it grew from eleven to twenty-nine worker-owners. But then the urban micro-credit agency developed serious financial difficulties. In a letter addressed to the cooperative, the agency director announced that it had been suddenly forced to cut all financial support and take back ownership of the building that housed the sewing cooperative.

Josefito's cooperative was completely caught off guard. Those involved in the project say the micro-credit agency cut ties for several reasons: they faced federal fines for failing to make payroll taxes, and they found it too costly to service this remote, rural colonia. Our experience shows this second challenge is common in rural colonias. Despite the best intentions, urban-based nonprofit organizations sometimes pull out when they find projects are too expensive and difficult to maintain without consistent revenue streams.

Yet, the workers of the local cooperative did not give up. After a hiatus of several months, the sewing cooperative reorganized as a nonprofit organization under management of a local business manager. The enterprise relocated to a leased facility and pared worker benefits to save payroll expenses. Within the year, the cooperative reopened. Soon, it obtained federal and local government grants and loans to purchase automated sewing machines and related capital equipment. The business manager had little financial training, however, and local residents soon began to complain about perceived improprieties and favoritism. A federal investigation revealed that the local director had allocated funding for unauthorized purposes. The manager was removed, and the cooperative has since reorganized under new management. Community trust has been badly damaged, and federal funding agencies have since monitored spending carefully.

These three cases show that colonia grassroots and nonprofit organizations struggle, often unsuccessfully, to achieve organizational competencies. Yet, these skills are essential if colonias are to build sustainable community development initiatives.

Building Community Partnerships

Finally, colonia residents find it difficult to build community partnerships. Alliances with local and nonlocal organizations are critical if colonia organizations are to leverage resources to improve the quality of life.

Colonia residents have trouble creating partnerships among local organizations for several reasons. First, there are few organizations and associations to work with. In addition, colonia organizations tend to work in isolation (Donelson 2005). High levels of suspicion, distrust, and competition for resources typically confound open communication and alliance-building among colonia organizations. As Earle (1999) observed from his research in Texas colonias, residents tend to doubt others' motivations and operate on the assumptions that others are "pulling something over" on them. This behavior is typical of environments with high poverty and competition for scarce resources, where leaders tend to create centralized hierarchies and fence off resources from one another (Milofsky 2003).

The colonias of Solano and San Cristobal are like many others that struggle to build local alliances. The only locally led organizations in Solano and San Cristobal, the fire department and water cooperative, respectively, rarely collaborate with their local school district, churches, or nonprofit organizations.

In Solano, the volunteer firefighters have also been frustrated with the school board's unwillingness to share resources. When the volunteers petitioned to use the local school for a community meeting space, the school board reportedly told them to post $1 million bond, give a month's notice of public meetings, and hire a security officer during meetings. They have also been upset that current leadership of their Catholic parish abandoned efforts of the previous priest to mobilize the local congregation for community development priorities. The volunteer fire district leaders have also worked in isolation from a local health organization that has complementary priorities. The health association has a pool of local lay workers (*promotores*) who could be mobilized for community development priorities.

Similar problems plague San Cristobal. The local health organization and a regional faith-based nonprofit have abandoned efforts to organize the community because they say it is difficult to get leaders to work together. Leaders of the community water cooperative have been frustrated in their efforts to engage their local Catholic parish. They believe the Catholic diocese considers them to be unimportant compared to the larger parish in the adjacent community. The leaders say they were recently misled to renovate the church's dilapidated town hall to serve as a community center. Later, they found that church leaders restricted its use to church functions.

Colonias also struggle to build alliances with nonlocal institutions because distrust of outside agencies runs high. Colonia residents are often angered because county officials, federal agencies, and regional nonprofit organizations fail to deliver on their promises due to changing priorities, new administrations, and funding constraints.

Colonia residents often disparage urban nonprofit organizations, in particular. Although these organizations obtain funding specifically for the purpose of making colonia improvements, their perceived lack of follow-through has prompted some colonia activists to label urban nonprofit organizations "poverty pimps." Thus, it should be no surprise that outside efforts to organize colonias and achieve regional economies of scale in development projects often fail. Empirical research shows Hispanic organizations are more likely than other types of nonprofits to be independent organizations, without links to larger affiliate nongovernmental organization networks with national, state, or regional ties (Cortés 1999).

Summary

This chapter explored the challenges to capacity building in Arizona and New Mexico colonias. Both physical and civic infrastructure problems confound efforts to improve the quality of life. We examined several reasons why physical infrastructure problems persist. First, inadequate state land-use laws and weak enforcement have led to the expansion of colonias. Second, colonia residents cannot afford to remedy community deficiencies, and their efforts to do so often trap them in deeper poverty. Finally, there are insufficient county, state, and federal resources, and those that are available are inefficiently distributed and thus unable to correct colonia infrastructure problems.

Next, we examined how the lack of a strong civic infrastructure makes it difficult for many colonias to build community capacity. We discussed three impediments to development of civic infrastructure. First, colonias have difficulties recruiting and retaining community development leaders. Second, colonia residents often find it difficult to create sustainable organizations to represent local interests. Finally, colonia leaders tend to resist resource and information sharing among local and nonlocal organizations, due to historical experiences with conflict, resource deprivation, and racial oppression that thwart community trust. With a better understanding of these challenges, in the next chapter we provide a framework for understanding community capacity building in the context of colonias.

8
Developing Community Capacity in Colonias

The last chapter examined structural barriers and challenges to development of civic infrastructure in Arizona and New Mexico colonias. In this chapter, we draw upon our understanding to examine how colonias can improve local conditions by building community capacity.

First, we examine the concept of community capacity and explore why it has gained favor among government agencies and community development institutions, especially since the 1990s. We also discuss some of the potential problems arising from this approach in poor, rural areas. Next, we propose a three-part framework for assessing and building capacity in colonias. The framework draws on the challenges outlined in chapter 7: developing strong leadership, creating sustainable organizations, and forging collaborations that bridge local and nonlocal networks. Each part of the framework addresses the roles and responsibilities of local colonia residents and capacity building institutions. Such institutions considered here include regional intermediary organizations; government institutions at the federal, state, and local levels; and community development organizations that can build the skills and capacities of colonia residents.

Why Community Capacity?
A Historical Perspective

The approach to getting things done in community development has shifted remarkably over the past four decades. Although social reformers have long recognized the need to improve living conditions of the poor, it was not until the early 1960s that the U.S. federal government focused on financing large-scale, regional community development initiatives as a means of poverty reduction (Glasmeier 2002). These initiatives, however, developed only superficial partnerships with local institutions. The 1980s was a period of neoliberalism, in which federal control was shifted to civil sector governance. Beginning in the 1990s, the emphasis became

building community capacity and the local management of resources. In the rest of this section, we discuss these shifts in thought.

Early community development efforts of the 1960s were mostly federally controlled and directed. President Kennedy created the Area Redevelopment Administration (later the Economic Development Administration) in 1961 to direct economic development assistance to Indian reservations and other rural, poverty-stricken areas (Duncan 1999). Four years later, the Johnson Administration created the Community Action Program, Special Impact Program, and Model Cities Program to improve infrastructure, housing, and the social environment. The first two programs granted funding to nonprofit institutions, while the third provided resources to municipalities. These early programs, however, essentially failed to produce their expected results. This was largely because the federal government controlled resources without giving proper authority and accountability to community-based institutions. Federal agencies also failed to enlist true community participation and concurrence with these organizations (Green and Haines 2002).

By the 1980s, approaches began to shift from direct federal control to activities directed by community-based organizations. These organizations comprise the civil sector of society, performing socio-cultural, economic, and political functions beyond those mobilized by the private sector, government, or individual households (Salamon 1994; Weaver et al. 1997; Kramer 2000). There were two reasons for this shift in responsibility. The first related to the rise of neoliberalism, which took hold in the early 1980s and has continued thereafter. One tenet of neoliberalism is limited government involvement, and a second urges the withdrawal of federal financial support from state and local issues. These ideological changes led to major cutbacks in the size of U.S. government agencies. Policymakers believed that resources for community development would be cheaper if undertaken by community-based institutions because they could compete for funds and provide services with fewer dollars and more volunteer efforts (Alexander 1998). Policymakers also believed that the nonprofit sector was more capable of managing programs because of their perceived ability to build broad-based networks and local trust (Wolch 1990; Fisher 1993, 1998; Salamon 1994).

By the 1990s, however, it was clear that civil society alone could not eradicate poverty. Community-based organizations have found it difficult to create collaborations that reflect the diverse needs of multiple stakeholders and leverage fragmented sources of government funding in

an era of declining resources (Powell and Friedkin 1987; Goodwin 1998; Murdoch and Abram 1998; Rakodi 2001; Takahashi and Smutny 2001). This prompted federal agencies and national foundations to examine ways to strengthen community-based organizations. This approach, known as capacity building, has become increasingly popular since the 1990s. It seeks to strengthen the skills and organizational capabilities of the civil sector, so that local leaders can better manage their own affairs (Murray and Dunn 1995; Edwards and Hulme 1996; Meyer 1997; Chaskin 2001; Linnell 2003). Capacity builders have increasingly recognized the critical role of nonlocal institutions, such as federal and regional governments and foundations, in providing financial and technical resources (Chaskin 2001). This differs from some earlier capacity building approaches that overemphasized asset-based development. This school of thought, which prioritizes the community's responsibility in its own development and mobilizing assets instead of identifying problems, often implies that government interventions are irrelevant to capacity, and that capacity development is only the terrain of the community itself (Simpson et al. 2003). This is particularly unrealistic for poor places, however, where local leaders cannot rely on their own scarce resources. They need external assistance from partners in government, foundations, and community institutions in building both physical and civic infrastructure.

In colonias, capacity building can improve the skills and capabilities of local leaders and organizations and leverage them with resources of government agencies, foundations, and community institutions to improve the quality of life. It can help colonia residents organize more effectively to meet basic needs and influence policy.

Problems with the Capacity Building Approach

Capacity building approaches have generated significant enthusiasm, and since the mid-1990s community development advocates in the United States have increasingly requested more financial resources for this purpose. These advocates believe—and federal institutions agree—that capacity building efforts will make existing federal investments more effective (U.S. General Accounting Office 2002; National Congress for Community Economic Development 2004).

However, capacity building institutions mostly have in mind the needs of urban, nonprofit institutions, not the unique needs of poor,

rural places like colonias. For example, the U.S. Department of Housing and Urban Development (HUD) provides more than $100 million in capacity building funds each year to legally incorporated organizations to expand existing housing, economic development assistance, and related services (U.S. General Accounting Office 2002). Agencies like HUD do not fund skill-building for individual leaders associated with grassroots associations, because informal associations lack legal nonprofit status and do not provide services. Yet, informal associations are more common than nonprofits in rural areas. Rural areas rarely have the human and fiscal resources or economies of scale needed to sustain nonprofit development organizations (McGuire et al. 1994; Fine et al. 2001). As such, the efforts led by these informal associations are often overlooked.

Rural leaders and the small associations they organize have more basic needs than professional nonprofit organizations. Therefore, organizational models and nonprofit concepts of efficiency cannot simply be transferred. By virtue of their smallness, grassroots associations often have unclear missions, undefined boundaries, no administrative staff, and no legal incorporation (Smith 1997; Milofsky and Messer 1998; Anheier and Themudo 2002; Milofsky 2003). Because of this, small, informal organizations may be unaccountable to any constituency. In the absence of representation, grassroots efforts can become self-serving, conforming to an "iron law of oligarchy" in which the elected rule over the electors (Powell and Friedkin 1987). The minority, feeling they alone are committed or competent to lead, make decisions to satisfy their own needs. In doing so, they subvert the interests of the larger community (Harris 1998).

Being small does not have to be a liability—it can be an asset, especially in colonias. Informal associations may be better able to exercise flexible and imaginative leadership, enabling them to develop a strong sense of shared purpose (Rochester 1999). These associations may also devote more time to building personal relationships, so they can gain trust more effectively and represent the collective interests of residents. In contrast, formal organizations are often forced to spend much of their time on organizational maintenance: tending to budgets, performing audits, updating bylaws, keeping minutes, and reporting to funding agencies. As Dolhinow (2005) and Lemos et al. (2002) noted from their research of nonprofit organizations in New Mexico colonias, focusing on resource acquisition and "professionalization" can disable community activism. Their findings echo those of other nonprofit scholars: donor

nonprofit organizations can easily become transformed into mere pass-throughs of government funding (Wolch 1990; Fisher 1998; Froelich 1999). Therefore, the smallness and informality of grassroots associations is worth preserving. Capacity building efforts in colonias should seek to build local leadership and protect the potential of grassroots associations for mobilizing and reversing historical patterns of isolation and discrimination.

Capacity Building Needs in Colonias

Colonias have relatively straightforward capacity building needs. These are divided into three elements: developing leadership for local autonomy, or self-determination; creating associations of leaders that can sustain community development efforts; and forging collaborative partnerships that can scale up or enhance the work of local community associations (fig. 8.1). This three-part strategy involves roles for both local associations and capacity building institutions. The roles for each are described in greater detail throughout the remainder of the chapter.

Building Leadership for Local Autonomy

Colonias need to cultivate strong leadership if residents are to effectively determine and act on community priorities and interests. Strong leadership, distributed broadly enough to reflect diverse community interests, helps the colonia become autonomous. That is, it ensures independence from local individuals or organizations who seek to dominate and/or satisfy self-interests (Powell and Friedkin 1987) as well as from external partners who may seek to control community activities (Wolch 1990; Fisher 1998; Warner 1999, 2001). As discussed in chapter 7, colonia residents often complain they lack both forms of independence.

Colonia leaders have basic needs, what De Souza Briggs (2004) termed the "skills of public life," such as learning how to run a meeting, to deliberate, and to define public issues, all of which help assimilate the poor and underserved into broader community participation. These skills are essential to breaking the strongholds of elites, who often gain the benefits of development. Development of these leadership skills motivates more than a few to define local needs and carry them forward, preventing leader burnout and ensuring that the community as a whole owns them (De Vita et al. 2001).

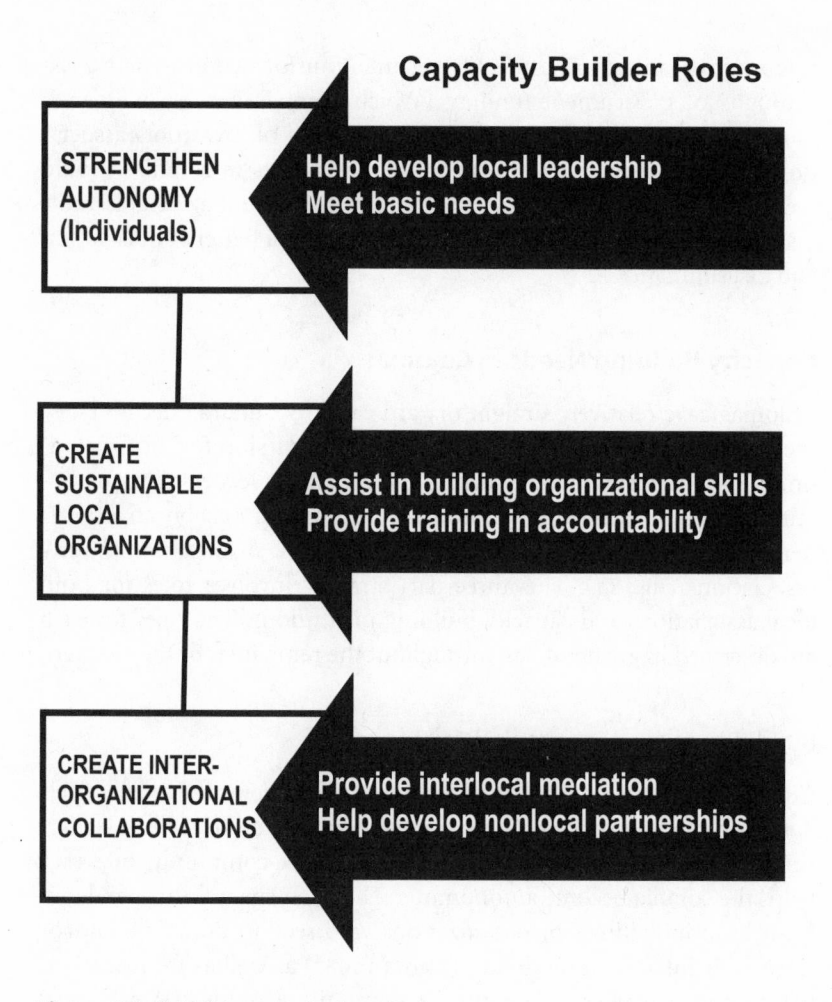

Figure 8.1 Building capacity in colonias

Given the constraints of the poverty, transient population, and class and generational divisions presented in chapter 7, it is unrealistic to expect colonias to cultivate a large and diverse pool of leadership. Therefore, residents must look to other means of building participation. Community brokers hold great potential as a means of assisting in this objective. These brokers are respected among colonia residents and able to bridge local interests with the assistance of outsiders. In areas marked by poverty and insufficient leadership, community brokers can be effective

advocates for mobilizing resources and making quality-of-life improvements possible (Eckstein 2001).

Our experience and those of other capacity builders reveals that even the poorest colonias have some form of brokers. Some are local residents who seek to bring in water, sewer, or other essential services. Others are former residents who have moved away but care deeply about the needs of their former community and extended families who still live there. Some are trusted outsiders, such as lay health workers (*promotores*) residing in nearby colonias. Several regional nonprofit organizations in the U.S.– Mexico border states, as well as in other parts of the country, have found it effective to hire lay health workers to conduct outreach on issues such as diabetes, prenatal health, lead-based paint hazards, HIV/AIDS, and services for women and children (May et al. 2003, 2005). Through their training, promotores learn to make public presentations, conduct community surveys, organize residents, and sometimes mediate conflicts. Research has found that promotores add value to the community in several ways, through information and referral services, education in specialized areas, capacity building that fosters leadership and connects residents, emotional support, and advocacy for local empowerment (May et al. 2004). These functions build a source of knowledge and expertise that remains in border communities, even when nonprofit agencies complete outreach projects or lose grant funding.

Brokers serve as an excellent source for colonia mobilization because they serve as a bridge between local and nonlocal organizations. Colonia residents tend to recognize community brokers as reputable sources of information and resources. Therefore, brokers are likely to have the trust of local residents. Regional nonprofit organizations and local governments also recognize these brokers as de facto leaders and consult with brokers when they want to know more about local concerns or assist a colonia.

Building Leaders for Local Autonomy:
The Role of Capacity Building Organizations

Government institutions, regional community development organizations, and foundations play important roles in developing the leadership skills of local residents. First, they can provide funding and training for basic skills needed to function in Anglo culture. These skills, such as

learning English and obtaining a general equivalency diploma, improve the level of human capital and reduce barriers to participation. Capacity builders also can provide residents with public skills leadership training, that is, how to advocate for their interests and work with local elected officials. Furthermore, they can strengthen the capabilities of existing brokers and help them cultivate new ones. Our experience shows that brokers probably most need training in mediation, community building, and mentorship.

Capacity building institutions, especially federal and local governments, also have the critical role of addressing basic physical and economic inequalities, a task that residents cannot do on their own. Physical infrastructure inequalities have become increasingly evident as colonias expand. As many communities have grown, the newest, poorest, most peripheral neighborhoods often lack infrastructure, while older, more established neighborhoods typically have acquired them (see chapter 4 for more on the morphology of colonias). Eliminating physical inequality is one of the most effective uses of federal assistance, because it responds to immediate basic needs while leveling the playing field so that the community can build unity and move ahead in the capacity building process. By directing resources to the most underserved places, government institutions can reduce patterns of inequality that concentrate poverty in the poorest neighborhoods. As the physically worst-off places improve, they can remain affordable to the poor through governmental subsidies, such as homeownership assistance and affordable housing land trusts.

Similarly, government agencies, foundations, and community development institutions can help remedy economic disadvantages by providing resources for entrepreneurship training and capital for creating small businesses. Entrepreneurship tends to be especially well suited to poor, ethnic communities, where language difficulties hinder local residents from accessing traditional employment and residents already engage in informal industry to make ends meet (Sanders 2002). Government institutions can help ethnic entrepreneurs build wealth and expand their economic potential by helping them reach markets for goods and services that extend beyond their community (Aldrich and Waldinger 1990). For example, the U.S. Small Business Administration helps certify minority- and women-owned businesses that can compete for federal contracts. By providing resources for more stable employment, government institutions can free residents for positions of leadership, because

stably employed residents are likely to have more time, energy, and capabilities to lead in local affairs.

Building Sustainable Organizations

As individuals obtain resources to meet basic needs and strengthen their leadership skills, they must also find ways to organize collectively. Organizing enables residents to distribute leadership and therefore better sustain community efforts to meet short- and long-term needs. Organizing efforts take different forms. Colonia residents often create loose-knit, grassroots associations to address advocacy needs on particular issues, such as lobbying the county for infrastructure improvements or a community center. Sometimes colonia leaders make their organizing efforts more formal—through incorporating as small nonprofit organizations—to be eligible for funding. Formal incorporation enables colonia associations to provide basic services such as water or a local fire department. Regardless of how they organize, colonia associations can sustain their work only if they are successful in attaining basic competencies.

For small colonia organizations, basic competencies require a balance between the formal and the informal and between the day-to-day and the long term (Rochester 1999). Small organizations need informality to develop relationships and forge a strong sense of shared purpose. At the same time, they need some formality to clarify responsibility, eliminate unclear or ill-defined roles, and avoid making arbitrary and inefficient use of resources (Rochester 1999). Yet, formality does not require the standard organizational criteria most capacity builders believe are required of effective nonprofit organizations. Items such as a written needs assessment, standard operating procedures, planning documents, appraisal process, and measurement criteria almost never apply. In fact, research has shown that there is only a weak relationship between nonprofit organizations that have these items in place and their effectiveness (Herman and Renz 1999).

What basic competencies are essential to small colonia associations, regardless of whether they are formally incorporated? First, small associations must have an agreed-upon set of strategic commitments. Most often these are reflected in a mission statement, along with clear priorities that members agree are necessary to carry out the mission. However, leaders of small nonprofits and grassroots associations find it difficult to build consensus on priorities because it simply takes excessive

resources and energy to establish and maintain communication with stakeholders. Local residents rarely attend public meetings. Most incorporated colonias also lack the means to survey the community, publish a newsletter, or gain feedback regarding community priorities. These constraints force colonia leaders to piece together a picture of community needs and priorities in creative, although time-intensive, ways. Leaders in colonias such as the predominantly farm-worker community of Cerrito (discussed in chapter 7) have surveyed needs by going door to door to talk to their neighbors. However, they say they have only done this once—at the very beginning of their eight years of work in the community. Because the process was slow and all consuming, they have not updated their assessment of needs, despite the changing needs of many new immigrants.

The strategy adopted by the Industrial Areas Foundation (IAF) is perhaps more promising. (The foundation's history and strategy are discussed in much more detail in chapter 9.) The IAF has built consensus for action in some colonias of Yuma County, Arizona, and Doña Ana County, New Mexico. The foundation has done so by organizing small groups of local residents in private homes to discuss their individual hopes, fears, and desires, as well as shared community concerns. However, the process that seeks to build confidence and trust among a group of residents is lengthy. It sometimes takes years to build a shared agenda for community action, and the process requires time and resources that many communities lacking IAF sponsorship cannot afford.

The second component critical to competency of small colonia organizations is the means to act upon strategic commitments. Leaders often cannot act because they do not know how to mobilize resources or access assistance. Many organizations we have worked with were unaware of potential resources or assistance. If they are aware, most lack the confidence or technical ability to apply for them. Volunteers with grassroots and small organizations also say they would like to approach county officials for assistance, but they do not know how to go about it. Even formal nonprofit organizations with paid staff working in the U.S.–Mexico border region struggle with developing basic organizational skills. As noted in chapter 7, a recent study of eighteen nonprofit housing organizations in El Paso found that all but one lacked the institutional capacity to carry out its core mission (Fredericksen and London 2000).

The third competency critical to colonia organizations is transparency and accountability. Research has shown that nonprofit organiza-

tions effective in carrying out their commitments prioritize accountability both with local stakeholders and with external organizations that provide resources (Avner and Van Hoomissen 1991; Edwards 1996; Edwards et al. 2000). Without accountability for resources, leadership can become self-serving, thereby fostering distrust and potentially destroying well-intentioned community projects.

Organizations can build transparency in two ways. First, they can maintain regular communications with their constituents, both informally through word of mouth as well as through more formal channels, such as holding meetings to discuss organizational goals, priorities, and activities. Second, organizations can maintain transparency of their activities through financial accountability. Small colonia nonprofit associations that accept resources tend to struggle with this issue. As discussed in chapter 7, colonia organizations tend to lack trained staff knowledgeable of good financial principles and practices. Yet, this type of training is essential to win public confidence.

Building Sustainable Organizations: The Role of Capacity Building

Capacity building institutions have important roles in helping colonias build associations that can identify strategic commitments, act on them, and remain transparent about their activities. First, capacity builders should provide resources to grassroots and small organizations to assess local needs. These resources are required on an ongoing basis, not as one-time projects. For example, funding can be directed for stipends to community brokers who regularly host small-group house meetings, similar to the IAF strategy, to determine local priorities.

Capacity builders can also help colonia associations act on commitments by providing training in community analysis, fundraising, negotiating with public officials, and similar activities. Perhaps the most effective way to do so is to fund a tiered mentoring program. Colonias with stronger associations can assist those seeking to build capacity. In turn, associations with slightly less capacity can mentor those with the least organizational capacity.

In addition, capacity builders can help colonias build greater transparency by directing funding and technical resources for accountability in both their activities and financial affairs. Greater transparency in organizational activities can be accomplished through subsidizing improved

communications, such as newsletters, surveys, and door-to-door outreach activities. Surprisingly, some urban social service organizations
have assumed that colonia leaders can do these things without financial
assistance. For example, colonia leaders in the poor, Hispanic colonia
of Mirasol said several service agencies asked them to disseminate information about social services without offering stipends to defray the
expenses of reaching the community's 5,000 residents. Community-
based organizations—especially those whose outreach efforts are conducted by lay health promotores—can provide information effectively
and survey resources and enhance the brokering capabilities of community leaders.

Finally, greater transparency in financial affairs can be accomplished
through better training in resource management, budgeting, bookkeep-
ing, and related skills. Without adequate controls for ensuring fiscal
accountability, donors are hesitant to invest resources for fear of man-
agerial incompetence or misuse of funds.

Building Community Collaborations

In addition to strong leadership and organizations, colonia associations
need collaborative partnerships with both local and nonlocal institutions
to generate and sustain quality-of-life improvements. As many community development scholars and sociologists have noted, both local and
nonlocal partnerships are critical (Warren 1963; Rogers 1974; Galaskiewicz 1979; Fisher 1993, 1998; Putnam 1993; Edwards and Hulme 1996; Wilson 1997; Duncan 1999). A broad base of relationships among local leaders
and community associations strengthens local skills and knowledge,
which, in turn, improves autonomy. At the same time, a network of relationships with nonlocal institutions provides access to external resources
and policy assistance that may improve the quality of life in colonias.

Working with local partners—those within the immediate community—includes building strategies for action among brokers and grassroots associations, as well as more formal local institutions, such as
schools, churches, and nonprofit organizations that provide programs or
services in the colonia. Local partnerships are essential because they help
coordinate and share the workload. Interorganizational partnerships
also create a rich network of social capital, which Putnam (1993), Coleman (1988), and others defined as norms, networks, and trust among
local leaders and institutions that facilitate collective action for mutual

benefit. That is, collective action builds social capital that creates a shared sense of purpose and priorities. As discussed in chapter 7, predominantly ethnic communities facing racial oppression and isolation find this task daunting because leaders tend to operate in an environment based on distrust, not sharing resources with one another (Earle 1999; Milofsky 2003). Trust among local associations is essential for advancing interests important to all members of the community.

Nonlocal partnerships are also essential, including collaborations with county, state, and federal agencies; foundations; and regional community development agencies. Nonlocal institutions can provide colonias with two types of assistance: fiscal/technical and policy/strategy assistance. The first form of assistance can resolve immediate resource needs. For example, fiscal resources can build a local wastewater system, while technical assistance can train individuals who will maintain it. Policy and strategy intervention is also essential, because it can enable colonias to forge politically strategic relationships and alter social relations that keep many poor and marginalized colonias from participation.

Building Community Collaborations: The Role of Capacity Building Organizations

Capacity builders have three critical roles in helping colonia organizations develop local and nonlocal collaborative partnerships to improve the quality of life. First, they can help local colonia institutions forge strong local networks by providing resources for consensus building. In community development planning, research has shown that consensus is often achieved through third-party mediation and dispute resolution. Mediation can improve the quality of stakeholder deliberation because more believe they are heard, respected, and included in community discussions (Innes 1996; Innes and Booher 1999). In turn, better stakeholder deliberation can produce participation and consensus on community agreements that result in both tangible benefits, such as plans, agreements, policies, and activities, as well as intangible ones, such as improved trust among diverse stakeholders with different power distributions and interests (Innes and Booher 1999).

Resources for mediation could be particularly helpful in colonias plagued by deep class and generational divisions. Our experiences and those related by other capacity builders reveal that external organizations, especially foundations and government organizations, rarely

venture into this territory. Donors often lack the political courage, skills, or resources to involve themselves in the messy business of community conflict. In our experience, however, residents often express a strong desire for third-party mediation. A volatile situation in the colonia of Josefito (described in chapter 7) illustrates how this type of assistance could be helpful. After a regional micro-credit agency abandoned the community's sewing cooperative, a minority of leaders rose up to take control. Leaders within several distinct sectors—some involved in the community food bank, others affiliated with the local community college—petitioned federal staff to intervene. However, federal staff held off for a year, until it was inevitable. At this point, evidence of financial impropriety surfaced. Early mediation might have averted many problems, but late action only deepened local divisions.

Second, capacity builders can help colonia associations build relationships with networks of funding institutions. Many colonia associations lack the time or knowledge to navigate the maze of government institutions and foundation grant programs. External institutions, such as HUD's Southwest Border Region, Colonias, and Migrant/Farmworker Initiative and community development intermediary associations, can bring resources and training to these communities. These capacity builders have sought to train grassroots associations on how to partner with federal networks on special border initiatives.

Third, external institutions, especially community-based organizations and foundations, can help colonias pool knowledge and resources in the form of regional network organizations that share similar resource constraints or policy interests. Creating networks helps grassroots associations scale up to expand their impact beyond the local level, while creating social and intellectual diversity and new knowledge (Fisher 1998; Uvin et al. 2000). Networks are important in developing a wider sense of community and advocacy among diffuse, heterogeneous colonia groups, which Ward (2001) appropriately observed "vary markedly in size, layout, mode of development, [and] mix of housing types." Networking enables smaller organizations to remain small, while collaborating with other agencies to lobby for specific policies or to implement programs (Uvin et al. 2000). Community-based organizations and foundations can be a powerful force in reversing policies that promote the marginalization of colonias and lead to the expansion of new ones.

Despite the potential of regional networks, many colonia grassroots

associations in Arizona and New Mexico have not built or joined these networks. Instead, colonia grassroots associations in these states tend to operate in isolation, focusing on the provision of basic service needs (Donelson 2004). Organizations are isolated because it takes political skill to organize networks, which colonia leaders often lack. In addition, it requires leaders who understand shared concerns and issues that rise above parochial interests. This is especially challenging, given that colonias find it difficult to organize their own community collective interests. Finally, organizing networks requires resources for alliance-building, which are scarce. Federal funding, for example, prohibits political activities and only allows organizations to use capacity resources for service-related organizational capacity. Therefore, private foundations and community-based organizations, in particular, should seek to direct resources for this purpose.

As capacity builders help develop network organizations, however, they must be wary of displacing colonia priorities with their own. For example, network building institutions like the IAF's Interfaith Sponsoring Committee (discussed in greater detail in chapter 9) are subject to this critique. The IAF operates on the assumption that residents will attain autonomy only if they are taught organizing skills that help access basic services. Yet, colonia residents may disagree. Many say they would like to see capacity builders help meet basic needs first. Some residents say they do not have time for extensive political mobilization strategies.

This goal displacement problem is apparent in the Hispanic colonia of Jacinto, an unincorporated community of nearly 5,000 residents, many of them former farm workers now employed in low-wage services. The community lacks sewer service, adequate roads, and street lighting. Many homes are dilapidated or in serious disrepair. A group of Hispanic women leaders reported that IAF turned down their request to help them legally incorporate their small association. The women hoped incorporation would give them greater recognition in the eyes of county officials, as well as access to federal infrastructure grants. However, the IAF reportedly declined to help because this activity was considered inconsistent with the network's political orientation.

This story illustrates why local colonias are wary of participating in network organizations. Although these organizations can provide great resources, capacity builders must be sensitive to and willing to assist in building progress toward locally directed priorities.

Summary

This chapter examined the concept of community capacity, especially as applied to poor, rural colonias. We first explored advantages of the capacity building approach, as well as potential problems with its application in poor areas. Next, we proposed a simple three-part framework for evaluating capacity in rural colonias. This framework emphasized the importance of building individual-level leadership for autonomy, community development associations that are sustainable, and collaborative local and nonlocal partnerships that improve access to and use of resources. As each factor of capacity was addressed, we discussed the important role for capacity builders in strengthening the local skills and ability of colonia leaders and organizations. The next chapter addresses how colonias have successfully applied principles of capacity building to improve their quality of life.

9
Strategies for Capacity Building in Colonias

This chapter illustrates how some Arizona and New Mexico colonias have adopted strategies of effective capacity building to improve their quality of life. We demonstrate how the three principles outlined in chapter 8—promoting local autonomy, sustainable organizations, and effective partnerships—are carried out in practice.

The chapter is divided in three sections, following these three principles. The first shows how colonia residents and capacity builders have built greater autonomy and self-determination through strengthening local leadership and meeting basic needs. Next, we discuss how colonia residents have worked with capacity builders to create sustainable community organizations, through improving both organizational skills and training in accountability. Finally, we consider how colonia associations have created partnerships that generate and sustain quality-of-life improvements. These interorganizational local collaborations address shared concerns and link to nonlocal networks that bring fiscal and technical assistance as well as policy and strategy support.

The principles of this chapter suggest six capacity building strategies for action (shown in fig. 8.1). We provide examples of how colonias have applied the six strategies. Where appropriate, we draw attention to the ways in which success in strategy implementation varies with the cultural context. That is, colonias with mostly Hispanic populations tend to approach community improvement efforts in more informal ways that build upon personal relationships, rather than formal organizational collaborations. Colonias with Anglo leadership, in contrast, tend to approach community building from a more structured framework that builds formal interorganizational partnerships. Capacity builders should keep in mind that both formal and informal approaches can be useful, as long as they are inclusive of and responsive to the unique needs of each colonia and their diverse populations.

Strengthening Community Autonomy

As discussed in chapter 8, colonias need autonomy to set and follow through on community development priorities. Autonomy depends on successful implementation of two strategies: developing strong local leadership and meeting basic needs. Yet, colonia residents may disagree about which takes precedence. Some emphasize leadership building as a precondition for obtaining basic needs. Its advocates assume leadership is the first step in the development process because it builds a pool of trained leaders who will advocate effectively for local improvements. Others, however, believe that meeting basic needs is the starting point in development. They contend that conditions of extreme poverty and economic instability undermine the potential for broad leadership. Only when basic needs are met, they argue, will residents have sufficient time and energy to pursue leadership training that advances local community development. Capacity builders need to be sensitive to these concerns and aware that one strategy is often a better fit than the other. Ultimately, however, both approaches are essential to development, as we show in the following two case studies.

Building Local Leadership for Autonomy

Perhaps the most successful example of the first strategy, building leadership as a precondition for development, is embodied in the work of the Industrial Area Foundation (IAF). The IAF has launched networks of mostly church-based organizers that have operated in Texas and New Mexico colonias since the 1980s and in some Arizona colonias since the 1990s (Ward 1999; Buckwalter 2003). The IAF seeks to identify the types of community brokers described in chapter 8 and to expand their leadership capacities so they can elicit participation from the wider community (Warren 1996; Ward 1999; Buckwalter 2003).

The IAF was founded in the 1930s by radical community organizer Saul Alinsky, who used controversy and conflict as a means for negotiating for the rights of the poor. Today, the IAF, with more than forty national community-based organizations, is perhaps the nation's most successful organizing network for community development issues (Warren 1996). Its professional organizers work with church leaders in local communities to recruit and train leaders, mostly women. IAF associations have attracted membership mostly from the Catholic Church, but

also some mainstream Protestant denominations, because they are polit-ically active but nonpartisan (Warren 2001).

These efforts are particularly well suited to colonias. Religious-based organizing capitalizes on the ties of many colonia residents to the Catho-lic Church. As Carl Milofsky (2003) noted, faith-based consensus build-ing in community development can break the tendency toward tight centralization and control of leadership in racially oppressed commu-nities. In addition, IAF efforts tend to be successful in colonias because they focus on building the leadership capacities of local residents. The IAF first dispatches paid community organizers (usually from outside the area) to work in a colonia. These organizers, in turn, train local colonia leaders who then become brokers for information, resources, and organizing. Community organizers look for specific qualities when they recruit leaders: those who can motivate others, commit to training additional leaders, and desire to bring about equity on economic, social, and political concerns within their communities (Warren 2001).

Through the IAF, local leaders receive two kinds of training. They learn technical leadership skills, such as how to chair a meeting, do research, or give a public presentation. Perhaps more importantly, they learn a set of skills known as the "art of politics": how to analyze commu-nity power dynamics, decide a course of action based on collective needs, and weigh alternatives (Warren 2001). Through their mentors, brokers learn how to negotiate with, and sometimes confront, local elected offi-cials. Once IAF gets elected officials to commit to common interests, the organization hosts accountability sessions. Officials are challenged to publicly commit to these needs.

Maria Torres is one of the brokers trained by the IAF. Like many who live in the colonia of Independencia, she is an immigrant farm worker. Nearly half of the 7,000 residents of her area live below poverty. The unemployment rate rises to 80 percent during the summer months be-cause the agriculture industry does not employ workers year-round. Working on her own for a decade, Maria struggled unsuccessfully to bring basic services to her rapidly growing colonia, especially parks and after-school recreational opportunities. Her efforts began to bear fruit after the IAF provided her with leadership training. In the late 1990s, she organized more than a hundred residents who took time off work to show up for county public hearings—held during weekday hours—to ensure that more funds are committed to colonias. Several years ago, the county pledged funding to build a park that would serve Independencia

and an adjacent colonia, and the local school district agreed to maintain the property. Local government also funded two after-school educational pilot programs designed by parents and teachers to provide a safe haven for children with no after-school activities.

While it offers great potential, the IAF leadership development approach is not well suited for all colonias. For one, the process is lengthy and expensive. It requires months and sometimes years of house meetings to build trust and consensus among individuals with different values and personal motivations and who are separated by class, generational, and religious differences (Buckwalter 2003). In Yuma County, for example, IAF's group of Catholic, Presbyterian, and Methodist member congregations hosted more than 1,000 conversations with 400 residents organized in small groups of about 10 people. This is what it took to create a broad coalition that agreed on a countywide "human/family development agenda" that includes health care, youth development, work and labor, education, and immigration issues. Clearly, the IAF does not have the resources to make such deep investments in all colonias. Most Arizona and New Mexico colonias have no such organizing effort.

Moreover, the IAF approach is not well suited to all colonias because local residents may resist externally imposed efforts. Colonia leaders sometimes disapprove of the IAF's political tactics, instead favoring less confrontational solutions. They may distrust IAF's paid organizers, who select local brokers and manage the training process. Colonia residents may be wary of faith-based organizing because the church, like any institution, is perceived as fallible. As discussed in chapter 7, colonia residents sometimes believe clergy selectively ignore their needs or manipulate leaders to serve church interests.

Therefore, the IAF's leadership development approach has both strengths and weaknesses. The strengths are in building upon existing religious ties in organizing to cultivate deep, lasting political and technical leadership skills. The weaknesses are the IAF's reliance on externally imposed decision-making and the time needed to develop consensus-based leadership.

Meeting Basic Needs for Autonomy

Given the shortcomings of the leadership development approach, colonias at times favor an alternative: addressing basic needs as the first step

in development. Often, a handful of local residents will take on this task and petition the county and regional nonprofit organizations to help resolve infrastructure and service deficiencies. They believe their efforts will lead to services that, down the road, can generate energy and support for participating in broader-based leadership.

By prioritizing basic needs, community improvements happen quickly and thus generate resident enthusiasm for further action. The weakness of this strategy, however, is in its tendency to build a narrow leadership base that struggles to achieve broad-based consensus on issues over time. Development in the Mirasol area has taken this path.

The Mirasol area includes a cluster of colonias with approximately 5,000 residents who are mostly low-income Hispanics. According to U.S. Census Bureau data for 2000, foreign-born immigrants made up nearly half of the population. Many of these immigrants came with the 1986 Immigration Reform and Control Act, settling in secondhand trailers set up in improperly platted subdivisions. In contrast, many residents of the oldest, most settled area have lived there for generations; their African American and Hispanic parents established the area as a farming community in the late 1800s. Residents mostly work in the service industry, at dairies, and at local farms. Only about one-quarter of the residents have a high school education.

To address the growing needs for infrastructure and services, a few Mirasol residents organized in the early 1990s. Blanca Silvestre, a 30-year resident, launched the effort. She had the confidence to do so, given her experiences: she had helped organize some Catholic Church bazaars, and she had received a little training from the IAF. Yet, Blanca was wary of outsiders. She wanted to work independently to set needs and organize her community. She and her husband, along with a handful of long-term residents, brought eighty residents to a county hearing. They also carried written petitions on behalf of other community members at that meeting to successfully petition for a community resource center. Several years later, Blanca led a local organizing effort to secure badly needed sewer and road improvements. These projects were recently completed with the assistance of federal and county funding.

After the community center was built, Blanca and her husband managed it on a volunteer basis, along with a small group of local residents. The center helped meet vital needs, and it continues to provide meals for senior citizens and low-income women and children, free

immunizations, English and citizenship classes, arts-and-crafts activities, and after-school sports activities for youth. For a time, it also housed training for a women's micro-business cooperative, along with child care for the trainees. (The micro-business cooperative has since expanded and moved to a larger location.)

As services at the Mirasol community center expanded, Blanca and the small group of volunteers became increasingly exhausted. While the center served hundreds in the late 1990s, it accommodated more than 1,000 residents by 2000 and more than 3,000 residents by 2003. The center volunteers wanted to provide additional services: child care, a Head Start Program, and an on-site health clinic. The capacity of the local board was overstressed, however, and volunteers could barely keep up with the cleaning duties and administrative management.

This stress hindered development of new leadership. Board members found they lacked the time, skills, and resources to train others, especially newcomers, so the workload could be spread more evenly. Although the community development board had originally intended to seek new members, their neglect created problems. New residents began to accuse existing board members of failing to include them in decision-making and of misrepresenting their top priorities.

It was at this point in 2004, when local needs outstripped capacity, that Mirasol received much-needed assistance in broadening its leadership base and building community consensus. A trusted staff member of a federal agency helped spearhead a multiple-agency effort that brought federal, state, and local resources to meet growing needs. The agencies worked with the community center board and local residents to design and implement a comprehensive community development plan. A federal agency hired a local bilingual planning contractor to coordinate the process. The contractor was familiar with local residents' concerns. The firm's staff had a track record of community advocacy and positive relationships with Mirasol's leaders. The contractor facilitated small group discussions that bridged conflicts, created better communications, and identified shared priorities among diverse stakeholders. These stakeholders included county elected officials and planners frustrated with rampant growth, long-term residents upset by changing conditions, and new immigrants moving into substandard housing in newly developed areas. The plan included an assessment and proposed improvements for the Mirasol economy, environment, infrastructure,

housing, land use, and educational system. It provided a means for relaxing county land-use codes to enable more residents to legally operate home-based businesses. At the same time, it identified the locations of rapidly spreading, unplanned housing, along with mechanisms by which county planners could better monitor and control development of slum housing.

In the case of Mirasol, capacity builders helped strengthen self-determination at a critical point in the process. The Mirasol plan galvanized new leadership, largely by incorporating the desires of various groups of local residents. It also resulted in tens of millions of dollars in state and federal investments. These included a new school, flood control, access to emergency services, water and similar infrastructure improvements, and a planned affordable housing project using self-help construction methods with native materials (such as adobe). The housing project is particularly innovative because as homes are built, the land-use codes and architectural design features will enable families to add on to their homes.

The planning process also has strengthened the existing leadership. With the colonia residents' consent, the county recently assumed management of the community center. They hired Blanca as a county employee to direct its activities and have invested in her leadership skills, along with about a dozen other women. The county has done so, in part, by creating a network of community center directors. These directors are rotated throughout the county, so the women can learn from each other more creative and effective ways to accomplish their work.

Building Sustainable Organizations

To sustain development efforts across a community, colonia residents organize collective interests through loose-knit grassroots associations and more formal incorporated organizations. As discussed in chapter 8, colonia associations that are effective and able to sustain their work pursue two distinct types of strategies. First, they develop strong organizational skills needed to set and meet strategic commitments. Second, they are transparent and accountable for their actions, both with constituents and agencies that provide funding and resources. In this section, we discuss how colonias have successfully applied both strategies for building sustainable organizations.

Building Organizational Skills for Sustainable Organizations

Whether loosely organized or formally incorporated, colonia organizations need to establish consensus for action and means for following through on priorities. Our experience reveals, however, that the way in which colonias do so varies with the cultural context. Colonias with mostly Anglo populations tend to use more formalized methods, while mostly Hispanic colonias appear to rely on more informal means of building and acting on strategic commitments.

These distinctions are clear when comparing the mostly Anglo colonia of Jackson with the Hispanic colonia of Cerrito. In Jackson, two local associations with Anglo leadership have organized to bring resources to the area's 5,000 residents. Although a growing number of Hispanic and African American residents have moved into the area, approximately three-quarters of the population are white, English-speaking residents. Most are low-income residents living in mobile homes with lots lacking proper easements, flood control, sewer systems, and adequate paving.

A group of about forty Jackson residents formed a community infrastructure advocacy association in 2002 to call for better law enforcement and infrastructure services. They have developed agreement on vision and action through formal communications: they publish and widely distribute a monthly newsletter to recruit new members and discuss their goals and priorities. The association also relies on grassroots, consensus-based leadership, and its members must vote unanimously at monthly board meetings to pursue action on specific issues. Within three years, the association has made good progress toward achieving its goals. Members have recruited more law enforcement to patrol the area and shut down two of the three known methamphetamine laboratories. They have also successfully lobbied county officials for a park and community swimming pool.

A second organization in Jackson, run mostly by Anglos, operates the community center. Like its sister organization, the community center board has used formal communications, including publicized meetings, flyers, and the area newspaper, to share its purposes and elicit feedback about issues important to the working poor. This two-way communication has refined the organization's purpose and strategic commitments, helping the community center mobilize resources with minimal staffing.

One paid staff member and the local board have brought an impressive array of services, including a free lunch program, emergency food boxes, a clothing bank, a diaper bank, a library, a mobile health clinic, an arts-and-crafts program, a sports program, and a children's program.

Both of Jackson's community organizations engage in formal processes to set strategic commitments. They each have a written, clearly defined mission statement that bounds their activities, and each hosts monthly meetings that are open to the public. Both organizations regularly communicate their vision and the means by which they carry it out through structured communications.

In contrast, mostly Hispanic organizations appear to use less formal methods. In the predominantly Hispanic community of Cerrito (described in chapter 7), only one organization—a loose-knit association of families—carries out development activities. In the mid-1990s, an IAF-trained community development broker and former farm worker, Adan Diego, began to organize local residents to address many needs. Over eight months, Adan and his wife, Sara, met informally in local homes. They explained the purpose of their work and recruited residents for leadership positions. After building awareness of their work through word of mouth, the organization mobilized eight families. All were recent immigrants, most of whom did not speak English. These families, in turn, informally surveyed residents about priorities for the community. They also hosted only one event, a community meeting to identify specific projects to ensure public safety, improve education and recreation opportunities, and bring in public services and infrastructure. The eight families then met as a group twice monthly to develop strategies to bring public services to their communities. Over eight years, they were successful in petitioning the county for a regional day care center, sewer and natural gas service, improved water and paving, and a multipurpose center.

The informal awareness-building activities of Cerrito's grassroots association are typical of successful organizing efforts in Hispanic colonias. They tend to engender trust and awareness through personal contacts and building relationships. In contrast, experience shows that Hispanic colonia organizations that rely solely on formal, written communications struggle to elicit participation. For example, volunteer fire departments and utility associations in several Hispanic colonias set priorities and carry out their business in English, without much community

awareness. They post notices of their meetings as a matter of law. Yet, many residents say they do not know what these organizations do, how they do it, or how to get involved.

Therefore, informal community-building activities, such as sponsoring community potlucks and events to engage the entire family in an ethic of civic service, are valuable for building a broad agenda to address local needs. For example, two associations in the remote, rural colonia of Abbeyville have done so very effectively. Volunteer firefighters sponsor an annual dinner that informs residents of their work and raises funds for costs not covered by the local fire district tax. The children of firefighters run their own junior fire department and participate in fire department training sessions. Abbeyville also encourages youth to participate with their mothers in the monthly meetings and ongoing activities of a community service organization. The association benefits the entire community by conducting public health education campaigns, addressing needs of the local indigent population and children in foster care, providing life skills training for women prisoners, and sponsoring college scholarships. By participating, youth learn about the value of community service as a means of building community. Therefore, even colonias with few organizations and scarce resources can develop their ability to set and meet strategic commitments by organizing informal events and mobilizing families for action.

Building Accountability and Transparency for Sustainable Organizations

Colonia associations that organize effectively not only build organizational skills to set and meet strategic commitments, they also promote accountability and transparency in their activities. If they are to generate trust and attract external resources, organizations must build transparency and accountability with both local residents and funding agencies. A handful of colonia organizations we have interviewed and worked with have done so very effectively.

In Abbeyville, a rural colonia with a population of approximately 500 residents, both the community service association and volunteer fire department have actively pursued transparency. They have promoted a sense of organizational openness by actively recruiting newcomers to work on shared priorities. For example, the thirty members of the community service organization track down and pursue newcomers, encour-

aging them to volunteer. Existing members mentor newcomers in their roles as committee chairs or special events coordinators. Several leaders say they have a great success rate, boasting that 90 percent of all residents join a local association. The community service organization also promotes transparency by ensuring their budget and leadership is accountable to its broader network. The organization is part of a county and state network, launched by the state university agricultural extension office in the 1930s.

Similarly, the Abbeyville fire department has pursued fiscal accountability. They have remained the only debt-free fire department of more than a dozen in the county. The fire chief, an accountant, has worked with the membership to carefully budget resources and purchase only necessary equipment. The fire department is answerable to county government, which approves the department's purchases and administers its funds. The fire department has publicized these facts, along with their annual budget, in the local newspaper and by word of mouth. This openness and proactive accountability recently enabled them to mobilize the local vote that successfully renewed the 0.25 percent sales tax dedicated to volunteer fire services.

Most colonias, though, struggle to build transparency. Most are not blessed with skilled financial managers savvy in resource management. Few colonia residents have been mentored in organizational leadership or trained to compile and manage budgets, financial statements, or audits. Yet, some colonia associations have overcome fiscal accountability problems by contracting with outside organizations to manage their fiscal resources. The range of fiscal agents varies widely. Leaders in Mirasol rely on the county to manage their community center's finances and required federal audits. In Cerrito residents turned to a regional nonprofit organization to manage grant funding. The local community college assists the residents in Josefito in managing a small food bank. This was made possible through grant funding from the U.S. Department of Housing and Urban Development, which assists community colleges and universities in building local capacity for development projects.

Many local community-based organizations, however, are wary of contracting for services for fear that others will take advantage of them. The community center in the colonia of Jackson has avoided this dilemma. The center's board serves as an outstanding example of how a small organization can safeguard local control, while partnering with an outside organization to properly administer finances. When the center

was built in the 1980s, a local nonprofit board of directors managed the community center, even though the county built the facility. In the late 1990s, the incoming county parks and recreation director sought to consolidate management of all county community centers. The board of the community center mobilized an appeal. Local residents argued the community center board was better qualified to provide a broader range of services than the county, given federal food bank regulations stipulating nonprofit management. As such, the local board successfully defeated the proposition and retained greater local control. Today, the county administers the budget and required audits, and it pays the local director's salary to run the center. Yet, the director, a resident of Jackson, is accountable to the local community center board. The board has greater control and has been able to expand services because they are now free to pursue long-term goals, not simply day-to-day management.

Thus, small colonia associations can be effective while remaining true to their purpose. They can retain their small size by partnering selectively with larger organizations that have in place fiscal accountability and controls. In this way, colonia associations can promote accountability and transparency.

Building Effective Community Collaborations

Colonias that have found ways to solve complex development problems have organized associations that leverage local and nonlocal resources. As discussed in chapter 8, both types of partnerships are essential. Local collaborations help coordinate and share the workload, thus strengthening colonia associations' skills and knowledge base, whereas nonlocal partnerships can improve the impact of local development projects by injecting fiscal and technical assistance as well as policy and strategy support.

Creating Interlocal Collaborations to Address Shared Quality-of-Life Concerns

A few Arizona and New Mexico colonias with which we have worked have built, on their own, strong collaborations among local leaders operating across different interest areas, such as local government, schools, churches, water cooperatives, and fire districts. For example, the volunteer fire department and women's community service organization

in Abbeyville have collaborated on fundraisers, which raise more than $10,000 each year for college scholarships and meals for on-the-job fire-fighters, who sometimes battle weeklong forest fires. Other community clubs and the congregations of three churches in Abbeyville also assist these local organizations with training, festivals, and similar projects, thereby helping build a spirit of shared interests. Similarly, in the colonia of Jackson, leaders of an informal grassroots association have lobbied for better roads, water and sewer services, and improved housing. They have achieved success by coordinating their efforts with a local school and micro-credit enterprise to plan for growth and bring in services.

Experience and research reveals, however, that these forms of strong local collaborations are rare. Research on rural community development has shown that collaborations are more likely in ethnically homogenous and isolated rural communities (Milofsky 2003). As discussed in chapter 7, interlocal collaboration is less likely in places marked by strong racial oppression and status deprivation. According to Milofsky, this is because oppressive environments deepen divisions across class and generations and hinder work toward shared local priorities.

The challenge of developing local collaborations is especially clear in the Hispanic colonia of Cerrito. Members of the Cerrito grassroots association, the sole local organization, have struggled to develop collaborations. They have been unsuccessful in attempts to join the volunteer regional fire department because the fire district cannot conduct fire-fighter training in Spanish. Similarly, they have not participated in the regional water cooperative because that entity also conducts its affairs solely in English. Surprisingly, they have also been excluded for opportunities to work with the regional school district and Catholic Church. According to area residents, a local activist, and several social service providers, the school district's Anglo and long-term Mexican American members have deliberately excluded new immigrants from participation in school board affairs by refusing to provide translation services, despite requests. Furthermore, local leaders believe they have been unable to rely on their local Catholic parish (located in the adjacent community) for help in integrating their needs with those of the larger surrounding community. Local leaders say they petitioned the parish for a bilingual mass only to have their idea dismissed.

Without the support and expertise of area cross-organizational collaborations, Cerrito leaders have struggled to succeed in these challenging and complex projects. For example, Cerrito's grassroots association

was unable to incubate a micro-business project intended to improve residents' economic prospects. Because they had no local partners, they were forced to seek the support of a regional development organization, which proposed a project ill-suited to local needs and imposed an inappropriate top-down structure that residents complained was "not respectful of the community." Residents felt betrayed, and the project simply proved too difficult for the small group.

Therefore, one of the most powerful external capacity building roles, particularly among those with limited English skills, is that of helping local grassroots associations develop their voice, legitimacy, and standing with other local organizations. As discussed in chapter 8, external capacity builders can provide essential third-party mediation and dispute resolution for this purpose. Mediation efforts have been successful in the predominantly Hispanic Mirasol area, described at the beginning of this chapter. The firm contracted to develop a plan for the Mirasol colonias spent much time in negotiation and arbitration activities. Initially, forums and meetings were contentious. Residents believed county institutions did not care about them, while county officials and staff believed that residents did not care about their own neighborhoods. The process provided a means for building consensus on community priorities. Discussions occurred first between the community center board and local residents. Once local agreements were achieved, talks proceeded with various departments of the county, and finally with the local school district and state agencies. Now the county is applying this model of resolving quality-of-life challenges in the rest of the county's colonias.

In minority communities with few resources, capacity builders have also strengthened cross-organizational collaborations by supporting public spaces for interaction. Field experience and other research indicate that shared public-use facilities can ease the task of community building (Wallis 1991; Green and Haines 2002; Donelson 2005). Colonias that have multipurpose centers use them to host a variety of religious groups, clubs, and community-based organizations. These spaces do not always require new construction: sometimes they simply call for stronger local partnerships. For example, a dozen residents have proven they could do this in La Palma, a Hispanic colonia of about 1,000 residents located a few miles from the border. In the late 1990s, the group created an infrastructure improvement association that developed agreements for two shared public-use facilities. First, they developed a partnership with the fire district to share local meeting space, free of charge. The

firehouse has become a de facto town hall for the area's 1,000 residents. The leaders also successfully lobbied the school district to use local school facilities for after-school activities and community events. The school playground is the community park, and its buildings have been the site for children's karate lessons, a baseball program, and a folkloric dance group. Local leaders were able to achieve this, in large part, because many work in public education; the infrastructure association board includes two teachers, a retired superintendent, and a support staff.

Unfortunately, the case of La Palma is unusual. Many colonias have struggled to obtain access to meeting space at their schools, which often represent the largest local public investments. As discussed in chapter 7, school boards and administrators are sometimes unwilling or unable to share space, due to legal liabilities or increased maintenance requirements. Therefore, capacity builders can work with schools to create a larger vision for their communities by developing arrangements like those in La Palma.

Texas legislators have recognized the importance of investing in shared public-use facilities. In the early 1990s, state and federal agencies directed funding to the Center for Housing and Urban Development at Texas A&M University to build or recondition community resource centers in sixteen colonias. These centers provide information and services to residents as well as space for training leaders and developing collaborative services (Ramos et al. 2003). Community centers and shared public-use facilities, then, can be a valuable resource. Unless adequate local support exists to sustain them, however, public-use facilities may become abandoned eyesores and harbingers for illicit activities. For example, the unincorporated colonia of Valle Verde, a former mining settlement, obtained funding from the U.S. Department of Housing and Urban Development to construct a community center. Just a few years later, the center fell into disrepair and closed when local volunteers failed to maintain it. Therefore, capacity builders must ensure that committed local leadership exists for this purpose, along with adequate county technical and financial management, before investing scarce resources.

Pursuing Nonlocal Partnerships That Enhance Resources and Impact Policy

Partnerships with nonlocal organizations are critical because they help colonias access resources and policy assistance. This helps them scale up

their efforts and influence. In this section, we share examples of two colonia associations (one with Hispanic representation, the other mostly Anglo) that have worked with capacity builders to create innovative networks of nonlocal associations that improve colonia conditions.

In the early 1990s, Melissa Smith, the director of the community center in the predominantly Anglo, low-income colonia of Jackson, had a vision. She wanted to bring the types of services to her community that would help the working poor get the stopgap assistance they needed to escape poverty. But while trying to lobby for services as a small, rural community within an urban county, she had little influence. Melissa realized the only way to enhance resources was to build political influence at the county and regional levels.

Melissa organized a network of more than forty like-minded rural community centers and service providers. She did so by sharing her passion and vision for the role of rural community centers to help the working poor get the resources, training, and assistance for a "hand up rather than a hand out." Today, Melissa serves as president of the network. It has no staff or overhead expenses, only a committed membership that meets monthly. Agency heads are invited to speak at meetings about ways they can partner with members. In addition, members discuss common problems and ways to organize for better, more cost-effective services. Over eight years, the network has obtained funding and resources from federal and county government agencies, the United Way, the local university health department, and the regional food bank. They have come to represent a respected, well-organized association that advocates for the working poor in the southern part of the state.

Regional organizing efforts took a different turn in the mostly Hispanic community of Cerro del Avila. These efforts grew out of the frustration of a group of residents who faced difficult infrastructure challenges. First, they were not initially recognized as a colonia in need of improvement. Somehow, the county failed to designate the area of 1,000 residents as a colonia, which was a requirement for funding eligibility. Cerro del Avila certainly had urgent needs: the local water supply was contaminated by nitrates and bacteria, and a sewer system was needed to replace inadequate septic tanks. The local domestic water association board mobilized about sixty residents, who convinced the county to designate the area a colonia. Next, they worked to obtain federal and state funding for infrastructure.

But they soon realized that advocacy work was a heavy burden. Like members of many other water and volunteer fire associations we have interviewed, these leaders volunteered an average of 25 to 40 hours per month on infrastructure board affairs alone. They needed help to petition for their interests. With assistance of a technical trainer hired by the U.S. Department of Agriculture–Rural Development (USDA-RD), the Cerro del Avila water association organized a network of like-minded mutual domestic water districts to amplify their voice and lighten their administrative burden. Since the late 1990s, USDA-RD has helped them obtain more than $6 million for colonia infrastructure, as well as free water meters from the WalMart foundation. Through a cooperative arrangement, the association has also purchased heavy machinery that members can rent, at reduced cost, for water operations and maintenance. The association has successfully lobbied the state legislature to obtain direct water infrastructure appropriations, rather than going through county government. Finally, the network is also seeking direct appropriations of community development block grant funding from the U.S. Department of Housing and Urban Development for water planning purposes, rather than having to go through county channels.

In both Jackson and Cerro del Avila, colonia associations have been successful in creating regional networks with nonlocal organizations to represent their interests. These associations have been successful for two reasons. First, they have focused on accomplishing narrow, well-defined objectives that benefit their particular membership. In the case of Jackson, the network has sought to improve the operations, services, and political influence of rural community centers. In Cerro del Avila, the network has sought to improve the effectiveness and advocacy of rural mutual domestic water associations. Second, they have carefully chosen nonlocal partners with which to work. Although Melissa Smith, the Jackson community center director, has developed connections with more than 300 resource contacts over the past 15 years, she has intentionally worked with only about 30 of those. She is aware that pursuing partnerships and funding with too many resources may overstress local organizational capacity and displace local priorities. Similarly, the Cerro del Avila board has only partnered with like-minded water associations and one federally funded technical assistance provider. They have maintained distance from other organizations, such as the IAF, which could provide needed leadership training but is motivated by different political

goals. They have also avoided the county, when possible, because they believe the county is motivated to manage and regionalize water and sewer services without taking into account local needs and priorities.

In sum, capacity builders have important roles in mediating both local and nonlocal partnerships. They can strengthen local interorganizational ties by helping broker partnerships that lead to improved communications and stronger local commitments for action. In addition, they can help local leaders strengthen ties to nonlocal partners by funding resources and administrative assistance to scale up the local political voice and effectiveness.

Summary

This chapter examined effective community improvement strategies adopted by colonias and the capacity builders that assist them. The chapter followed the three-part framework outlined in chapter 8, specifying six capacity building strategies. We first examined how some Arizona and New Mexico colonias have built greater autonomy by enhancing residents' leadership capabilities and basic needs. Next, we discussed how colonias have developed effective associations by building organizational skills as well as transparency and accountability. Finally, the chapter explored how colonias have enhanced their impact by creating partnerships with both local and nonlocal institutions to improve access to resources and technical assistance as well as policy and strategy support.

10

The Road Ahead

Colonias differ from most other towns and cities across the country because they confront numerous development problems that receive little attention from the outside world. Thus, the fate of colonias rests mainly in the hands of the people who live in them. While we acknowledge the numerous contributions made by nongovernmental organizations (NGOs) and government agencies, the relative obscurity of colonias means that making things better often requires local activism and community organizing. There is no doubt that colonias require outside assistance, but it is local leaders who often set community development in motion.

This final chapter continues with the theme of community development, which holds the most promise for improving the lives of colonia residents. First, we present a generalized plan for colonia community development in support of local activists and organizers, as well as NGOs and government agencies. The plan builds on the capacity building approach and ties together a sequence of steps that can guide community development over an extended time horizon.

But even the best of development plans can be derailed by factors that lie beyond the control of community organizers. These filter down to colonias from national, state, and local governments. Thus, the second objective is to identify programs, policies, and initiatives at all levels of government that have been instrumental in local community development. We point to programs now in place so that community organizers can monitor these programs' activities in the years ahead. This is not an attempt to forecast the future, as such efforts are complicated, perhaps impossible, given the fickle nature of policy-making. Instead, our goal is to inventory policies and programs that have contributed to successful colonia community development efforts thus far. We do not attempt an exhaustive treatment but rather point to policies and programs that have provided the most support.

Finally, the chapter concludes by highlighting the book's themes and

objectives. This includes a summary of our motives and a brief overview of the book's content.

The Colonia Community Development Plan

Improving colonias' quality of life requires a community development plan that guides the mobilization of human and financial resources. It is convenient to think of the plan as an organizing framework that lays out a sequence of steps or actions. This framework coordinates activities so that the plan unfolds logically and sequentially (Levy 2002).

Figure 10.1 provides a development plan for Arizona and New Mexico colonias. The plan is tailored to colonias but should be modified according to local needs, which are expected to vary due to the heterogeneity of colonias (see chapter 4). The plan divides the development path into three time horizons: immediate, 5 years, and longer term. This division follows from traditional planning practices in which activities are sequenced logically over time. Immediate actions, for example, target critical problems that demand attention. Health care, child care, adult education, and fire and safety all influence quality of life in the short term and should be dealt with swiftly. In addition, these factors require comparatively less investment because they can sometimes be shared by many colonias (mobile health/dental clinics), with nearby communities (fire and safety), or through local cooperatives (child care). In the short term, education may not be locally available, but arrangements can be made with nearby communities, in which case the problem involves transportation of colonia residents. Immediate actions, therefore, focus on the provision of essentials that can be obtained or shared with minimal cost or investment. County government and NGOs can provide the contacts needed to arrange these facilities.

The most critical component of immediate action deals with getting the capacity building process off the ground. In the short term, this requires an inventory of community needs and assets so that organizers can implement the more formal and longer-term development plan. The capacity inventory often requires the assistance of federal organizations (e.g., colonia specialists from the U.S. Department of Housing and Urban Development, HUD), county and local government agencies, and/ or NGOs.

The ultimate objective of the development plan is to guide the community beyond immediate needs and secure permanent and long-term

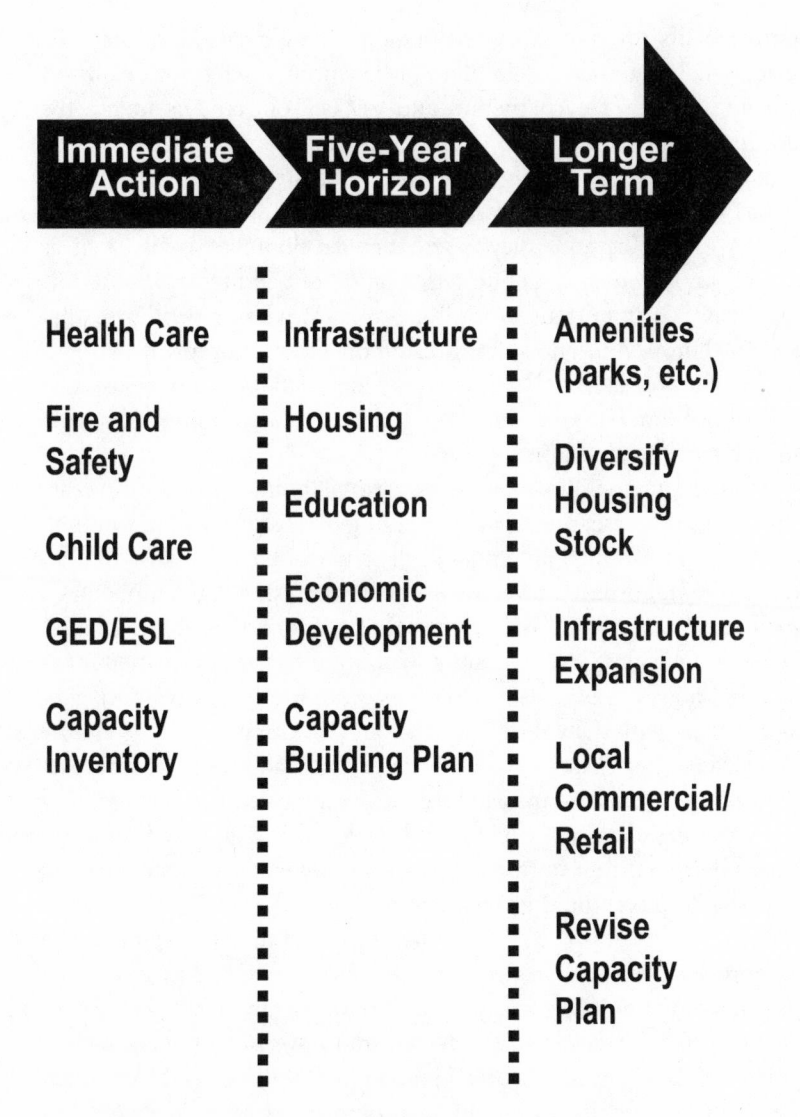

Figure 10.1 A community development plan for colonias

improvements through capacity building. As figure 10.1 indicates, the capacity building plan should be in place within 5 years (for details on capacity building, see chapters 8 and 9). The objective is to use the capacity building approach to facilitate construction of large-scale and more costly projects. At the 5-year stage, infrastructure improvements such as water delivery and waste treatment systems should receive the highest priority because they ease other development goals, such as housing improvements, public parks, and recreation centers. At this stage, it is also important to resolve problems with land titles so that individual property owners can invest in on-site improvements without the risk of loss or eviction (see chapters 7 and 8). Subsequent goals, such as housing upgrades, educational programs, and job training can be met through targeted programs.

Finally, figure 10.1 illustrates a long-term planning horizon of 20 years or more. In this case, the capacity building plan promotes local growth and expansion through amenities such as parks, bicycle paths, and pedestrian trails. Fostering diversity in the housing stock accommodates a broad range of the population by providing a variety of housing types, from high-density apartments and townhouses to formally platted manufactured housing subdivisions. Expansion of local infrastructure goes hand in hand with these developments but also complements economic development. For example, commercial, retail, and industrial land uses require more specialized infrastructure, which is essential for promoting local economic development. In the longer term, plans need to be revised and kept current so that they respond to changing inventories and assets and keep communities on track.

There is every reason to believe that quality of life in all colonias can be improved given local leadership, adequate resources, and a plan that lays out a development strategy. Figure 10.1 presents such a plan for the benefit of local leaders and the NGOs and government agencies that work with them. The plan is broad in scope and thus should be modified to meet the unique needs of individual colonias.

The Role of Federal, State, and Local Governments

Community development plans rely on resources that lie beyond the control of colonias, especially funding opportunities and technical assistance provided by federal, state, and local governmental agencies. But the

reliance on external resources means that even the best of plans are vulnerable to shifts in funding priorities, budget cuts, and even the termination of programs altogether. For this reason, community organizers must be attentive to the policy environment and revise plans accordingly. To ease this task, we discuss several policies and programs of the federal, state, and local government.

Federal Programs and Initiatives

Three federal agencies have played an important role in colonia community development: HUD, the Environmental Protection Agency, and the U.S. Department of Agriculture–Rural Development (USDA-RD). In many ways, HUD has taken the lead in colonia community development in Arizona and New Mexico (U.S. Department of Housing and Urban Development 2003, 2004a).[1] For example, HUD's Set-Aside Program targets community development by requiring that states (Arizona, New Mexico, California, and Texas) reserve 10 percent of their community development block grants for colonias. These funds are used for housing, water, and sewer improvements, and eligibility requires recognition as a federally designated colonia. HUD also makes available colonia specialists who provide outreach to local communities, including assistance in capacity building, leadership training, and grant writing. The colonia program is closely associated with HUD's Migrant/Farmworker Initiative, which benefits many colonias, especially with low-income housing and renter assistance. But the future of these programs is unclear, especially in view of reduced support for programs that aid unauthorized immigrants.

HUD also provides housing assistance, especially for minority-owned low-income housing. Programs that target homeowner down payments and neighborhood redevelopment are available through HUD's block grant programs. Many of these are reserved for urban areas (especially inner-city neighborhoods), but some also apply to colonias and homeowners in general. As the Housing Assistance Council (2006a, 2006b, 2006c) indicated, however, the future of HUD housing assistance programs is unclear, and local organizers are advised to monitor the agency's funding opportunities closely. The Housing Assistance Council is an excellent source for current information on low-income housing.

The Environmental Protection Agency has been instrumental in funding border infrastructure projects through two of its agencies (U.S.

Environmental Protection Agency 2003a, 2003b), the North American Development Bank and the Border Environmental Corporation Commission. Both programs came into effect in 1994 with the passage of the North American Free Trade Agreement. Over the years they have provided funding and technical assistance for many large-scale projects, including storm-water management, water and sewer systems, and waste treatment facilities. The Environmental Protection Agency's Clean Water State Revolving Fund is also important because it targets wastewater systems, which are a critical problem for many rural colonias. These programs have made significant contributions in years past, but it is difficult to say what the future holds.

USDA-RD has also played a role in colonia community development by providing funds for rural development more generally, and many colonias are eligible for support. The agency makes funds available in the form of loans, loan guarantees, and grants. Programs improve quality of life in rural areas through housing assistance, economic development, water delivery, waste treatment systems, and other infrastructure. These programs are especially important for colonias, where the lack of basic infrastructure remains a critical problem. The USDA's Rural Community Development Initiative holds much potential because it targets capacity building in the areas of housing as well as community and economic development in rural areas. While funding for these programs is currently available, colonia community organizers are cautioned to monitor future developments.

The U.S. Department of Health and Human Services, through its Health Resources and Services Administration, has played a vital role in delivering health services to colonias. But recent federal budget cuts have hampered the agency's programs, and future prospects are unknown. This means that community organizers and NGOs should watch developments closely in the years ahead.

Despite the contributions of these agencies and their programs, a fundamental problem rests in the federal government's uncoordinated approach to the border, as the federal response to border problems has been cyclical and fragmented. In May 2000, for example, the Clinton Administration released the *First Annual Report of the President's Interagency Task Force on the Economic Development of the Southwest Border*, which outlined a multiple-agency strategy for reinvestment for sustainable development in the U.S. border region. The report asserted that prior planning efforts had been piecemeal, uncoordinated, and charac-

terized by crisis management.[2] Yet, this situation had not arisen due to lack of attempts to develop border strategies, for many of the report's recommendations echo those outlined decades earlier. The Southwest Border Regional Commission, chartered in 1977, intended for domestic agencies to devise a framework for analyzing conditions that inhibit growth and a development strategy for the border region. The barriers to development identified in that study are much the same as those that exist today: a shortage of skilled labor, a lack of private financing and a poor tax base for local revenue bond financing, and psychological resistance, as border states "have been slow to recognize or admit that problems exist along the border which are unique to the region."[3]

The federal government's inability to launch a consistent and long-term development plan for the border region speaks to many of the challenges that confront colonias. While the federal government acknowledges the need for a comprehensive approach to the region's problems, such a program has not appeared. Instead, individual agencies offer assistance with the best of intentions, but they often act alone without coordination or cooperation. For this reason, community development approaches that coordinate efforts across organizations are critical to scaling up their action and policy influence at regional and national levels (see chapters 8 and 9). Federal agencies need to engage these networks in a more meaningful dialogue over extended periods to craft effective long-term solutions.

The federal government's inconsistent approach to the border carries over to perhaps the most important issue of all: immigration reform and border security. As discussed in chapters 5 and 6, immigration reform has led to dramatic temporal changes in colonia demographics. These challenge the foundation of community development plans because the needs and wants of the population are always in flux. Long-term plans build on a shared vision of the future, but this vision changes as new arrivals reveal a different set of problems and preferences.

Little can be said about the future of immigration reform and border security. As with the federal government's overall approach to the border, immigration reform is illusive. There is every reason to believe that more changes are ahead. The recent buildup along the border, including construction of 700 miles (1,120 km) of walls and the addition of 6,000 more U.S. Border Patrol agents by 2008 (U.S. Customs and Border Protection 2006), may signal the end of recent reforms but, more likely, it is only one step among a stream of reforms yet to come. In any event, the

consequences for colonias are clear. They can anticipate continued community instability as the characteristics of colonia populations continue to change in response to immigration reform. For this reason, local leaders, NGOs, and government agencies must be mindful of programs and policies that affect immigration.

State Programs and Policies

Programs and policies coming down from state governments in Arizona and New Mexico also affect local planning efforts. In contrast to those of the federal government, few programs at the state level target colonia development directly. Nevertheless, the indirect effects of land subdivision regulations, border security, and education have significant implications for long-term development goals.

In Arizona, lax land subdivision regulations are perhaps most important because they are largely responsible for the growing number of colonias in southern Arizona. Competition for federal resources increases as the number of colonias grows, and wildcat subdivisions spring up seemingly overnight and seldom have basic infrastructure such as water and sewer systems, fire protection, and paved roads (see chapter 7 for a discussion of wildcat subdivisions).

Without revisions to land subdivision codes at the state level, the proliferation of colonias in southern Arizona will continue as the cost of land and housing in urban areas continues to rise. This often forces low-income segments of the population to rural areas, where living costs are more affordable. But the prospects for revising state statutes do not look good. For several years now Arizona legislators have proposed lowering the number of lot-splits (thus eliminating the wildcat problem), but legislation has not been ratified. Moreover, there is little evidence to suggest that such legislation will make its way through the Arizona state legislature in the near future.

There are at least two ways that colonia organizers and NGOS can respond to the proliferation of wildcat subdivisions. First, they must be mindful of the situation, especially in their area. County government monitors these subdivisions and can provide information without cost. Second, colonias can work with organizations to push for revised land subdivision regulations at the state level. There are several organizations working for reforms, including environmental groups, county gov-

ernments, and professional associations such as the Arizona Planning Association.

The situation in New Mexico is different because land-use regulations do not promote the formation of wildcat subdivisions. Even so, competition among colonias for federal assistance is likely to grow as additional communities apply for recognition as federally designated colonias. In addition, inadequate enforcement of land-use laws in rural areas of the state contributes to the unregulated growth of communities already designated as colonias. The lack of enforcement means that development often occurs with substandard infrastructure and housing, which intensifies competition for federal assistance as communities seek to remedy these problems. For these reasons, New Mexico colonias should expect an increasingly competitive funding environment during the years ahead.

The entrance of state government into the border security arena brings an added layer of complexity to development planning in colonias. In recent years, both Arizona and New Mexico have passed legislation that applies to the border, including funding for health care facilities in border communities and the mobilization of the National Guard. As with federal immigration policy, legislation at the state level will likely alter the characteristics of colonias. This means that local organizers, NGOs, and government agencies should keep an eye on state governments as border security legislation is revised and new legislation comes on board.

State funding for education is also important in long-term colonia community development. This is a hot issue in Arizona, because voters have rejected a bilingual (bicultural) approach in favor of designating English as the state's official language. State legislation also excludes unauthorized immigrants from receiving publicly provided health care and education. This reflects the sentiments of Californians, who also voted to prohibit assistance to unauthorized immigrants. For these reasons, the future looks bad for health care and adult and bilingual education in Arizona.

Education is critical for improving quality of life over the long term, especially for Hispanic students, who traditionally do not perform well in public schools. Thus, state agencies need to support local public schools in helping low-income Hispanics become well educated and prepared for the workforce. Schools must become an essential link tying

community development networks together. Such a program has been implemented in twelve Hispanic schools across Arizona with remarkable results. The program helped students overcome poverty and English language difficulties to make the list of top performing schools in the state. Each of these schools overcame challenges by collaborating to find solutions, having a strong principal, devising student-tailored educational plans, and establishing a clear bottom line (Center for the Future of Arizona 2006). Thus, colonia leaders and the development community (NGOs and government agencies) should consider similar programs and develop multiple strategies for meeting educational, as well as health care, needs. Such efforts are required to prevent new immigrants from becoming trapped in a permanent underclass.

In contrast, New Mexico is an official bilingual state, which means that funding for bicultural education is sanctioned and even encouraged. The state's public schools support education for all students, regardless of whether they come from immigrant or American families or of household income level (Dominguez and Contreras 2005). New Mexico supports education for all students because it opens doors to higher education and equips the population for employment opportunities. For this reason, New Mexico colonia residents face a different educational future than those in Arizona.

Local Government

Local governments can play a critical role in colonia community development plans. Colonia organizers should be especially aware of the impacts and benefits that come from county planning and local economic development opportunities. As discussed in chapter 3, several counties in southern Arizona and New Mexico have put in place long-range comprehensive plans and planning devices that seek to improve quality of life in rural communities. In Arizona, for example, Cochise County has approved plans for unincorporated areas that apply to several colonia communities. The first was approved in 1998 and the rest in 2005. The same holds for Yuma County, which also recently approved several regional comprehensive plans. In New Mexico, Doña Ana County has taken the lead in planning initiatives that apply to rural areas, including colonias. Their use of a Village District zoning designation holds much promise for the preservation and improvement of older colonia communities, such as the village of Doña Ana. In addition, their Performance

Zone designation complements rural community development by imposing land development standards. Much of Doña Ana County is rural and encompasses the fertile Rio Grande Valley, where agricultural preservation is an important issue. The Performance Zone designation targets preservation, which carries over to rural communities throughout the region.

Because nearly all of these planning initiatives are new, the long-term consequences are unknown. Much of their potential benefit depends on the ability of county planners, administrators, and elected officials to carry out the intent and purpose of plans and zoning designations. Given the current emphasis on rural area planning in these counties, we project a brighter future. This is a new opportunity for colonias, and every effort should be made to bring residents and county officials closer together.

Economic development in colonias is perhaps the largest obstacle to long-term growth and development. Much of this difficulty is rooted in the small size of many colonias and their remoteness. As discussed in chapter 3, over 50 percent of Arizona and New Mexico colonias house fewer than 2,000 residents. Attracting employers is challenging because colonias lack amenities, educational infrastructure, physical infrastructure (roads, sewer, water), and a skilled labor force. Although federal programs and initiatives respond to some of these problems, competition for resources is fierce.

This points to the importance of the community development plan, which calls for the sequencing of activities over a long-term horizon (fig. 10.1). Colonias are perhaps best served by first accommodating immediate needs, then using the capacity building approach to secure funding for large-scale projects that provide infrastructure, housing improvements, and amenities, which are critical for attracting employers. In the absence of such improvements, economic development is difficult. The community development plan responds to the need for economic development by devising long-term plans for colonias.

Summary

It is easy to overlook poverty along the U.S.–Mexico border because it is lost in the turbulence of unauthorized immigration, border security, and drug trafficking. Poverty fades from view as Congress and the popular media stir the cauldron of discontent, then race for quick-fix solutions to deal with complex and long-term issues. Although Massey et al. (2002),

Nevins (2002), Massey (2005), and others have noted the failures of such stopgap measures, few in Congress or the popular press have heeded their words. Given the rush to solve the "border problem," it comes as no surprise that few are aware of the pressing issues of poverty and deprivation that color life in the entire region along the border.

Some of the United States' most deprived communities are located in the border region. These colonias claim some of the country's highest levels of poverty, most severe housing problems, and, in many cases, a lack of basic infrastructure. Colonia residents are well aware of these problems, which is why the future is more important than the past. Like people everywhere, they seek basic human needs and look to the future for better lives.

We have written this book in the same spirit—hopeful and optimistic that the future holds opportunities for improving the quality of life in colonias. Our approach builds on the understanding that awareness and knowledge bring power and power brings solutions. For this reason, we have attempted to provide readers with a thorough understanding of colonias in Arizona and New Mexico.

We began by tracing the border's history and then looked more narrowly at economic development during the past century. This economic history is important because it explains why and how colonias emerged. We then turned to urbanization and the social and economic characteristics of colonias with the objective of documenting their diversity, morphology, and current circumstances. We also examined policies that affect quality of life and community development in colonias and provided an assessment of community development initiatives. Capacity building was presented as a practical approach to colonia community development. Finally, we provided a framework for guiding colonia community development and summarized policies, programs, and initiatives of the federal, state, and local government that contribute to colonia development efforts.

In the end, we hope the book offers assistance to colonias and the organizations and people who work tirelessly to improve the lives of colonia residents. We hope others, after reading the book, are motivated to do the same.

Appendix
Arizona and New Mexico Colonias

Arizona County	Incorporated	Unincorporated
Cochise	Benson	Bowie
	Bisbee	Cochise County Northwest
	Douglas	Sunnyside
	Huachuca City	Fry Townsite
	Tombstone	Naco
	Willcox	Pirtleville
		Palominas
		Pomerene Water District
		Saint David
		San Simon
		Sulphur Springs Valley
		Whetstone
Gila		Canyon Domestic Water District
Graham	Pima	Bonita
	Safford	Bryce-Eden
	Thatcher	Central
		Fort Thomas
		Klondyke
		Solomon
		Sanchez
		San Jose
		North of Gila River/South
Greenlee	Duncan	Safford/Artesia
La Paz	Parker	
	Quartzsite	
Maricopa	Gila Bend	Mobile

Arizona County	Incorporated	Unincorporated
Pima	South Tucson	Ajo
	Marana	Avra Valley Water Cooperative
	Sahuarita	Littletown/Canoa Hills
		Marana Domestic Water District
		Rancho del Conejo
		Red Hill Water Company
		Rillito
		Sierrita Mountain Water Co-op
		Three Points
Pinal	Coolidge	Colonia del Sol
	Eloy	Maricopa
	Kearney	Palo Verde Mountain
	Mammoth	Saddleback Vista subdivision
		Villa Grande Domestic Water District
Santa Cruz	Nogales	Carmen
	Patagonia	Chula Vista subdivision
		Firestone Gardens subdivision
		Pete Kitchen subdivision
		Tumacacori
Yuma	San Luis	Antelope Acres and Antelope Heights
	Somerton	Avenue B&C
	Wellton	Dateland
	Yuma	Del Sur subdivision
		Donovan Estates, units 1 and 2
		Drysdale and Wall Lane
		El Prado Estates and Speece Addition
		Gadsden
		Orange Grove Mobile Manor
		Padre Ranchitos subdivision
		Rancho Mesa Verde, units 1–3
		Tacna

New Mexico County	Incorporated	Unincorporated
Catron	Reserve	Alma
		Apache Creek
		Apache Park subdivision
		Beaverhead
		Cruzville
		Datil
		El Caso Ranch subdivision
		Escudilla Bonita subdivision
		Five Ranch Bar
		Frisco-Middle
		Frisco-Lower
		Glenwood
		Horse Peek Ranch
		Horse Springs
		Ignacio Creek
		Lost Cabin
		Luna
		Mogollon
		Old Thomas Place
		Pie Town
		Pleasanton
		Pueblo Largo
		Quemado
		Quemado Lake Estates
		Rancho Grande
		Rimrock Hills
		San Cristobal*
		TeePee Ranch
		The Homestead
		The Last Frontier
		The Rivers
		Top of the World
		Willow Creek
Chavez	Lake Arthur	Catfish Farms
		Franklin
		Keeler Farm Road
		Sunshine

New Mexico

County	Incorporated	Unincorporated
Doña Ana	Sunland Park	Abbeyville*
		Anthony
		Berino
		Brazito
		Cattleland
		Chamberino
		Chaparral
		Del Cerro
		Doña Ana
		El Milagro
		Fairacres
		Fort Selden
		Garfield
		Hill
		Joy Drive subdivision
		La Mesa
		La Union
		Las Palmeras
		Leasburg
		Mesquite
		Montana Vista
		Moongate
		Old Picacho
		Organ
		Placitas
		Radium Springs
		Rincón
		Rodey
		Salem
		San Isidro
		San Miguel
		San Pablo
		Tortugas
		Vado
		Winterheaven
Eddy	Hope	Malaga
		Ottis/Livingston/Wheeler
		Riverside
		Happy Valley

New Mexico County	Incorporated	Unincorporated
Grant	Bayard	Arenas Valley
	Santa Clara	Bear Mountain
		Buckhorn
		Carlisle
		Cliff
		Cottage San
		Dwyer
		Faywood
		Fierro
		Gila
		Gila Hot Springs
		Hachita
		Hanover
		Lake Roberts
		Mangas
		Mimbres
		Mockingbird Hill
		Mule Creek
		Pinos Altos
		Redrock
		Riverside
		Rosedale
		San Juan
		San Lorenzo
		Santa Rita
		Separ
		Sherman
		Turnerville
		Vanadium
		White Signal
		Whitewater
Hidalgo	Lordsburg	Cotton
	Virden	Del Sol
		Glen Acres
		Rodeo
		Windmill
Lincoln	Ruidoso Downs	
Luna	Columbus	

New Mexico

County	Incorporated	Unincorporated
Ortero	Tularosa	Bent
		Boles Acres
		Chaparral
		Cloudcroft
		Dog Canyon
		Dungan
		High Rolls
		La Luz
		Mayhill
		Orogrande
		Pinon
		Sacramento
		Timberon
		Twin Forks
		Weed
Sierra	Butte City	
Socorro	San Antonio	

*Pseudonym

Notes

Introduction

1. Most colonias in Texas are unincorporated and fall under the jurisdiction of county government, whereas a few Texas colonias are incorporated jurisdictions. See the "Colonias Facts" listed by the Texas Department of State (2006) for details on the definition of colonias. Likewise, in Arizona and New Mexico colonias are either incorporated or unincorporated jurisdictions. Chapter 3 discusses the definition of Arizona and New Mexico colonias in greater detail.

2. Although some research has sought to understand poverty in rural Texas colonias (Chapa and Eaton 1997; Wilson 1997; Ward 1999, 2001; Texas Department of Housing and Community Affairs 2006), only a few studies have examined these communities in other states (Henkel 1998; Donelson and Holguin 2001a, 2001b; Huntoon and Becker 2001; Koerner 2002; Lemos et al. 2002). The limited research is due to the fact that colonias outside of Texas have only been recognized since 1989, when federal legislation was passed to improve conditions in these communities.

Chapter 1

1. Arizona counties that contain colonias include Cochise, Gila, Graham, Greenlee, La Paz, Maricopa, Pima, Pinal, Santa Cruz, and Yuma. New Mexico counties that contain colonias include Catron, Chavez, Doña Ana, Eddy, Grant, Hidalgo, Lincoln, Luna, Otero, Sierra, and Socorro. In our analysis of demographic trends throughout this book, we exclude Maricopa and Pima Counties because they have mostly large urban centers that mask the demographic conditions in colonias.

2. Although they exerted little economic influence, Arizona and New Mexico did what they could to gain it. Economic boosters, subsidized by territorial legislatures, often greatly exaggerated the virtues of the territories in the press (Lyon 1968). Territorial lawmakers also offered lucrative incentives to potential investors. For example, in 1885 the Arizona legislature authorized so many bonding issues for outright subsidies of four railroads and two wagon roads that it put the state into precarious debt for a decade (Lyon 1968). In 1903, the Arizona legislature also exempted the railroad and dams from taxation to encourage development (Wagoner 1970).

Chapter 2

1. Government-related employment refers to all persons employed in local, state, and federal government (e.g., including the military, border patrol personnel), as well as persons employed in social services and education. Data was calculated from U.S. Census Bureau (2000) Summary File 3 data for southern Arizona and New Mexico rural counties bordering Mexico. Counties considered include Yuma, Santa Cruz, and Cochise in Arizona and Hidalgo, Grant, Luna, Doña Ana, Otero, and Eddy in New Mexico. Pima County was excluded because it is an urban county, with more residents than all the nine rural border counties combined.

2. Census-reported unemployment rates in colonias and border towns do not fully reflect economic problems. Residents in colonias and border communities, like many poor communities, tend to be underemployed. Many take two to three jobs in low-wage positions to make ends meet.

Chapter 3

1. We acknowledge several problems in using the U.S. Census Bureau data, which can underreport socio-economic problems. First, the census geography does not always correspond perfectly with colonia boundaries identified by counties and local governments. That is, some colonias comprise only a fraction of the smallest census geography units, while other colonias encompass portions of multiple census areas. Because of this limitation, we were forced to consider all areas in which a colonia subdivision lies in our analysis. However, using this method sometimes picks up nearby settlements that are wealthier than the colonia, skewing the true level of socio-economic problems. Second, census workers are likely to have undercounted colonia residents in some communities, especially those with large numbers of unauthorized immigrants. Therefore, we believe the true levels of socio-economic problems are greater than that reported by the U.S. Census Bureau. Despite these limitations, we use census data because it provides the best currently available picture of conditions.

Total population data for the states of Arizona and New Mexico were obtained from the U.S. Census Bureau's (2006a) annual population estimates. All other data for 2005 reported in tables 3.1–3.4 are estimated from a linear extrapolation of 1990 and 2000 census data. The U.S. Census Bureau has not yet provided population or socio-economic data for unincorporated places for 2005.

2. Estimates of the number of Hispanics in Texas colonias are difficult to come by, and government sources typically indicate that nearly all or a preponderance of the colonia population is Hispanic. See, for example, the Texas Department of Housing and Community Affairs (2006) and the "Colonias Facts" listed by the Texas Department of State (2006).

3. Data for 2005 are unavailable, but the spatial patterns shown in figure 3.2 would likely reveal little change from 2000 to 2005.

4. It should be noted that housing assistance at the state level is far more prevalent in Texas, where state agencies have been involved with colonia housing for many years. This is an indication of the larger number of colonias in Texas, as well as the overall poor quality of housing in these places. In contrast, Arizona and New Mexico state governments have been less active in colonia housing development.

Chapter 4

1. The U.S. Census Bureau defines urban and rural places according to population size and land-use density. Urban places consist of "urban clusters" that range in size from 2,500 to 49,999 persons, and "urban areas" that have a population of at least 50,000. Rural places consist of all settlements that do not qualify as either urban clusters or urban areas (populations are less than 2,500). The Census Bureau also defines "census designated places," which are unincorporated settlements with an identifiable core and a mixture of land uses. There are no minimum or maximum size classifications for census designated places. Many colonias are classified as census designated places and, for present purposes, are considered urban places. For additional information, see U.S. Census Bureau (2006b).

2. Hatch, New Mexico, the self-proclaimed chile capital of the world, is the most recognizable community in the region but is not an officially designated colonia.

3. The 1980 population data for San Luis are available from the U.S. Census Bureau but are not comparable with 2005 data because boundary definitions have changed over time. For 1980 the Census Bureau indicated a population of 1,946 residents (U.S. Census Bureau 2003b).

4. Urbanization refers to the growth of urban places over time. It is measured by population size and physical expansion, which is identified by changes in density and the mix of land uses. Urbanization is an important indicator of the changing social, economic, and infrastructure characteristics of urban places. See Cadwallader (1996) for a fuller discussion of urbanization.

5. In Arizona, colonia counties include Cochise, Gila, Graham, Greenlee, Pinal, Santa Cruz, and Yuma. Pima and Maricopa counties are not considered because populations exceed 1 million, and La Paz County is excluded from this analysis because data were not available until 1990. New Mexico colonia counties include Catron, Chavez, Doña Ana, Eddy, Grant, Hidalgo, Lincoln, Luna, Otero, Sierra, and Socorro.

6. Population data for individual colonias were obtained from historical U.S. Census Bureau data (1950–2000). Data for 2005 were obtained from the Census Bureau's annual population estimates (U.S. Census Bureau 2006a).

Chapter 5

1. Controversy remains about the racist basis of the 1986 Immigration Reform and Control Act and more recent immigration legislation. Much of this concern rests in the public's perception of Mexican nationals living in the United States. See Espenshade and Calhoun (1993), DeLaet (2000), and Hing (2004) for a closer look at attitudes toward unauthorized immigrants.

2. Zúñiga and Hernández-León (2005) provide a comprehensive look at the diffusion of Mexican workers across the United States. In addition to a numerical count of workers across the country, they profile many communities where unauthorized immigrants live and discuss problems and solutions to the integration of workers in these communities.

Chapter 6

1. Chapters 7–9 concentrate on colonia community development. These chapters discuss communities in which development has proven successful and provide examples where efforts have fallen short of expectations. They also discuss the capacity building approach to community development as it applies to colonias.

2. In recent years Mexican nationals claim nearly all apprehensions along the country's southern border. According to the U.S. Department of Homeland Security (2004), they accounted for 95 percent of total apprehensions in 1970, 97 percent in 1980, 96 percent in 1990, and 95 percent in 2003. The rest come mainly from other countries in Central and South America.

3. The Department of Homeland Security was organized in 2002 as part of the government's response to the terrorist threat. Prior to this, the Immigration and Naturalization Service was responsible for border security (U.S. Border Patrol) and the compilation of apprehension data. Formerly a branch of the U.S. Department of Justice, the U.S. Border Patrol now falls under the jurisdiction of Customs and Border Protection, a division of the Department of Homeland Security.

4. In 2006 the 109th Congress continued the emphasis on deterrence by passing legislation that called for building 700 miles (1,120 km) of walls along the U.S.–Mexico border. Under Operation Jump Start, Customs and Border Protection, a division of the Department of Homeland Security, will also employ 6,000 more U.S. Border Patrol agents by 2008 to further deter immigrants from crossing the border. See U.S. Customs and Border Protection (2006) for details.

5. An alternative approach calls for a detailed assessment of the foreign-born population by citizenship status, origin country, and year of entry to the United States, but these data are unavailable for many colonias. Even if these data were available, they are self-reported and there is no guarantee of accuracy, especially given the unauthorized status of many foreigners.

6. Data for 1990 and 2000 are used because we target policies of the 1980s and 1990s.

Chapter 7

1. Subprime lending includes a range of lending practices that promise borrowers quick credit and cash, including home mortgage loans, check cashing for payday loans, car title loans, tax refund loans, and rent-to-own loans (Carsey Institute 2006). This market is often termed "predatory" because lenders market loans to low-income borrowers who lack access to other means of credit and have little or no ability to repay the high interest fees and terms. The Carsey Institute (2006) found that predatory lending practices are becoming more common in rural areas, especially among minority populations. For more information about subprime lending and strategies to combat it, see the U.S. Department of Housing and Urban Development (2004b) and a special edition on predatory lending by the Housing Assistance Council (2002).

2. There is an array of land-use schemes other than "contract for deed" in colonias. Some subprime lenders offer financing to prospective homebuyers who purchase land without clear title. That is, some colonia residents in Arizona and New Mexico cannot prove they legally own land they acquired through quitclaim and warranty deeds because previous sellers may never have had clear title to the property. Therefore, these residents are excluded from federally financed infrastructure or housing improvements.

3. New immigrants in some colonias, such as San Cristobal, also express concern about the increasingly militarized presence along the border. They believe the U.S. Border Patrol unfairly detains Mexican residents, creating an environment of intimidation for families and children. However, other groups of residents see it differently. Many claimed that the border patrol needed to step up its presence and expand monitoring efforts. Long-term residents, in particular, say they would like a greater police presence; in fact, a group of families in San Cristobal offered the county sheriff space for an expanded police presence. Nongovernmental organizations working in the area have a different, mixed view of the impact of the border patrol presence, depending upon their political orientation. Thus, there is little consensus on this issue, illustrating the difficulty of setting community development priorities.

Chapter 10

1. The programs of the U.S. Department of Housing and Urban Development (HUD) apply to Texas as well. In Texas, however, there are state-sponsored programs that complement HUD's efforts, but this is not the case in Arizona and New Mexico, which provide far less state support. Little work has been done in California colonias because there has been much less documentation of where

they are located, their needs, and their development concerns. Moreover, urban counties, such as San Diego County, are excluded from using HUD funding according to the 1989 Cranston-Gonzales Act.

2. See the President's Interagency Task Force on the Economic Development of the Southwest Border (2000, p. 69).

3. See the Southwest Border Regional Commission (1978, p. 8).

Works Cited

Adams, John. 1997. *Mexican Banking and Investment in Transition*. Westport, Conn.: Quorum Books.

Aghevli, Bijan, Mohsin Khan, and Peter Montiel. 1991. *Exchange Rate Policy in Developing Countries*. Washington, D.C.: International Monetary Fund.

Aguirre, Yjino. 1975. Echoes of the conquistadores: stock raising in Spanish-Mexican times. *Journal of Arizona History* 16: 267–86.

Aldrich, Howard, and Roger Waldinger. 1990. Ethnicity and entrepreneurship. *Annual Review of Sociology* 16: 111–35.

Alexander, Jeffrey. 1998. *Real Civil Societies: Dilemmas of Institutionalization*. Thousand Oaks, Calif.: Sage.

American Friends Service Committee. 1992. *Sealing Our Borders: The Human Toll*. Philadelphia: American Friends Service Committee.

Andreas, Peter. 2000. *Border Games*. Ithaca, N.Y.: Cornell University Press.

Anheier, Helmut, and Nuno Themudo. 2002. Organisational forms of global civil society: implications of going global. In *Global Civil Society*, Helmut Anheier, Marlies Glasius, and Mary Kaldoor, eds., pp. 191–216. Oxford: Oxford University Press.

Anonymous. 2005. Drug trade on the border. *The Economist* 376(8433): 35–36.

Arendt, Randall. 1994. *Rural by Design: Maintaining Small Town Character*. Chicago: Planners Press.

Arizona Department of Mineral Resources. 1957–1958. *Historical Data and Special Articles Relating to the Copper Industry in Arizona, the United States, and the World, Showing the Need for Copper Tariff, and Addenda I and II*. Compiled from reports of the U.S. Bureau of Mines, U.S. Census Bureau, American Bureau of Metal Statistics, Arizona Employment Security Commission, and Arizona State Tax Commission. Phoenix: Arizona Department of Mineral Resources.

Arizona Statistical Review. 1952–1980. Phoenix: Valley National Bank, Economic Research Department.

Arizona Workforce Development. 2000. Decennial census population of Arizona, counties, cities, places: 1860 to 1990. Available via http://www.workforce.az.gov/admin/uploadedPublications/1601_census_decennial.pdf.

Arreola, Daniel, and James Curtis. 1993. *The Mexican Border Cities: Landscape Anatomy and Place Personality*. Tucson: The University of Arizona Press.

Audley, John, Demetrios Papademetriou, Sandra Polaski, and Scott Vaughan. 2003. *NAFTA's Promise and Reality: Lessons from Mexico for the Hemisphere.* Washington, D.C.: Carnegie Endowment for International Peace. Available via http://www.carnegieendowment.org/publications.

Austin, Mary. 1992. Arizona: the land of joyous adventure. In *These United States: Portraits of America from the 1920s*, Daniel H. Borus, ed., pp. 37–44. Ithaca, N.Y.: Cornell University Press.

Avner, Ben-Ner, and Theresa Van Hoomissen. 1991. Nonprofit organizations in the mixed economy: a demand and supply analysis. *Annals of Public and Cooperative Economics* 62: 519–50.

Baerrensen, Donald. 1971. *The Border Industrialization Program of Mexico.* Lexington, Mass.: Lexington Books.

Bailey, Linda. 2004. *Three Essays on Skill, Racial, and Ethnic Labor Market Differences.* Ph.D. diss., Department of Economics, Michigan State University, East Lansing.

Bancroft, Hubert. 1962. *History of Arizona and New Mexico, 1530–1888.* Albuquerque: Horne and Wallace.

Blecker, Robert. 1997. *NAFTA and the Peso Collapse: Not Just a Coincidence.* Briefing Paper no. 66. Washington, D.C.: Economic Policy Institute.

Bond, Marian. 1980. Exchange rates, inflation, and the vicious cycle. *Finance and Development* 17: 27–31.

Buckwalter, Paul. 2003. Building power: finding and developing leaders in Arizona congregations. *Social Policy* 33: 2–8.

Burns, Carol. 1996. *Permeable Boundaries and the Construction of Place.* Berkeley, Calif.: International Association for the Study of Traditional Environments.

Bustamante, Antonio. 1998. As guilty as hell: Mexican copper miners and their communities in Arizona, 1920–1950. In *Border Crossing: Mexican and Mexican American Workers*, John Hart, ed., pp. 163–83. Washington, D.C.: Scholarly Resources.

Cadwallader, Martin. 1996. *Urban Geography.* Upper Saddle River, N.J.: Prentice-Hall.

Calavita, Kitty. 1992. *Inside the State: The Bracero Program, Immigration, and the INS.* New York: Routledge.

Campoli, Julie, Elizabeth Humstone, and Alex MacLean. 2002. *Above and Beyond: Visualizing Change in Small Towns and Rural Areas.* Chicago: Planners Press.

Carroll, Susan. 2006. Colonia problem growing in Arizona. *Arizona Republic*, 23 January, p. A1.

Carroll, Susan, and Daniel González. 2005. Napolitano taps disaster funds for border counties. *Arizona Republic*, 16 April. Available via http://www.azcentral.com/arizonarepublic/news/articles/0816borderemergency16.html.

Carsey Institute. 2006. *Subprime and Predatory Lending in Rural America.* Policy

Brief no. 4. Durham: University of New Hampshire. Available via http://www.carseyinstitute.unh.edu

Center for the Future of Arizona. 2006. *Why Some Schools with Latino Children Beat the Odds While Others Don't*. Phoenix: Center for the Future of Arizona and the Morrison Institute for Public Policy, Arizona State University. Available via http://www.asu.edu/copp/morrison/LatinEd.pdf.

Chapa, Jorge, and David J. Eaton. 1997. *Colonia Housing and Infrastructure*. Austin: University of Texas, LBJ School of Public Affairs.

Chaskin, Robert. 2001. Building community capacity: a definitional framework and case studies from a comprehensive community initiative. *Urban Affairs Review* 36(3): 291–323.

Chávez, Sergio. 2005. Community, ethnicity, and class in a changing rural California town. *Rural Sociology* 70: 314–35.

Clark, William, and Freya Schultz. 1997. Evaluating the local impacts of recent immigration to California: realism versus racism. *Population Research and Policy Review* 16: 475–91.

Cochise County. 2006. Comprehensive plan and area and neighborhood plans. Available via http://www.cochisecounty.com/P&Z/Comprehensive.htm.

Coleman, James. 1988. Social capital in the creation of human capital. *American Journal of Sociology* 94: S95–120.

Conover, Ted. 1987. *Coyotes*. New York: Vintage Books.

Copp, Nelson. 1963. *Wetbacks and Braceros: Mexican Migrant Laborers and American Immigration Policy*. Ph.D. diss., Department of History, Boston University.

Cortés, Michael. 1999. A statistical profile of Latino nonprofit organizations in the United States. In *Nuevos Senderos: Reflections on Hispanics and Philanthropy*, Diana Campoamor, William Díaz, and Henry Ramos, eds., pp. 17–54. Houston: Arte Publico Press.

Crane, Keith, Beth Asch, Joanna Heilbrunn, and Danielle Cullinance. 1990. *The Effect of Employer Sanctions on the Flow of Undocumented Immigrants to the United States*. Santa Monica, Calif.: Rand Corporation.

Davidson, Miriam. 2000. *Lives on the Line: Dispatches from the U.S.–Mexico Border*. Tucson: University of Arizona Press.

Davila, Alberto. 1990. The impact of the 1982 peso devaluations on maquiladora profits. *Journal of Borderlands Studies* 5: 39–49.

Davis, Tony. 2000. Wildcat subdivisions fuel fight over sprawl. *Arizona Daily Star*, 24 April, p. A1.

De Gennero, Nat. 1987. The need for diversification in bordertown economies. In *Arizona and Mexico: Changing Patterns of Socioeconomic Relations—The Third Annual Policy Forum*, Gary Woodard, ed., pp. 40–42. Tucson: University of Arizona, College of Business and Public Administration, Division of Economic and Business Research.

DeLaet, Debra. 2000. *U.S. Immigration Policy in an Age of Rights*. Westport, Conn.: Praeger.

de la Madrid, Miguel. 1984. Mexico: the new challenges. *Foreign Affairs* 63: 62–76.

De Long, Bradford, Christopher De Long, and Sherman Robinson. 1996. The case for Mexico's rescue. *Foreign Affairs*, 75: 8–14.

De Souza Briggs, Xavier. 2004. Social capital: Easy beauty or meaningful resource? *Journal of the American Planning Association* 20: 151–58.

De Vita, Carol, Cory Fleming, and Eric Twombly. 2001. Building nonprofit capacity: a framework for addressing the problem. In *Building Capacity in Nonprofit Organizations*, Carol De Vita and Cory Fleming, eds., pp. 5–30. Washington, D.C.: The Urban Institute.

Dolhinow, Rebecca. 2005. Caught in the middle: the state, NGOs and the limits to grassroots organizing along the U.S.–Mexico border. *Antipode* 37: 558–80.

Dominguez, Debra, and Russell Contreras. 2005. N.M. schools aim to educate all students. *Albuquerque Journal*, 4 November. Available via http://www.abqjou rnal.com/border2005/404955nm11-04-05.htm.

Doña Ana County. 1987. *Las Cruces Extra-Territorial Zoning Ordinance*. Las Cruces, N.M.: Doña Ana County Department of Community Development.

Doña Ana County. 2005. *Doña Ana County Land Use Regulations and Zoning Ordinance*. Las Cruces, N.M.: Doña Ana County Department of Community Development.

Donato, Katherine, Jorge Durand, and Douglas Massey. 1992. Changing conditions in the U.S. labor market: effects of the Immigration Reform and Control Act of 1986. *Population Research and Policy Review* 11: 93–115.

Donelson, Angela. 2004. The role of NGOs and NGO networks in meeting the needs of U.S. colonias. *Community Development Journal* 39: 332–34.

Donelson, Angela. 2005. *Social Networks, Poverty, and Development: An Analysis of Capacity Building in Arizona and New Mexico Colonias*. Ph.D. diss., Department of Geography and Regional Development, University of Arizona, Tucson.

Donelson, Angela, and Esperanza Holguin. 2001a. Homestead subdivision/ colonias and land market dynamics in Arizona and New Mexico. In *Memoria of a Research Workshop: Irregular Settlement and Self-Help Housing in the United States*, Peter Ward, ed., pp. 39–41. Cambridge, Mass.: Lincoln Institute of Land Use Policy.

Donelson, Angela, and Esperanza Holguin. 2001b. Social infrastructure in colonias in Arizona and New Mexico. In *Memoria of a Research Workshop: Irregular Settlement and Self-Help Housing in the United States*, Peter Ward, ed., pp. 91–93. Cambridge, Mass.: Lincoln Institute of Land Use Policy.

Driesen, Kevin, and Amanda Aguirre. 2000. Evaluating medical outreach networks in the U.S.–Mexico border region. *Journal of Border Health* 5: 19–27.

Duncan, Cynthia. 1999. *Worlds Apart: Why Poverty Persists in Rural America.* New Haven, Conn.: Yale University Press.

Durand, Jorge, Douglas Massey, and Emilio Parrado. 1999. The new era of Mexican migration to the United States. *Journal of American History* 86: 518–36.

Earle, Duncan. 1999. The border colonias and the problem of communication: applying anthropology for outreach. In *Life, Death, and In-between on the U.S.–Mexico Border*, Martha Loustaunau and Mary Sanchez-Bane, eds., pp. 23–38. Westport, Conn.: Bergin and Garvey.

Eastman, Clyde. 1991. Impacts of the Immigration Reform Act of 1986 on New Mexico agriculture. *Journal of Borderlands Studies* 4: 103–29.

Eckstein, Susan. 2001. Community as gift-giving: collectivistic roots of volunteerism. *American Sociological Review* 66: 829–51.

Edwards, Michael, and David Hulme. 1996. Too close for comfort? The impact of official aid on nongovernmental organizations. *World Development* 24: 961–73.

Edwards, Michael, David Hulme, and Tina Wallace. 2000. Increasing leverage for development: challenges for NGOs in a global future. In *New Roles and Relevance: Development NGOs and the Challenge of Change*, David Lewis and Tina Wallace, eds., pp. 1–14. Bloomfield, Conn.: Kumarian Press.

Edwards, Sebastian. 1996. Exchange rates, inflation, and disinflation: Latin American experiences. In *Capital Controls, Exchange Rates, and Monetary Policy in the World Economy*, Sebastian Edwards, ed., pp. 301–38. Cambridge: Cambridge University Press.

Elac, John. 1972. *The Employment of Mexican Workers in U.S. Agriculture, 1900–1960: a Binational Economic Analysis.* Los Angeles: University of California–Los Angeles Press.

Esparza, Adrian, and John Carruthers. 2000. Land use planning and exurbanization in the rural Mountain West: evidence from Arizona. *Journal of Planning Education and Research* 20: 23–36.

Esparza, Adrian, and Andrew Krmenec. 2000. Large city interaction in the United States urban system. *Urban Studies* 37: 691–709.

Esparza, Adrian, Brigitte Waldorf, and Javier Chavez. 2004. Localized effects of globalization: the case of Ciudad Juárez, Chihuahua, Mexico. *Urban Geography* 25: 120–39.

Espenshade, Thomas, and Charles Calhoun. 1993. An analysis of public opinion toward undocumented immigration. *Population Research and Policy Review* 12: 189–224.

Fine, Alison, Nancy Kopf, and Colette Thayer. 2001. *Lessons from the Field: Proven Capacity Building Strategies for Nonprofits.* Washington, D.C.: Innovation Network. Available via http://www.innonet.org/files/view/Echoes_Full.pdf.

Fisher, Julie. 1993. *The Road from Rio: Sustainable Development and the Nongovernmental Movement in the Third World*. Westport, Conn.: Praeger.

Fisher, Julie. 1998. *Nongovernments: NGOs and the Political Development of the Third World*. West Hartford, Conn.: Kumarian Press.

Ford, D'Lyn. 2000. Peppers under pressure. Las Cruces: Department of Agricultural Communications, New Mexico State University. Available via http://cahe.nmsu.edu/pubs/resourcesmag/spring00/PepperPressure.html.

Franke, Paul. 1950. *They Plowed Up Hell in Old Cochise! A Blazing Saga of Cochise County, Arizona, America's Last Frontier*. Douglas, Ariz.: Douglas Climate Club.

Fredericksen, Patricia, and Rosanne London. 2000. Disconnect in the hollow state: the pivotal role of organizational capacity in community-based development organizations. *Public Administration Review* 60: 230–39.

Froelich, Karen. 1999. Diversification of revenue strategies: evolving resource dependence in nonprofit organizations. *Nonprofit and Voluntary Sector Quarterly* 28: 246–68.

Frontera NorteSur Online. 2005. *The Battle of the Border: Round 2*. Compilation of U.S.–Mexico border news reports. Las Cruces: New Mexico State University. Available via http://www.nmsu.edu/frontera.

Galarza, Ernesto. 1964. *Merchants of Labor: The Mexican Bracero Story—An Account of the Managed Migration of Mexican Farm Workers in California, 1942–1960*. Charlotte, S.C.: McNally and Loftin.

Galaskiewicz, Joseph. 1979. *Exchange Networks and Community Politics*. Beverly Hills, Calif.: Sage.

Galbis, Vincent. 1982. Inflation: the Latin American experience, 1970–1979. *Finance and Development* 19: 22–26.

Gauthiez, Bernard. 2004. The history of urban morphology. *Urban Morphology* 8: 71–89.

Geffert, Garry. 2002. H-2A Guestworker Program: a legacy of importing agricultural labor. In *The Human Cost of Food*, Charles Thompson Jr. and Melinda Wiggins, eds., pp. 111–35. Austin: University of Texas Press.

Glasmeier, Amy. 2002. One nation, pulling apart: the basis of persistent poverty in the USA. *Progress in Human Geography* 26: 155–73.

Gonzales-Berry, Erlinda, and David Maciel. 2000. *The Contested Homeland: A Chicano History of New Mexico*. Albuquerque: University of New Mexico Press.

Goodman, David. 1969. *Arizona Odyssey: Bibliographic Adventures in Nineteenth-Century Magazines*. Tempe: Arizona Historical Foundation.

Goodwin, Mark. 1998. The governance of rural areas: some emerging research issues and agendas. *Journal of Rural Studies* 14: 5–12.

Green, Gary, and Anna Haines. 2002. *Asset Building and Community Development*. Thousand Oaks, Calif.: Sage.

Griffith-Jones, Stephany, and Osvaldo Sunkel. 1986. *Debt and Development Crises in Latin America: The End of an Illusion*. Oxford: Oxford University Press.

Gurría, José. 2000. Mexico: recent developments, structural reforms, and future challenges. *Finance and Development* 37: 23–26.

Hamnett, Brian. 1999. *A Concise History of Mexico*. Cambridge: Cambridge University Press.

Harrell, Louis, and Dale Fischer. 1985. The 1982 Mexican peso devaluation and border area employment. *Monthly Labor Review* 108: 25–32.

Harris, Margaret. 1998. Doing it their way: organizational challenges for voluntary associations. *Nonprofit and Voluntary Sector Quarterly* 27: 144–58.

Hart, John. 1998. *The Rural Landscape*. Baltimore, Md.: Johns Hopkins University Press.

Hawley, Chris. 2005. Shared goal, different motive. *Arizona Republic*, 21 August, p. A1.

Henkel, David. 1998. Self-help planning the colonias: collaboration and innovation in southern New Mexico unincorporated areas. *Small Town* Nov/Dec: 16–21.

Herman, Robert, and David Renz. 1999. Theses on nonprofit organizational effectiveness. *Nonprofit and Voluntary Sector Quarterly* 28: 107–26.

Heyman, Josiah. 1993. The oral history of the Mexican American community of Douglas, Arizona, 1901–1942. *Journal of the Southwest* 35: 186–206.

Hing, Bill. 2004. *Defining America through Immigration Policy*. Philadelphia: Temple University Press.

Housing Assistance Council. 2002. Predatory lending. *Rural Voices* 7(2): 1–24.

Housing Assistance Council. 2006a. *Rural Housing in the Administration's FY 2007 Budget*. Washington, D.C.: Housing Assistance Council. Available via http://www.ruralhome.org.

Housing Assistance Council. 2006b. *Administration Housing Budget Proposals Resemble 2006 Requests*. Washington, D.C.: Housing Assistance Council. Available via http://www.ruralhome.org.

Housing Assistance Council. 2006c. *Information on Rural Low-Income Housing Issues*. Washington, D.C.: Housing Assistance Council. Available via http://www.ruralhome.org.

Huntoon, Laura, and Barbara Becker. 2001. Colonias in Arizona: a changing definition with changing location. In *Memoria of a Research Workshop: Irregular Settlement and Self-Help Housing in the United States*, Peter Ward, ed., pp. 34–35. Cambridge, Mass.: Lincoln Institute of Land Use Policy.

Innes, Judith. 1996. Planners as consensus builders. *Journal of the American Planning Association* 62: 460–72.

Innes, Judith, and David Booher. 1999. Consensus building and complex adaptive systems: a framework for evaluating collaborative planning. *Journal of the American Planning Association* 65: 412–23.

James, Daniel. 1991. *Illegal Immigration: An Unfolding Crisis*. Lanham, Md.: University Press of America.

Jordan, Lara. 2005. 500 agents to be added to Arizona border. Available via http://sfgate.com/cgi-bin/article.cgi?file=/n/a/2005/03/29/national/wo8495 9S80.DTL.

Kalter, Eliot, and Hoe Khor. 1990. Mexico's experience with adjustments. *Finance and Development* 27: 22–25.

Kearney, Milo, and Anthony Knopp. 1995. *Border Cuates: A History of the U.S.–Mexican Twin Cities*. Austin, Tex.: Eakin Press.

Kent, Robert. 1983. Agriculture and ranching. In *Borderlands Sourcebook: A Guide to the Literature on Northern Mexico and the American Southwest*, Ellyn Stoddard, Richard Nostrand, and Jonathan West, eds., pp. 136–43. Norman: University of Oklahoma Press.

Kessell, John. 2002. *Spain in the Southwest: A Narrative History of Colonial New Mexico, Arizona, Texas, and California*. Norman: University of Oklahoma Press.

Koerner, Mona. 2002. Colonias in New Mexico: rethinking policy approaches to substandard housing problems. Paper presented at the colloquium Constructing Urban Space, 6 April. Austin: University of Texas, Urban Issues Program.

Kramer, Ralph. 2000. A third sector in the third millennium? *Voluntas: International Journal of Voluntary and Nonprofit Organizations* 11: 1–23.

Krikorian, Mark. 2005. *Downsizing Illegal Immigration*. Washington, D.C.: Center for Immigration Studies. Available via http://www.cis.org.

Krmenec, Andrew, and Adrian Esparza. 1999. City systems and industrial market structure. *Annals of the Association of American Geographers* 89: 267–89.

Langham, Thomas. 1992. Federal regulation of border labor: Operation Wetback and the wetback bills. *Journal of Borderlands Studies* 7: 81–91.

Lemos, Maria, Dianne Austin, Robert Merideth, and Robert Varady. 2002. Public-private partnerships as catalysts for community-based water infrastructure development: the border water works program in Texas and New Mexico colonias. *Environment and Planning C: Government and Policy* 20: 281–95.

Levy, John. 2002. *Contemporary Urban Planning*. Upper Saddle River, N.J.: Prentice-Hall.

Linnell, Deborah. 2003. *Evaluation of Capacity: Lessons from the Field*. Washington, D.C.: Alliance for Nonprofit Management.

Linton, April. 2002. Immigration and the structure of demand: Do immigrants alter the labor market composition of U.S. cities? *International Migration Review* 36: 58–80.

Livingston, Gary. 1993. Racism and the passage of the Immigration Act of 1924: the beginning of the quota system. *Journal of Borderlands Studies* 8: 73–89.

Lorey, David E. 1990. *U.S.–Mexico Border Statistics since 1900*. Los Angeles: University of California–Los Angeles, Latin American Center.

Lorey, David E. 1999. *The U.S.–Mexican Border in the Twentieth Century*. Wilmington, Del.: Scholarly Resources.

Lustig, Nora. 1998. *Mexico: The Remaking of an Economy*. Washington, D.C.: Brookings Institution Press.

Lyon, William. 1968. The corporate frontier. *Journal of Arizona History* 9: 1–2.

MacDonald, Scott, Jane Hughes, and Uwe Bott. 1991. Latin America in the 1990s: Democracy or debt? In *Latin American Debt in the 1990s*, Scott MacDonald, Jane Hughes, and Uwe Bott, eds., pp. 1–13. New York: Praeger.

Magaña, Lisa. 2003. *Straddling the Border*. Austin: University of Texas Press.

Maquila Portal. 2005. Number of persons employed in maquiladoras in the binational border states, 2000–2004. Available via http://www.maquil apor tal.com.

Marek, Angie. 2005. Border wars. *U.S. News and World Report*, 28 November, p. 47–56.

Marizco, Michael. 2005. Sasabe, Sonora, has turned into a smugglers' haven. *Arizona Daily Star*, 2 October, p. A1.

Martin, Philip. 1999. California farm labor market and immigration reform. In *Foreign Temporary Workers in America*, Briant Lowell, ed., pp. 179–207. Westport, Conn.: Quorum Press.

Martin, Philip, and David Martin. 1994. *The Endless Quest*. Boulder, Colo.: Westview Press.

Martinez, Oscar. 1990. Transnational fronterizos: cross-border linkages in Mexican border society. *Journal of Borderlands Studies* 5: 79–93.

Martinez, Ruben. 2001. *Crossing Over*. New York: Picador Press.

Massey, Douglas. 2005. *Backfire at the Border: Why Enforcement Without Legalization Cannot Stop Illegal Immigration*. Washington, D.C.: Center for Trade Policy Studies, The Cato Institute.

Massey, Douglas, Jorge Durand, and Nolan Malone. 2002. *Beyond Smoke and Mirrors*. New York: Russell Sage Foundation.

Massey, Douglas, and Zai Liang. 1989. The long-term consequences of a temporary worker program: The U.S. bracero experience. *Population Research and Policy Review* 8: 199–226.

May, Marlynn, Gloria Bowman, Kenneth Ramos, Larry Rincones, Maria Rebollar, Mary Rosa, Josephine Saldana, Adelina Sanchez, Teresa Serna, Norma Viega, Gregoria Villegas, Maria Zamorano, and Irma Ramos. 2003. Embracing the local: enriching scientific research, education, and outreach on the Texas-Mexico border through a participatory action research partnership. *Environmental Health Perspectives* 111: 1571–76.

May, Marlynn, Richard Contreras, Linda Callejas, and Elvia Ledezma. 2004. *Mujer y Corazón: Community Health Workers and Their Organizations in*

Colonias on the U.S.–Mexico Border—An Exploratory Study. Report to the Office of Rural Health Policy, Health Resources and Services Administration. College Station: Texas A&M University Colonias Program, Center for Housing and Urban Development.

May, Marlynn, Bita Kash, and Ricardo Contreras. 2005. *Community Health Worker (CHW) Certification and Training: A National Survey of Regionally and State-Based Programs*. Report to the Office of Rural Health Policy, Health Resources and Services Administration. College Station: Texas A&M University Colonias Program, Center for Housing and Urban Development.

McGuire, Michael, Barry Rubin, Robert Agranoff, and Craig Richards. 1994. Building development capacity in nonmetro communities. *Public Administration Review* 54: 426–33.

Melody, Michael. 1989. *The Apache*. New York: Chelsea House.

Meyer, Caroline. 1997. The political economy of NGOs and information sharing. *World Development* 25: 1127–40.

Meyer, Michael, and John Garcia. 1987. *Arizona's Relations with Northern Mexico: Arizona's 51st Town Hall*. Tucson: University of Arizona, Latin American Area Center.

Meyers, Dowell, William Baer, and Seong-Youn Choi. 1996. The changing problem of overcrowded housing. *Journal of the American Planning Association* 62: 66–84.

Miller, Willard, and Ruby Miller. 1996. *United States Immigration*. Santa Barbara, Calif.: ABC-CLIO.

Milofsky, Carl. 2003. Transorganizations as a focus for study in nonprofit organizational research. Paper presented in May 2003 at the School of Business and Social Sciences, University of Surrey Roehampton, Southlands College, London.

Milofsky, Carl, and John Messer. 1998. Building social capital with community: a case study of a virtual organization. Paper presented at the Southern Sociological Society, 4 April, Atlanta, Ga.

Morgan, David. 1979. Fiscal policy in the oil exporting countries, 1972–1978. *Finance and Development* 16: 14–17.

Murdoch, Jonathan, and Simone Abram. 1998. Defining the limits of community governance. *Journal of Rural Studies* 14: 41–50.

Murray, Michael, and Larry Dunn. 1995. Capacity building for rural development in the United States. *Journal of Rural Studies* 11: 89–97.

Myrick, David. 1967. The railroads of Arizona: an approach to Tombstone. *Journal of Arizona History* 8(3): 156–57.

Nash, Gerald. 1990. *World War II and the West: Reshaping the Economy*. Lincoln: University of Nebraska Press.

Nash, Kate. 2005. Counties to get emergency aid: governor finds ruin, violence along border. *Albuquerque Tribune*, 12 August. Available via http://www1

.abqtrib.com/albq/nw_local_state_government/article/0,2564,ALBQ_19
859_3997751,00.html.

Nashashibi, Karim. 1983. Devaluation in developing countries: the difficult
choices. *Finance and Development* 20: 14–17.

Nathan, Robert. 1968. *Industrial and Employment Potential of the U.S.–Mexico
Border*. Washington, D.C.: EDA Technical Assistance Project.

National Congress for Community Economic Development. 2004. The Community Economic Development Expertise Enhancement Act: fact sheet.
Available via http://www.ncced.org/policy.

Nevins, Joseph. 2002. *Operation Gatekeeper*. New York: Routledge.

North, David. 1987. *Immigration Reform: Its First Year*. Washington, D.C.: Center
for Immigration Studies. Available via http://www.cis.org.

North American Development Bank. 2006a. Projects with NADB financing in
Arizona: fact sheet. Available via http://www.nadbank.org/projects/projport
folio.html.

North American Development Bank. 2006b. Projects with NADB financing in
New Mexico: fact sheet. Available via http://www.nadbank.org/projects/proj
portfolio.html.

Orrenius, Pia, and Madaline Zavodny. 2001. *Do Amnesty Programs Encourage
Illegal Immigration? Evidence from IRCA*. Working Paper no. 0103. Dallas,
Tex.: Federal Reserve Bank of Dallas.

Pagán, José. 2004. *Worker Displacement in the U.S.–Mexico Border Region*. North-
hampton, Mass.: Edward Elgar.

Patch, Joseph. 1962. *Reminiscences of Fort Huachuca, Arizona*. Published by the
author.

Patrick, Michael, and William Renforth. 1996. The effects of the peso devaluation on cross-border retailing. *Journal of Borderlands Studies* 11: 25–41.

Pavlakovich-Kochi, Vera. 2006. The Arizona-Sonora region: a decade of transborder region building. *Estudios Sociales, Revista de Investigación Científica*
14(27): 25–55.

Peach, James. 1997. Income distribution along the United States border with
Mexico, 1970–1990. *Journal of Borderlands Studies* 12: 1–16.

Peña, Sergio. 2005. Recent developments in urban marginality along Mexico's
northern border. *Habitat International* 29: 285–301.

Pew Hispanic Center. 2005. Unauthorized migrants: numbers and characteristics. Available via http://pewhispanic.org.

Powell, Walter, and Rebecca Friedkin. 1987. Organizational change in nonprofit
organizations. In *The Nonprofit Sector*, Walter Powell, ed., pp. 180–92. New
Haven, Conn.: Yale University Press.

President's Interagency Task Force on the Economic Development of the Southwest Border. 2000. *First Annual Report of the President's Interagency Task Force
on the Economic Development of the Southwest Border: Empowering Southwest*

Border Communities to Meet the Challenges of the 21st Century. Washington, D.C.: Government Printing Office.

Proffitt, Thurber. 1994. *Tijuana: The History of a Mexican Metropolis*. San Diego, Calif.: San Diego State University Press.

Putnam, Robert D. 1993. *Making Democracy Work*. Princeton, N.J.: Princeton University Press.

Rakodi, Carole. 2001. Urban governance and poverty: addressing needs, asserting claims—an editorial introduction. *International Planning Studies* 6: 343–56.

Ramírez, Rogelio de la O. 1996. The Mexican peso crisis and recession of 1994–1995: Preventable then, avoidable in the future? In *The Mexican Peso Crisis*, Riordan Roett, ed., pp. 11–32. Boulder, Colo.: Lynne Rienner.

Ramos, Irma, Marlynn May, and Kenneth S. Ramos. 2003. Evaluation of the Texas Health and Human Services Commission's colonias initiative. Available via http://www.hhsc.state.tx.us/hhsc_projects/colonias/082003_HHSC_Eval.html.

Ratcliffe, Michael. 2001. Identification of colonia-type settlements in census 2000. In *Memoria of a Research Workshop: Irregular Settlement and Self-Help Housing in the United States*, Peter Ward, ed. Cambridge, Mass.: Lincoln Institute of Land Use Policy.

Richardson, Chad. 1996. Building strength from within: colonias of the Rio Grande Valley. *Journal of Borderlands Studies* 11: 51–68.

Rochester, Colin. 1999. *Building the Capacity of Small Voluntary Agencies: Juggling on a Unicycle*. London: Centre for Civil Society, London School of Economics and Political Science. Available via http://www.lse.ac.uk/Depts/ccs/Small-Agencies-pubs/small-agencies.htm.

Rogers, David. 1974. Toward a scale of interorganizational relations among public agencies. *Sociology and Social Research* 59: 61–70.

Rothenberg, Daniel. 1998. *With These Hands: The Hidden World of Farmworkers Today*. New York: Harcourt Brace and Co.

Saenz, Rogelio, and Marie Ballejos. 1993. Industrial development and persistent poverty in the Lower Rio Grande. In *Forgotten Places: Uneven Development in Rural America*, Thomas Lyson and William Falk, eds., pp. 102–24. Lawrence: University of Kansas Press.

Salamon, Lester. 1994. The rise of the nonprofit sector. *Foreign Affairs* 73: 109–23.

Sanborn Map Company. 1886–1939. *Maps of Arizona Cities*. New York: Sanborn Map Co.

Sanders, Jimy. 2002. Ethnic boundaries and identity in plural societies. *Annual Review of Sociology* 28: 327–57.

Schweikart, Larry. 1981. You count it: the birth of banking in Arizona. *Journal of Arizona History* 22(3): 349–68.

Seltzer, Raymond. 1959. Analysis of national beef production. *Arizona Cattlelog*, p. 26.

Simmons, Marc. 2001. *Spanish Pathways: Readings in the History of Hispanic New Mexico*. Albuquerque: University of New Mexico Press.

Simpson, Lyn, Leanne Wood, and Leonie Daws. 2003. Community capacity building: starting with people not projects. *Community Development Journal* 38: 277–86.

Sklair, Leslie. 1989. *Assembling for Development: The Maquila Industry in Mexico and the United States*. Boston: Unwin Hyman.

Smith, David Horton. 1997. The rest of the nonprofit sector: grassroots associations as the dark matter ignored in prevailing "flat Earth" maps of the sector. *Nonprofit and Voluntary Sector Quarterly* 26: 114–31.

Smith, Hoval. 1934. An analysis of the United States copper mining industry and its relationship to the National Industrial Recovery Act. Paper presented at the Copper Code Hearing, 12 March, Washington, D.C.

Southwest Border Regional Commission. 1978. *Southwest Border Regional Commission Seminar on Federal Border Activities*. Washington, D.C.: Southwest Border Regional Commission.

Stoddard, Ellwyn. 1989. Amnesty: functional modifications of a congressional mandate. *Journal of Borderlands Studies* 6: 103–29.

Takahashi, Lois, and Gayla Smutny. 2001. Collaboration among small, community-based organizations: strategies and challenges in turbulent environments. *Journal of Planning Education and Research* 21: 141–53.

Taylor, Lawrence. 2001. The mining boom in Baja California from 1850 to 1890 and the emergence of Tijuana as a border community. *Journal of the Southwest* 43: 463–93.

Texas Department of Housing and Community Affairs. 2006. Background on the colonias. Available via http://www.tdhca.state.tx.us/oci/background.jsp.

Texas Department of State. 2006. Colonias FAQs. Available via http://www.sos.state.tx.us/border/colonias/faqs.shtml.

Thacher, Proffitt, and Wood, LLP. 2001. Consumer lending alert. Available via http://www.tpw.com/Page.aspx?Doc_ID=2185.

Trafzer, Clifford. 1980. *Yuma: Frontier Crossing of the Far Southwest*. Wichita, Kans.: Western Heritage Books.

Trennert, Robert. 1988. A different perspective: Victorian travelers in Arizona, 1860–1900. *Journal of Arizona History* 29(4): 349–70.

Twin Plant News. 1990, 1995, 2000. *Monthly Maquila Score Board: January*. El Paso: Nibbe, Hernandez and Associates.

U.S.–Mexico Border Counties Coalition. 2002. Report on uncompensated emergency health care. Available via http://www.bordercounties.org.

U.S. Census Bureau. 1920–1980. *Arizona and New Mexico: Land Area and Population, Population of Counties*. Washington, D.C.: Government Printing Office.

U.S. Census Bureau. 1990. Summary file 3. Available via http://factfinder.census

.gov/servlet/DatasetMainPageServlet?_program=DEC&_tabId=DEC2&
_submenuId=datasets_1&_lang=en&_ts=164469979687.

U.S. Census Bureau. 2000. Summary file 3. Available via http://factfinder.census
.gov/servlet/DatasetMainPageServlet?_lang=en&_ts=164469939906&_ds
_name=DEC_2000_SF4_U&_program=.

U.S. Census Bureau. 2003a. *2000 Census of Population and Housing, Population
and Housing Unit Counts, PHC-3-33, New Mexico*. Washington, D.C.: Government Printing Office.

U.S. Census Bureau. 2003b. *2000 Census of Population and Housing, Population
and Housing Unit Counts, PHC-3-4, Arizona*. Washington, D.C.: Government
Printing Office.

U.S. Census Bureau. 2006a. Annual population estimates. Available via http://
factfinder.census.gov/servlet/DatasetMainPageServlet?_program=PEP&_
submenuId=datasets_3&_lang=en.

U.S. Census Bureau. 2006b. Census 2000 urban and rural classification. Available via http://www.census.gov/geo/www/ua/ua_2k.html.

U.S. Customs and Border Protection. 2006. More border patrol agents move to
the frontline as the first contingent of National Guard arrives at southern
border. Available via http://www.cbp.gov/xp/cgov/newsroom/commission
er/messages/bpa_frontline.xml.

U.S. Department of Health and Human Services. 2006. The 2000 HHS Poverty
Guidelines. Available via http://aspe.hhs.gov/poverty/00poverty.htm.

U.S. Department of Homeland Security. 2004. *Southwest Border Apprehensions
by Sector*. Washington, D.C.: Undersecretary for Management, Office of Immigration Statistics.

U.S. Department of Housing and Urban Development. 2003. Community Planning and Development Division directors notice: use of HUD resources to
assist colonias. Available via http://www.hud.gov/offices/cpd/lawsregs/not
ices/2003/03-10.doc.

U.S. Department of Housing and Urban Development. 2004a. Delivering results
to colonias and farmworkers. Available via http://www.hud.gov.

U.S. Department of Housing and Urban Development. 2004b. *Outreach Efforts
Target Fair Lending in Arizona*. HUD Research Works March 2004. Washington, D.C.: U.S. Department of Housing and Urban Development. Available via http://www.huduser.org.

U.S. Department of Labor. 2006. Bureau of labor statistics, quarterly census of
employment and wages. Available via http://www.bls.gov.

U.S. Environmental Protection Agency. 2003a. Colonias fact sheet. Available via
http://www.epa.gov/OW-OWM.html/mab/mexican/clnfcts.pdf.

U.S. Environmental Protection Agency. 2003b. Border 2012: U.S.–Mexico Environmental Program. Available via http://www.epa.gov/usmexicoborder/pdf/
2012_english.pdf.

U.S. General Accounting Office. 1999. *U.S.–Mexico Border: Issues and Challenges Confronting the United States and Mexico*. U.S. GAO report NSIAD-99-190. Washington, D.C.: General Accounting Office.

U.S. General Accounting Office. 2002. *HUD Management: Impact Measurement Needed for Technical Assistance*. U.S. GAO report 02-1109T. Washington, D.C.: General Accounting Office.

U.S. General Accounting Office. 2004. *Treaty of Guadalupe Hidalgo: Findings and Possible Options Regarding Longstanding Community Land Grant Claims in New Mexico*. U.S. GAO report 04-59. Washington, D.C.: General Accounting Office.

U.S. Office of the Border Patrol. 2004. *National Border Patrol Strategy*. Washington, D.C.: U.S. Customs and Border Protection.

Uvin, Peter, Pankaj Jain, and David Brown. 2000. Think large and act small: toward a new paradigm for NGOs scaling up. *World Development* 28: 1409–19.

Vernez, Georges, and Kevin McCarthy. 1996. *The Costs of Immigration to Taxpayers*. Santa Monica, Calif.: Rand Corporation.

Wagoner, Jay. 1970. *Arizona Territory, 1863–1912: A Political History*. Tucson: University of Arizona Press.

Wallis, Alan. 1991. *Wheel Estate: The Rise and Decline of Mobile Homes*. New York: Oxford University Press.

Ward, Evan. 2000. *The Irrigated Oasis: Transformation of the Colorado River Delta, 1940–1975*. Ph.D. diss., Department of History, University of Georgia, Athens.

Ward, Evan. 2003. *Border Oasis: Water and the Political Ecology of the Colorado River Delta, 1940–1975*. Tucson: University of Arizona Press.

Ward, Peter. 1999. *Colonias and Public Policy in Texas and Mexico: Urbanization by Stealth*. Austin: University of Texas Press.

Ward, Peter. 2001. Dysfunctional Residential Land Markets: Colonias in Texas. *Landlines* 13(1). Available via http://www.lincolninst.edu.

Warner, Mildred. 1999. Social capital construction and the role of the local state. *Rural Sociology* 63: 373–93.

Warner, Mildred. 2001. Building social capital: the role of local government. *Journal of Socio-Economics* 30: 187–92.

Warren, Mark. 1996. Creating a multi-racial democratic community: case study of the Texas Industrial Areas Foundation. Paper prepared for the Conference on Social Networks and Urban Poverty. Available via http://www.tresser.com/iafin.htm.

Warren, Mark. 2001. *Dry Bones Rattling: Community Building to Revitalize American Democracy*. Princeton, N.J.: Princeton University Press.

Warren, Roland. 1963. *The Community in America*. Chicago: Rand McNally.

Weaver, James, Michael Rock, and Kenneth Kusterer. 1997. *Achieving Broad-Based Sustainable Development: Government, Environment, and Growth with Equity*. Bloomfield, Conn.: Kumarian Press.

Weaver, Thomas. 2001. Time, space, and articulation in the economic development of the U.S.–Mexico border region from 1940 to 2000. *Human Organization* 60: 105–20.

White, Michael, Frank Bean, and Thomas Espenshade. 1990. The U.S. Immigration Reform and Control Act and undocumented migration to the United
States. *Population Research and Policy Review* 9: 93–116.

Whitt, Joseph. 1996. The Mexican peso crisis. *Economic Review* 81: 1–20.

Wilson, Robert. 1997. *Public Policy and Community*. Austin: University of Texas
Press.

Wilson, Robert, and Miguel Guajardo. 2000. Capacity building and governance
in El Cenizo. *Cityscape: A Journal of Policy Development and Research* 5: 101–23.

Wolch, Jennifer. 1990. *The Shadow State: Government and Voluntary Sector in
Transition*. New York: Foundation Center.

Wolf, Daniel. 1988. *Undocumented Aliens and Crime: The Case of San Diego
County*. San Diego, Calif.: University of San Diego, Center for U.S.–Mexico
Studies.

Yuma County. 2001. Yuma County 2010 Comprehensive Plan. Available via
http://www.co.yuma.az.us/dds/ord/2010/main.htm.

Zúñiga, Victor, and Rubén Hernández-León. 2005. *New Destinations: Mexican
Immigrants in the United States*. New York: Russell Sage Foundation.

Index

Naco, Arizona, 30–31
National Affordable Housing Act of
    1990, 42, 112
nativist immigration policies, 78
neoliberalism, 125–26
Nogales, Arizona, 29, 43, 61, 68
North American Development Bank,
    41–42, 112, 164
North American Free Trade Agree-
    ment (NAFTA), 3, 42, 87

Old Nogales, Arizona, 72–73

Pima Indians, 16
Pirtleville, Arizona, 30–31
predatory lending, 110–11
Programa Nacional Fronterizo
    (PRONAF), 21, 23, 35
promotores, 131

Quartzsite, Arizona, 59

railroad industry: Atchison, Topeka
    and Santa Fe, 30; and regional de-
    velopment, 29–31; Southern Pacific,
    19, 29
Reagan Administration: and drug
    trafficking, 82
Replenishment Agriculture Workers
    Program (1986 IRCA), 80
Rincon, New Mexico, 60, 69
Rural Community Assistance Corpo-
    ration, 107
Rural Poverty Research Center, 108

Salem, New Mexico, 60, 69
San Diego, California, 15, 20–21
San Luis, Arizona, 61
San Miguel, New Mexico, 60
Santa Cruz Valley, Arizona, 17
Seasonal Agricultural Workers Pro-
    gram (1986 IRCA), 80

services economy: in Arizona and
    New Mexico, 35–36
Somerton, Arizona, 67–68
southern Arizona and New Mexico:
    definition of, 13
Southwest Border Regional Commis-
    sion, 165
Spanish explorers: Coronado, 16;
    Oñate, 15
statehood: Arizona and New Mexico,
    20
subprime lenders. *See* predatory lend-
    ing
Sunland Park, New Mexico, 43, 61, 63

territories: Arizona and New Mexico,
    18–20
Texas colonias, 6, 111–12
Texas Department of Housing and
    Community Affairs, 111
Thatcher, Arizona, 67–68
Tombstone, Arizona, 29

unauthorized immigration: and bor-
    der apprehensions, 79, 82–84, 92–
    96; and employer sanctions, 81; and
    informal labor markets, 80; and la-
    bor contractors, 81; timing and vol-
    ume of, 94–96
urbanization: definition of, 64
urban morphology: of colonias, 70–
    74; definition of, 68–69
U.S. immigration and border se-
    curity: border patrol, 78; Hart-
    Cellar Immigration Act of 1965, 79;
    Illegal Immigration Reform and
    Immigrant Responsibility Act
    (IIRIRA) of 1996, 82, 96, 99–104;
    Immigration Act of 1917, 33, 78; Im-
    migration Act of 1924, 78; Immi-
    gration Act of 1990, 82; Immigra-
    tion and Naturalization Act of 1952,

About the Authors

Angela Donelson completed her doctorate at the University of Arizona and her master's degree at Kansas State University. Until recently, she worked as the U.S. Department of Housing and Urban Development's representative to Arizona's colonias and has worked as an urban and regional planner in both the public and private sectors. She is the president of Donelson Consulting, a firm that assists small nonprofit organizations with housing and community development capacity building. Her research targets housing policy, rural poverty, and community development in intercultural contexts and small and grassroots organizations. Her publications have appeared in leading housing and community development journals.

Adrian Esparza is an associate professor in the School of Natural Resources at the University of Arizona. He completed his doctorate at the University of Illinois–Urbana and previously held a faculty position at Indiana University–Bloomington. His research deals with urbanization along the U.S.–Mexico border, rural community development, and suburban and exurban land conversion in the Southwest. He has published widely in a range of urban planning, regional science, and border studies journals.

Colonias in Arizona and New Mexico